Phil

D1738030

PRAGMATISM WITH PURPOSE

AMERICAN PHILOSOPHY

Douglas R. Anderson and Jude Jones, series editors

PRAGMATISM WITH PURPOSE

Selected Writings

PETER HARE

*Edited by Joseph Palencik, Douglas R. Anderson,
and Steven A. Miller*

FORDHAM UNIVERSITY PRESS   NEW YORK   2015

Library of Congress Cataloging-in-Publication Data

Hare, Peter H.
[Essays. Selections]
 Pragmatism with purpose : selected writings / Peter Hare ; edited by Joseph Palencik, Douglas R. Anderson, and Steven A. Miller. — First edition.
    pages cm. — (American philosophy)
 Includes bibliographical references and index.
 ISBN 978-0-8232-6432-2 (cloth : alk. paper)
 1. Pragmatism. 2. American philosophy. I. Palencik, Joseph, editor. II. Title.
 B944.P72H37 2015
 144'.3—dc23

                                                                2014047802

Printed in the United States of America

17 16 15   5 4 3 2 1

First edition

Contents

Acknowledgments

We would like to acknowledge the following for their generous contributions to this book: Susan Howe, Vincent Colapietro, John Shook and the Center for Inquiry, and Ethan Traman for his help with the final drafts. We would also like to thank The State University of New York at Buffalo Philosophy Department and the Society for the Advancement of American Philosophy for help with funding of the project. Finally, we would like to acknowledge the following journals and publishers for granting us permission to reprint some of Peter Hare's previously published essays: *Transactions of the Charles S. Peirce Society, Canadian Journal of Philosophy, Prometheus Books*, Columbia University Press, *Southern Journal of Philosophy, Sats: Nordic Journal of Philosophy, Philosophy and Phenomenological Research, Pacific Philosophical Forum, Process Studies, Journal of the History of Behavioral Sciences, Handbook of Whiteheadian Process Thought, Fulcrum: An Annual of Poetry and Aesthetics*, and *Journal of Value Inquiry*.

Mr. Charles Sanders Peirce

introduced "practice" and

"practical" into philosophy

as when someone planning a

journey blind-eyed solitary

prepares a lamp and fastens

linen screens and the fine

linens from that moment end

·with a question of fire in

flight the word "pragmatism"

spread pleading particulars

—Susan Howe, from *Pierce-Arrow*

INTRODUCTION

Present at the End? Who Will Be There
When the Last Stone Is Thrown?

Vincent Colapietro

P eter H. Hare was prone emphatically to remind me, from time to time, that he was drawn to William James not only because of James's literary gifts but also because of his philosophical insights. While Peter[1] was throughout his life appreciative of James's efforts to articulate an ethics of belief, he was not willing to grant so readily to James and his followers the right to believe in the context of religion.[2] He felt compelled to hound the gods and their defenders.[3] Even so, the ethics of belief outlined and partly filled in by James provided Peter with the insights, and indeed inspiration, to develop a distinctive form of what in contemporary analytic philosophy is called epistemic responsibilism[4] (or, more often, simply responsibilism).[5]

In addition to the ethics of belief, James's reconstruction of experience provided, Peter argued, an invaluable resource for mounting an effective defense of such commonsensical notions as causality, selfhood, autonomy, and temporality.[6] Whereas *traditional* empiricism tended to undermine our confidence in the cogency of such conceptions (think here of David Hume's analysis of the self as a bundle of perceptions, or causality as *merely* a habitual conjunction of temporally discriminable factors within the experiential flux), pragmatic empiricism[7] underwrote many of the basic convictions of what James and (following him) Peter did not hesitate to call natural realism. Peter interpreted James's pragmatism to drive in the direction of such realism, not subjectivism, idealism, or antirealism. Peter's account of James's relationship to such realism is summed up in this way: "Although James throughout his life believed in natural realism, for many years he felt intensely his inability to marshal convincing arguments for such an epistemology. Only late in life, when he had fully developed both his radical empiricism and his theory of truth, did he feel that he possessed adequate justification for the realism to which he had always been committed."[8] One irony here is that while others saw in James's radical empiricism and pragmatist approach a decisive break with natural realism, Peter saw in these distinctively Jamesian doctrines the resources for a defense of such realism.[9]

As much as anything else, however, James's pluralism won Peter's allegiance. Much like James himself, Peter's writings and, indeed, his life itself were an eloquent plea for cooperative effort.[10] But the ideal of pluralism exemplified, as much as articulated, by James and Peter was what Richard J. Bernstein has called an *engaged pluralism*.[11] "In our day of philosophical pluralism," Peter noted, "tolerance of other traditions too often leads to scattered effort and consequent lack of philosophical progress."[12] A concerted rather than scattered effort alone holds the promise of advancing our understanding of the issues to which we, as philosophers, devote ourselves.[13] Without such effort and the ongoing engagement of diverse traditions with one another resulting from cooperative endeavor, we have not so much pluralism as parallelism. Such parallelism is, by definition, the failure or refusal of the representatives of different traditions to address overlapping concerns in a cooperative manner. Cooperative effort as envisioned by Peter would cut across not only the boundaries of different philosophical traditions but also those of distinct academic disciplines and research programs. "If Peirce and James were alive today, they surely would have immersed themselves," he rightly suggested, "in the relevant technical literature in neuroscience."[14] For some of the questions in which Peirce and James were most deeply interested, a working knowledge of this often highly technical literature would be indispensable.

There might, however, appear to be a tension between natural realism and any truly robust form of Jamesian pluralism (i.e., Jamesian pluralism in its authentic guise). That is, there seems to be an irreconcilable conflict within Peter's philosophical soul. The realism in question would appear to preclude a multiplicity of valid answers to the same question, whereas the pragmatic meaning of the form of pluralism championed by James and Peter is nothing less than heuristic tolerance of rival positions. On this occasion, then, I want to explore Peter's creative appropriation of the Jamesian doctrines of natural realism *and* heuristic pluralism, with the hope of showing them to be interwoven strands of a single tapestry. In this essay, however, I cannot do anything more than sketch, in broad, bold strokes, what these doctrines, at bottom, mean. Yet, in doing so, I hope to have rendered plausible my claim that they are far from incompatible.

James's Ambivalence toward "Naturalism"

I want, first, to say a word or two about naturalism, for James characteristically expressed misgivings about this orientation toward the universe while Peter consistently identified himself as a naturalist. In the opening chapter of *Pragmatism*, James observed:

> For a hundred and fifty years past the progress of science has seemed to mean the enlargement of the material [or natural] universe and the diminution of man's importance. The result is what one may call the growth of naturalistic or positivistic feeling. Man is no law-giver to nature, he is an absorber. She it is who stands firm; he it is who must accommodate himself. Let him record truth, inhuman tho it be, and submit to it! The romantic spontaneity and courage are gone, the vision is materialistic and depressing. Ideals appear as inert by-products of physiology [or some other mechanistic source]; what is higher is explained by what is lower and treated forever as a case of "nothing but"—nothing but something else of a quite inferior sort. You get, in short, a materialistic universe, in which only the tough-minded find themselves congenially at home.[15]

Such a universe is, however, one in which James felt anything but at home. Later in this same work, James suggests,

> Philosophical materialism is not necessarily knit up with belief in "matter," as a metaphysical principle. One may deny matter in that sense, as strongly as Berkeley did and yet one may still be a materialist in the wider sense, of explaining higher phenomena by lower ones, and leaving the destinies of the world at the mercy of its blinder parts and forces. It is in this wider sense of the word that materialism is opposed to spiritualism or theism. . . . This is the complexion of present day materialism, which may better be called naturalism.[16]

This position might even be better called reductivism or reductive naturalism, since what is for James objectionable is the reduction of the higher to the lower (e.g., the reduction of consciousness as apparently a fighter for ends to the operation of mechanisms governed by purely blind laws, not normatively structured forethought).

In *The Varieties of Religious Experience,* James asserts:

> The fact that we *can* die, that we *can* be ill at all, is what perplexes us; the fact that we now for a moment live and are well is irrelevant to that perplexity. We need a life not correlated with death, a health not liable to illness, a kind of good that will not perish, a good in fact that flies beyond the Goods of nature.[17]

That to which we devote ourselves must not be merely transitory, purely ephemeral. It is, for James, not so much that *we* must escape annihilation as that our ideals, those in and through which we define our selves, must be in some sense eternal. This is nowhere more eloquently expressed than in the concluding chapter of James's *The Principles of Psychology.* At one point he personally addressed his readers, asking them to take "those aspects of phenomena which interest you as a human being most, and class the phenomena as perfect and imperfect, as ends and means to ends, as high and low, as beautiful and ugly, positive and negative, harmonious and discordant, etc."[18] "What is precious should be," from the perspective of each one of us as humans, "preserved; unworthy things should be sacrificed for its sake."[19] From the perspective of reductive naturalism, however, the "sentimental facts and relations are butchered at a blow." For many, the theoretical compensations for such an austere outlook warrant pronouncing these "facts and relations" to be purely illusory: They reconcile "the thinker to the notion of a purposeless universe, in which all things and qualities men [and women] love, *dulcissima mundi nomina,* are but illusions of our fancy attached to accidental clouds of dust which will be dissipated by the eternal cosmic weather as carelessly as they were formed."[20] But, contra James, the *ultimate* ephemerality of our animating ideals and the most cherished objects of our defining loves does not, in itself, render the cosmos purposeless, for the cosmos is a matrix in which such ideals assume their myriad guises and exert their distinctive influence.[21] While naturalism might properly be taken to entail temporalism, temporalism in turn need not lead to the nightmare vision of a purposeless universe.

In "The Will to Believe," James suggests: "Science says things are; morality says some things are better than other things; and religion says essentially two things." The first is more relevant to our discussion, but the second is also worth recalling. *First,* religion "says that the best things are the more eternal things, the overlapping things, the things in the universe that throw the *last stone* . . . and say the final word."[22] *Second,* religion insists that we are better off in the present if we acknowledge the truth (even if it is only a possible truth) of its first affirmation. To live our lives as though the higher is not reducible to the lower, as though the objects of our defining allegiances are affairs of abiding significance, as though the death of our finite selves does not entail the annihilation of the ideals on which we have staked our lives, is to open our purely natural existence to transfigurative forces. James's defense of the right to believe was as much as anything else animated by his conviction that the transformative power of what might legitimately be identified as spiritual forces ought to have ample opportunity to exert themselves upon human life. To browbeat individuals, in the name of science or truth, out of their seemingly instinctual craving for a higher life than natural existence seemed to James an illicit denial of our human birthright.

From these and other texts, James's misgivings regarding naturalism are unmistakably evident. But there is a terminological question and also there are pivotal texts suggesting a more harmonious relationship between the naturalistic outlook and James's most basic philosophical convictions. The terminological question is (as I have already hinted at) whether James's antipathy is toward naturalism or, rather, toward reductionism. Would he be as strenuously opposed to a *nonreductive* naturalism in which emergent ideals exert an irreducibly normative force and authority? Indeed, are there not passages in his writings that drive in the direction of such a naturalism?

Moreover, there are a number of very important texts in which James clearly espouses a thoroughgoing temporalism in which the traditional conception of an eternal order, extending to our understanding of God, is called into radical doubt. For example, James in *A Pluralistic Universe* asserts: "We humans are incurably rooted in the temporal point of view. The eternal's ways are utterly unlike our ways."[23] James's pluralism is of a piece with his temporalism. "For pluralists . . . time remains as real as anything, and nothing in the universe is great or static or eternal enough not to have some history. But the world that each of us feels most intimately at home with is that of beings with histories that play into our history, whom we can help in their vicissitudes even as they help us in ours."[24] To remove divinity from time, to locate God in eternity is, in James's judgment, to erect "a bar to intimacy between the divine and the human";[25] "in representing the deepest part of reality of the world as static and without a history," the Hegelian (and all kindred outlooks) loosens "the world's hold upon our sympathies and leaves the soul of it foreign."[26] Accordingly, James insists: "God is not the absolute, but is himself a part when the system is conceived pluralistically [as James insists it must be], his function can be taken as not wholly dissimilar to those of the other smaller parts— as similar to our functions consequently."[27] God is *either* eternal and thus so utterly unlike us as to be absolutely foreign to our experience; *or* God is finite and hence deeply akin to us (so much so that relationships of an increasingly intimate character are an omnipresent possibility). The possibility of such intimacy with the divine prompted James to deny some of the traditional attributes of the divine being(s), and encouraged him to insist upon the finitude of God. "Having an environment, being in time, and working out a history just like ourselves, he [God] escapes," James argued, "from the foreignness from all that is human, of the static timeless perfect absolute."[28]

Insofar as naturalism does not encompass reductivism (the necessity always and everywhere to explain the higher in terms of the lower), also insofar as James's own religious pluralism drives in the direction of a thoroughgoing temporalism (a view calling into radical doubt an eternal order over and above the temporal world in which finite agents are so manifestly situated), James's misgivings about naturalism might be more terminological and more qualified than would appear to be the case. In psychoanalytic terms, we might say that, in the development of James's thought, we witness the achievement of ambivalence, at least a movement in the direction of such an achievement.[29] In any event, contemporary philosophers such as Peter Hare find in James's lifelong struggle to articulate a defensible form of natural realism some of the resources for formulating a compelling contemporary version of this philosophical stance. It is time to turn to the resources in James upon which Peter so heavily drew in his own work, but not without first insisting that his creative appropriation of Jamesian insights is far from being altogether at odds with some of the deepest intentions of his pragmatist predecessor. This is so because James's own intentions were, to some extent, at odds with each other.

Human Knowing as a Natural Process

If the emphasis on temporality and history is warranted in the case of our attempts to put forth a conception of divinity rooted in the legitimate cravings of the human psyche, then all the more is this emphasis justified in the case of elaborating a naturalistic account of human knowing. Such an account is emphatically temporal and, in a sense, historicist. "Why insist," James asks rhetorically, "that knowing is a static relation out of time when it practically seems so much a function of our active life?"[30] "The fundamental fact about our experience is," James also insists, "that it is a process of change."[31] "But, owing to the fact that all experience is a process, no point of view can ever be *the* last one. Every one is insufficient and off its balance, and responsible to later points of view."[32] James's temporalism thus underwrites his pluralism.

The human knower is a social *actor* who inescapably acquires an ethics of belief in the context of others. The pressures and prompting of others in the formation of one's own beliefs cannot, at least for James and Peter, be gainsaid. As social actors, human knowers form their beliefs (or opinions) in the rough-and-tumble give-and-take of social experience set in a natural context, and thus in a process in which both other human agents and natural objects are disposed to object to our attributions, descriptions, and conjectures. What is often missed is that the pluralistic form of Jamesian humanism insures that this pluralistic humanism is "essentially a social philosophy, a philosophy of 'co,' in which conjunctions [especially ones of an ambulatory character] do the work," at least most of the most critical work.[33]

The critics of James's pragmatism, however, deny what cannot truly be discounted or ignored (also, what James never dreamt of denying)—the irreducibly social context in which human knowing not only takes its more-or-less determinate shape but also alone has its point and pertinence. "The anti-pragmatist . . . immediately falls foul," James contends, "of the word 'opinion' here, *abstracts it from the universe of life,* and uses it as a bare dictionary substantive, to deny the rest of the assumptions which it coexists withal."[34] So understood, an opinion is simply "what some one thinks or believes"; it is more often than not taken to mean whatever anyone just happens to suppose, regardless of whatever one's experience (communal as well as personal or individual) suggests about the truth of the matter at hand. "This definition leaves everyone's opinion to be autogenous, or unrelated either to what anyone else may think or to what the truth may be."[35]

This is, however, anything but how the pragmatist understands this work. Nowhere is James's characterization of pragmatism as a "concrete way of seeing"[36] more evident than in his description of what the term *opinion* means in the mouth of pragmatists: When such a theorist

> speaks of opinions, does he mean any such insulated and unmotivated abstractions as here are supposed [by the antipragmatist?]. Of course not, he means men's opinions in the flesh, as they have really formed themselves, opinions surrounded by their grounds and the influences they obey and exert, and along with the whole environment of social communication of which they are a part and out of which they take their rise. Moreover the "experience" which the pragmatic definition postulates *is* the independent something which the anti-pragmatist accuses him of denying.[37]

Lest anyone miss the thrust of this rejoinder to the antipragmatist or abstractionist James, first, italicizes his main conclusion and, then, draws out its polemical implications:

When the pragmatist talks of opinions, it is opinions as they thus con-
cretely and livingly and interactively and correlatively exist that he has
in mind; and when the anti-pragmatist tries to floor him because the
word "opinion" can also be taken abstractly and as if it had no environment, he simply ignores the soil out of which the whole discussion grows. His weapons cut the air and strike no blows. No
one gets wounded in the war against caricatures of belief and skel-
etons of opinion. . . . Refuse to use the word "opinion" abstractly,
keep it in its real environment, and the withers of pragmatism remain unwrung.[38]

To situate human knowing in the concrete contexts in which it actually
has arisen and continually unfolds, often in extremely convoluted forms,
is at the heart of James's account of knowledge, meaning, and truth. Far
from being an insulated and unmotivated affair, human knowing is a natural process animated and guided by the interests, passions, and purposes
of situated agents whose cognitive exertions, undertakings, and successes
as well as failures are inextricably bound up with environing forces.

Consider, for a moment, the example of truth, as conceived by James.
"If there is to be truth, it [pragmatism] says, both realities and beliefs
about them must conspire to make it; but whether there ever is such a
thing [as truth], or how anyone can be sure that his own belief possesses it,
it never pretends to determine."[39] Truth depends upon the world as much
as it depends upon us. It is a relationship established in an incredibly intricate nexus of countless other relationships, a nexus in which objects and
events assume additive and, in some respects, transformative roles and
functions.

It hence ought to be no surprise that Peter Hare approvingly quotes
Frederick Will, another theorist who is committed to articulating a defensible form of pragmatic realism.[40] In "Thoughts and Things," his 1969
presidential address to the Western (now Central) Division of the APA,
Will asserts: "Thinking is an activity which we engage in not only in the
world of things, but by means of things in the world, supported and sustained by them. And when these things fail us in certain ways, as they
sometimes do . . . words literally fail us, because our thoughts fail us."[41]
Later in this same essay, he adds: "In our thoughts themselves, things are
implicated and in a variety of subtle ways make their characters known."

This is so massively, intricately, and inescapably true that "the grand philosophical project" of devising a connection "between altogether independent thoughts and things . . . is a gratuitous one."[42] What takes the place of this project is "the difficult task of achieving *understanding in detail* of the way things are implicated in our thoughts" (emphasis added). "It is," Will realizes, "not the end, but the mere beginning of the story, to say that our thoughts are what they are by virtue of our relations with things, that their very roots lie in things." One way to conceive natural realism, in the sense espoused by Peter, is that this philosophical orientation imposes the arduous task of formulating in its most salient details the complex story of just how our thoughts are intertwined with things.[43]

Long before Will, James worked strenuously to begin anew the story of how human thought is inseparably connected to the experiential world in which it arises and unfolds—and he was acutely conscious that his own best efforts were a mere beginning. Even so, he appeared to be confident, especially in his later years, that these efforts pointed decisively in the direction of concreteness. "The whole originality of pragmatism, the whole point in it, is," James readily conceded, "its use of the concrete way of seeing. It begins with concreteness, and returns and ends with it."[44]

For James, the concreteness from which pragmatism commences and at which it aims is obtained, first and foremost, through the appreciation or acknowledgment of *context* (as we have already seen in the case of opinions). Perhaps somewhat misleadingly, he used the term *experience* to identify the context of contexts,[45] the enveloping situation in which all more or less circumscribed situations are themselves to be situated or located. "For pluralistic pragmatism, truth grows up," James suggests, "inside of all the finite experiences." These experiences "lean on each other, but the whole of them, if such a whole there be, leans on nothing else. All 'homes' are in finite experience; finite experience as such is homeless."[46] That is, there is, for him, no context beyond that of experience, such that the character or disclosures of our finite, perspectival, and ongoing processes of experience are beholden to anything more real, fundamental, or ultimate. Whatever is disclosed in and through our experience is, at bottom, deeply (though perhaps widely) akin to this medium of disclosure.[47]

What is most pertinent for our purposes is James's insistence that the relation of truth, "like all relations, has its *fundamentum*, namely, the matrix of experiential circumstance, psychological as well as physical, in which the correlated terms are found embedded."[48] He goes some way toward unpacking the significance of this claim when he adds: "What *constitutes the relation* known as truth . . . is just the *existence in the empirical world of this fundamentum of circumstance surrounding object and idea* and ready to be either short-circuited or traversed at full length."[49] James's understanding of the experiential matrix in which our cognitive endeavors have their seemingly miraculous origin and their ongoing evolution recalls our earlier point regarding the inseparable connection between human thought, thinking, and their objects, on the one hand, and environing, objects, events, and histories, on the other. "The nature and place and affinities of the object [of our epistemically satisfactory ideas, i.e., our pragmatically true conceptions] . . . play as vital a part in the particular passage possible as do the nature and associative tendencies of the idea."[50] In other words, the objects as objects, and not merely as objects of our thoughts, play an ineliminable role in our epistemic successes—and failures, so much so that "*both* realities and beliefs about them must conspire" together to establish, maintain, or revise the relationship of truth.[51]

The relationship in question encompasses more than how a mind stands to reality or reality to the mind, this relationship being but one strand or, more accurately, an interwoven cable of various strands themselves intricately connected to a nexus of other relationships (far too numerous to identify). Though it is in many contexts singularly important or vital, the relationship of truth is (at least, on this account) not ontologically singular or isolatable. James is quick to point out how fundamentally mistaken, then, are those critics of pragmatism who associate it with waywardness or subjectivity: If one comprehends the "nature and place and affinities of the object"—if one appreciates its omnipresent role in our epistemic endeavors—then "the notion that truth could fall altogether inside of the thinker's private experience and be something purely psychological" (moreover, something over which an allegedly isolated thinker might exercise unbridled control) must be seen for what it is—"absurd."[52]

Human knowing is, thus, a natural process taking place not only alongside but also in and through other natural processes.[53] It is anything but a self-contained process, the success of which resides in the ingenuity or resourcefulness, the tenacity or stubbornness, of what, in effect, turns out to be some otherworldly being (i.e., some unsituated agent whose actions miraculously carry no consequences or repercussions). For all of its flaws and distortions, Herbert Spencer's excessively vague formula of our mental life no less than our bodily one ("the adjustment of our inner and outer relations") "takes into account the fact that minds inhabit environments which act on them and on which they in turn react." Indeed, "it takes mind in the midst of all its concrete relations" or goes some distance in doing so.[54] To a far greater degree, and hence in a much thicker manner, James, beginning with his critique of Spencer himself, strove to take the human mind and all kindred forms in the midst of its concrete relations.[55]

To do so means parting company with those who separate thoughts and things. It involves turning our backs on those theorists who conceive the relationship between cognition and object to be saltatory, rather than ambulatory. The alleged gap or gulf between thoughts and things requires, on this account, a leap; hence, James uses the word *saltatory* to designate the view he rejects. In his judgment, no leap is required, since we are always already connected to the world in which cognition emerges, evolves, and transforms itself. To alter the metaphor, epistemic relationships always ride on the back of other kinds of relationships, even if once they are instituted and augmented they significantly add to other kinds of connections.[56] Put positively, then, to take the human and all kindred minds in the midst of their concrete relationships means joining company with those who insist a vast network of conjunctive relationships is not only always already in place but also provides more or less adequate resources for increasing, instituting, and in other ways enhancing the heuristic functions of this intricate web of potentially cognitive connections.

Human knowing is a *discursive* process and, as the adjective implies, it is one best described in terms of movement rather than architecture.[57] "Cognition, whenever we take it concretely means determinate 'ambulation,' through intermediaries, from a *terminus a quo* to, or toward, a *terminus ad quem*. As the intermediaries are other than the termini, and connected with them by the usual associative bonds . . . , there would appear to be nothing especially unique about the processes of knowing. They fall wholly within experience."[58] From this and numerous other texts, it is clear why James proclaims: "My own account of this relation is ambulatory through and through."[59] The apparent gap between the knower and the known is an illusion generated by an abstract portrait of our onto-logical condition as human knowers. There is, in truth, no chasm to be leaped or bridged, only innumerable connections whose epistemic perti-nence remains to be plumbed. Yet, it is not altogether illicit or always mis-leading to construe the processes of experiences of knowing in abstract terms, at least insofar as we are attentive to the results being the residues of selective emphasis for particular purposes. But, then, "we have no right to oppose static essences . . . to the moving processes in which they live embedded."[60] The only concrete way of depicting the ambulatory processes of human knowing, with their multilevel intermediaries and dynamic con-junctions, however, is as open-ended processes.

Any step holds the possibility of a misstep, any movement into the un-known entails the possibility of the all-too-familiar human experience of realizing, painfully or otherwise, we are not only lost but also do not know how to find our way out of our ignorance or confusion. In other words, James's ambulatory portrayal of human knowing carries fallibilistic im-plications. "Our errors are," James counsels, "surely not such awfully sol-emn things. In a world where we are so certain to incur them in spite of all our caution, a certain lightness of heart seems healthier than this ex-cessive nervousness on their behalf. At any rate, it seems the fittest thing for the empiricist philosopher."[61]

James is acutely aware that such conclusions regarding our knowledge occur at a more self-conscious level than the one where the overwhelm-ing bulk of our epistemic ventures take place. More generally, he is keenly conscious that his "whole inquiry into knowing grows up on a reflective level. In any real moment of knowing, what we are thinking of is our ob-ject, not the way in which we ourselves are momentarily knowing it. We at this moment, as it happens, have knowing itself for our object."[62] It is one thing to know, quite another to know that we know, and yet another again to offer, on a reflexive level, an adequate account of human know-ing. James and, following him, Peter are striving to offer an account of what knowing is *known as* and, even more basically, *experienced as.*[63] Our *experience* of knowing is of the utmost relevance in fashioning a convinc-ing explication of our epistemic procedures, practices, and achievements as well as frustrations, failures, and delusions. In the end, such an account in effect offers a more or less recognizable portrait of human agency, in one of its most important guises or roles. It is a portrait of a self-accountable and self-critical actor who is deeply enmeshed in a vast nexus of actual relationships, including fateful ones with other social actors. A naturalistic account of human knowing locates this process in such a nexus and abstracts from this incredibly vast, intricate network of relationships only in a provisional and circumspect manner.[64] So understood, then, *naturalistic* tends to become synonymous with *thick* in James's sense.[65]

Despite his ambivalence toward "naturalism," James undeniably took human knowing to be a *natural* process. His "naturalistic realism" is bound up with his indefatigable efforts to provide a thick account of this ambulatory process, as it emerges and indeed evolves in the context of experience. In this account, the most salient features of human knowing (besides being a natural and ambulatory *process*) are, at the risk of being overly explicit, its experiential, thus its temporal,[66] social, situated, normative, discursive, fallible, potentially self-corrective, and inevitably open-ended character.[67] Our experience of our own epistemic endeavors, achievements, and failures provides the basis (the *fundamentum*), enabling this account to be truly one of knowing *as it is experienced* (as *humanly* experienced).

As a philosopher and scholar conversant with contemporary epistemology and current developments in various scientific fields, Peter H. Hare has done as much as anyone to show, on the one side, the relevance of James's "naturalistic" account of human knowing to contemporary debates, especially within analytic philosophy, and, on the other, the resources within contemporary thought for articulating an even-thicker *Jamesian* account of our epistemic practices. Each side should, in his judgment, heed the other. For pragmatists to insulate themselves from the contemporary debates within analytic philosophy would be, he was convinced, for these pragmatists to betray their own tradition. In turn, for contemporary philosophers trained in the analytic tradition to continue ignoring classical pragmatism is almost certain to doom their accounts of human knowing as a natural process to be unduly narrow and superficial.

In "Classical Pragmatism, Recent Naturalistic Theories of Representation, and Pragmatic Realism," Peter opened his treatment of these topics by recalling:

When I started graduate study at Columbia University in the late 1950s, the department was still dominated by a Deweyan outlook. Ernest Nagel, Herbert W. Schneider, John Herman Randall Jr., and others in the department had been students of Dewey. We often called our viewpoint "pragmatic naturalism." At that time Columbia was the only remaining graduate department dominated by that outlook, an outlook considered outmoded by the rest of the profession. To use a more recent turn of phrase, we felt ourselves "marginalized."[68]

Looking back forty years later (the time when he presented this paper at the Twentieth International Wittgenstein Symposium), he observed: "In the 1980s and 1990s it has been interesting but sometimes unsettling to witness pragmatic naturalism becoming more and more once again a major player in the profession." On the one hand, he was convinced, "the basic program of classical American pragmatism has . . . been genuinely advanced in recent philosophical research" and, in this context, he means by such research primarily work done by analysts. On the other, Peter remained convinced that, without a direct, sustained, and detailed engagement with the rich resources of the pragmatic tradition, such advancement would be severely limited.[69] Among his various and important contributions, his efforts to facilitate a critical dialogue between these two intellectual traditions certainly stands out as especially noteworthy and, indeed, praiseworthy.[70]

Peter was somewhat quirky, even after he had shorn his mutton chops and shed his bowtie, but he was never flamboyantly or aggressively idiosyncratic. In turning to William James as much as John Dewey, G. H. Mead, or other more unabashed naturalists, this facet of his character is on display. In a gentle, thoughtful, imaginative, and innovative manner, he drew heavily upon Jamesian insights to articulate a thick account of human knowing as a natural process. In this and countless other respects, we are the richer for his painstaking labors and unostentatious quirkiness.

Conclusion: Who Will Be There When the Last Stone Is Thrown?

For the special issue of the *Transactions* dedicated to his lifetime friend and cherished coeditor, Peter contributed a piece entitled "Richard S. Robin: Present at the Creation."[71] For the purpose of this foreword, however,

I am inclined to muse about who might be present, in some guise, at the eschaton. Of course, we cannot know who will be there when the last word is uttered and the last stone is thrown. We can nonetheless hope, without much or any warrant for supposing this to be a realistic aspiration. Whatever the character of such hope, however, it might serve as nothing less than a regulative ideal: Even a wild hope, if it be such, might serve effectively as a regulative ideal for our present pursuits.[72] At least this much seems implicit in James's 1907 talk at Radcliffe College: "A small force, if it never lets up," he urges there, "will accumulate effects more considerable than those of much greater forces if these work inconsistently." He adds: "The ceaseless whisper of the more permanent ideals, the steady tug of truth and justice, give them but time, *must* warp the world in their direction."[73] The life and work of Peter H. Hare, however, increase the likelihood that in the far, far distant future a number of pluralists committed to facilitating a critical dialogue among especially the most exemplary representatives of diverse traditions will be present for the foreseeable future and, we might hope, also the unforeseeable time after that (if not also in the eschaton). If so, they may be counted among Peter's possible progeny or, at least, his distant kin.

Peter Hare's intellectual life was animated by the Jamesian conviction that "there can be no final truth in ethics any more than in physics, until the last man has had his experience and [on the basis of this experience] said his say."[74] Indeed, there can be no final truth in any field of inquiry until the last persons have enjoyed, endured, and suffered the world from their singular angles of vision—and, thereafter, until they have had an opportunity to give voice to the revelations of their experience. Moreover, even at this point, there cannot be any absolutely final or certain judgment, only an arbitrarily interrupted process.

Such pluralism might be ultimately rooted in naturalism, at least the vision of nature quickly sketched by James in *A Pluralistic Universe*. James suggests there, "nature is but a name for excess; every point in her opens out and runs into the more; and the only question . . . is how far into the rest of nature we may have to go in order to get entirely beyond its overflow"—if indeed there is any place beyond the overflowing excess of the diverse natural settings in which we are ineluctably situated.[75] Nature as a name for a self-transcending and self-transforming excess, at every point opening out and running into the more (the more than has yet been achieved, the more than has yet been experienced or observed, recorded or investigated), as much as anything else, underwrites "the ever not yet," "ever not quite!"[76]

"We live," James arrestingly asserts, "upon the front edge of an advancing wave-crest, and our sense of a determinate direction in falling forward is all we cover of the future of our path. . . . Our experience, inter alia, is of variations of rate and of direction, and lives in these transitions more than in the journey's end."[77] At the journey's end,[78] either in the sense of an individual's life or in that of the cosmos's ceasing to be, I imagine that such an understanding of experience and, intimately allied to this understanding, a naturalistic account of human knowing might be reaffirmed without reservation. Looking back upon the course of one's personal or cosmic history, one need not necessarily feel cheated by anything so invincibly partial, provisional, and perspectival. "The pragmatism or pluralism which I defend," James readily acknowledged, "has to fall back on a certain ultimate hardihood, a certain willingness to live without assurances or guarantees"[79] This makes the ethics of belief and, more generally, a fallibilist approach to human knowing[80] all the more urgent. Accordingly, it makes the exemplarity of Peter H. Hare's work and life all the more worthy of timely celebration. Finally, it makes the renewed recollection, into a far distant future shrouded in impenetrable darkness, of this exemplary individual and ones akin to him all the more important and fitting.

But Peter's work is not only worthy of mindful celebration. It is also deserving of careful study. He was no less an exemplary philosopher than an exemplary person, not least of all in his creative appropriation of Jamesian insights into natural realism and heuristic pluralism. This collection of essays bears eloquent witness to this—and much more.

AUTOBIOGRAPHICAL OCCASIONS

A Brief Autobiography

Deep maternal and paternal roots in American intellectual history going back to the earliest settlers have influenced me since childhood. Most directly, my grandmother's work in American cultural history and my father's desire to combine philosophy, religion, physics, mathematics, and the arts have motivated my career. With a temperamental craving for inclusiveness and connectedness, I tried as a Yale undergraduate to integrate these influences by majoring in philosophy while slaving on the board of *The Yale Literary Magazine*. Arthur Pap's seminar in contemporary empiricism and John E. Smith's course in Kant engaged me as much as the teachings of Brand Blanshard and Paul Weiss. I wrote a thesis on Alfred North Whitehead, an exemplar of the multidisciplinary integration I sought. It is no accident that in the mid-1950s I had many of the same Yale teachers as Richard Rorty, Richard Bernstein, John Lachs, Andrew Reck, and Donald Sherburne.

As a graduate student at Columbia, where the philosophy department was still dominated by Deweyan and Woodbridgean thought, I struggled to graft Columbia naturalism and realism on to what I learned at Yale. My irenic impulse worked overtime, and I championed "polarity" and "sociality" as ways of coping with philosophical conflict. After contemplating a dissertation in philosophy of science under Ernest Nagel, I was drawn to Justus Buchler, especially to his work on Peirce and Santayana. I saw Buchler as another exemplar of the integration I had found earlier in Whitehead. After writing an MA thesis under Joseph Blau on Wilmon Sheldon's philosophy of polarity, it was Buchler's suggestion that I write a dissertation on G. H. Mead's metaphysics of sociality in order to integrate Columbian naturalism and realism with the process philosophy of my undergraduate thesis.

Receiving in 1962 an appointment at the State University of New York at Buffalo, I found myself in a rapidly expanding and congenial philosophy department. So much so that at the age of thirty-six I became a full professor and chair of a department of thirty-eight full-time faculty—perhaps more pluralistic than any department before or since. Several members of the department shared my interest in the American philosophical tradition, but I was also attracted to the mathematical logicians, various Marxists, linguistic analysts, specialists in continental philosophy, and assorted other sorts of philosophers, including a distinguished Buddhist. Although sometimes frustrating, twelve years of leading such a heterogeneous group was also immensely satisfying.

Edward Madden became my closest collaborator in the department. In addition to authoring jointly numerous books and articles, in the late 1960s I briefly assisted Madden in editing the *Transactions of the Charles S. Peirce Society: A Quarterly Journal in American Philosophy*. From the early 1970s until 2000 I edited the *Transactions* with Richard Robin and since 2000 have done so with Randall Dipert. My aim in this editorial work has been to encourage historical scholarship that reflects and advances the rich diversity of the American tradition. Working with *Transactions* contributors from outside the United States has been especially rewarding.

In my current work I am connecting philosophy to other disciplines (e.g., poetry, biology, cognitive science) and diverse subject matter (e.g., photography, TV drama). Long term, I hope to complete a book about the *Somers* Mutiny, a celebrated 1840s event in US naval history. Interwoven with a gripping sea story will be literary history (e.g., Herman Melville,

James Fenimore Cooper), cultural history, political history, theories of criminal, civil, and military law, pragmatist epistemology, theories of moral responsibility, history of naval architecture, and political figures today.

Editing American Philosophy

What have I been trying to achieve in my role as coeditor of the *Transactions* quarterly? A clear answer to that question may be of interest to others as well as to myself, and sorting out what have *not* been my goals will likely be as helpful as explaining what they have been.

(1) I have not sought to increase circulation by publishing only material accessible to readers with little prior knowledge of the history of philosophy in America. Although today book publishers, including university presses, believe that they are financially constrained to find a general readership for most, if not all, of their titles, I have not felt such a constraint. I have thought that the journal could survive financially as a publication aimed at specialists. That is not to say that I wished to tolerate poor writing. I have wanted the writing to be as clear and graceful as is consistent with scholarship of interest to specialists.

(2) I have wished the journal to reflect heterogeneities and discontinuities in the American tradition as well as the homogeneities and continuities. I have tried to avoid promoting one "ism" at the expense of other philosophical orientations. I have discouraged efforts to establish, for example, the hegemony of pragmatism. I have been suspicious of fashions in scholarship.

Reflections on the Career of John J. McDermott

Anyone who is familiar with John McDermott's writings or has heard him give talks knows that "nectar" is one of his favorite words—both as a noun and as a verb. Accordingly, it seems appropriate for me to begin my comments today with a story about nectar—the literal kind as well as the metaphorical kind of nectar. It is doubly appropriate because in recent years it has been John's pedagogy (another of his favorite words) that has inspired me to incorporate stories in my philosophizing much more than I used to.

Here is my story about nectar, a story that stars my grandmother, the matriarch of the family and the chief source of my interest in American history.

Before World War II, when I was four years old, my grandmother—always alert to "teaching moments" where her grandchildren were concerned—explained to me the wonders of the trumpet vine that grew in abundance on one side of her barn, from the ground all the way up to the eaves. From a branch of the vine at my shoulder level, she pulled off a reddish-orange trumpet bloom. Holding out the trumpet, she instructed me to suck on the end of it. As I obediently did so, she asked, "Doesn't that taste good?" After I nodded with pleasure, she delivered the lesson she had in mind in this exercise in pedagogy. "What you taste is nectar," she said as she pulled off another trumpet bloom from a branch at her own shoulder level, and sucked on it with a smile. "All trumpet vine blooms have sweet nectar in them. This summer you can reach only the blooms near the ground, but as you grow older and taller, each year you will be able to reach more and more blooms and more and more nectar, until"—she pointed to the eaves—"you can reach almost to the top of the vine as your father can."

This nectar incident, emblematic of my relationship with my grandmother, is relevant to the topic of our discussion today because it was this matriarch—active in numerous historical societies—whose approach to and fascination with American history I absorbed in my earliest memories. Throughout my childhood she took every opportunity to introduce me to historians who came to dinner or cocktails, and when I got a driver's license she paid me to drive her in the performance of her many duties as president of a society concerned with the history of Long Island.

But before I return to my grandmother's distinctive approach to American history that so influenced me and a discussion of how that bears on the way I respond to McDermott's ideas, I want to address directly some aspects of John's philosophy as expressed in the two books that are the subject of our meeting this morning.

Although I had been aware since the 1960s of McDermott's sympathy for such existentialists as Camus, it was only in the early 1990s, when I heard him deliver his Patrick Romanell Lecture, "Ill-at-Ease: The Natural Travail of Ontological Disconnectedness," that I seriously confronted the question of whether John's existentialist themes were compatible with his advocacy of what are commonly thought to be radical empiricist, pragmatist, and naturalist themes. It happens that John's lecture was one of the few attended by the person who endowed the lecture series in naturalism, Pat Romanell. As John may remember, Pat, who earned his PhD at Columbia in the 1930s while it was still dominated by the naturalism of Dewey, expressed puzzlement about what appeared to be McDermott's rejection of naturalism in favor of existentialism. Since he had established the lecture series to promote philosophical naturalism, Romanell was understandably concerned. I don't now recall whether Romanell seemed satisfied by McDermott's responses to his questions on that score. I'm sure that John remembers his exchange with Pat much better than I do. I was myself so flummoxed by the lecture that I rashly went up to John and asked whether his talk was intended to be ironical. John, who seemed as puzzled by my question as I was by the lecture's alleged naturalism, assured me that irony was not what he intended.

Fortunately, in the years following my asking John that rash question, I have come to understand why that lecture and other of his writings in the same vein can be fairly described as expressions of a naturalistic philosophy of experience. Reading *The Drama of Possibility*, especially Part 3 of that book, and McDermott's "Afterword: You Are Really Able," his response to the contributors to the Festschrift, has deepened my understanding of McDermott's distinctive way of incorporating existentialist themes in his naturalism. To put it simply and crudely, John has explored more fully than anyone has before the *dark* dimensions of experience within an American naturalistic framework. To be sure, he points to dark passages in James, Royce, and Dewey, as well as in the work of such earlier American thinkers as Emerson. But in many of his writings John has foregrounded that dark side of American naturalism in a way that no American philosopher has done before. That foregrounding is, in my view, one of his most original contributions to the American philosophical tradition. That is not to deny that he has often foregrounded the *nectar* in experience. The way he vividly *juxtaposes* the nectar and the dark in their complex interdependencies may be his most important contribution.

Part of the reason that it took me some time to understand this aspect of McDermott's work is that my approach to the relations between existentialism and the American tradition has been different, though in my own way I have been as fascinated by existentialism as John. In the 1960s and 1970s I regularly taught an undergraduate course in existentialism. I was eager to teach the subject because I recognized that in 1950s and 1960s existentialist authors were being widely read outside professional philosophy. I regarded existentialism as an important set of what I like to call "immigrant ideas." In my teaching of Kierkegaard, Heidegger, Camus, Sartre, and Marcel I often highlighted what the American tradition and existentialism had in common. I also stressed that the genuine differences between the two types of philosophy did not always entail contradictions between the two. The viewpoints could be complementary. In the Peter Hare brand of pedagogy, I was trying to build bridges between existentialism and the American tradition. I emphasized that the American philosophical tradition welcomes, to a greater degree than any other philosophical tradition, the influence of immigrant ideas. Just as we have always recognized that American culture in general has developed thanks to wave after wave of immigrants, we should understand, I argued, that America's *philosophical* tradition can and should develop similarly.

Although I applauded the existentialists' vivid portrayal of the contingencies of the human condition, in an important respect I qualified my endorsement of existentialism as a welcome immigrant to the shores of American philosophy. In journal articles as well as in class, I presented as "over the top" some of the things Heidegger said about death, what Camus wrote about suicide, Sartre's pronouncements on the subjects of nausea and freedom, and what Kierkegaard had to say about "sickness unto death," "the teleological suspension of the ethical," and "truth is subjectivity." While acknowledging that such claims had some basis in fundamental truth, they were, I insisted, melodramatic exaggerations—and potentially harmful exaggerations. They were overstatements that, if taken at face value, would threaten the core of the American tradition.

At that time, if John had told me, as he does tell us in his Romanell Lecture, that "we find ourselves in a situation which, in its most profound sense, *does not work*. In short, I believe that the being of being is to be disconnected, ontologically adrift," I would have told him (tactfully I hope) that he was exaggerating and that his recent remark in the afterword, that we are all "ontologically disconnected," was unhelpful melodrama.

Today my response to such existentialist claims made in the context of American philosophy is radically different from what it was thirty or forty years ago, and, I trust, wiser. While acknowledging that there are commonalities in "the American experience" so richly discussed by McDermott from the beginning of his career, I recognize now that, despite those commonalities, philosophers working within the American tradition can have experiences in their personal lives that differ in philosophically significant ways. I'm someone who has never had the experience of being "ontologically disconnected," as McDermott often has. Note the contrast between my trumpet-vine story and John's afterword story of a woman run over by a trolley and the "lonely," "disconnected" potatoes rolling out of her shopping bag to come to rest at John's five-year old feet. "Those potatoes taught me," John says, "that our journey, stellar or impoverished, ultimately goes nowhere. Addressing that baleful news is a central motif of our journey philosophically taken."

I'm not sure why I have never had the experiences of "ontological disconnectedness" that John takes to be of such philosophical significance. Is it because the circumstances of my family background and childhood were different from John's? McDermott describes himself as a "proletarian ethnic." Though I share with John a New York City birth and childhood in the 1930s, I come from a family background of many centuries of Protestant privilege—colonial governors, colonial lords of the manor, members of the Constitutional Convention, colonial mayors of Philadelphia and New York City, Episcopal bishops, admirals and generals, university professors and presidents, and so on. It seems to me entirely understandable for my grandmother to present American history to me in such a way that family history and American history in general were inseparably intertwined. She took it for granted that I would come to share her intimate personal connection with the course of American history. By osmosis as much as by overt instruction I came to feel deeply connected with American culture and its history. Perhaps because I was so deeply rooted culturally, I was unlikely to feel the "ontological disconnectedness" that the "lonely" potatoes evoked in McDermott.

Another explanation for my never having the sort of dark existentialist experiences that John describes occurs to me. My matriarch grandmother and her family felt meliorism in their very bones. To be sure, meliorism is also a crucial part of John's outlook. But for my grandmother, meliorism was central to her very being. She had an awesomely powerful faith that organized effort could bring more nectar into the American world. During the Progressive Era her family was deeply involved in reform politics in New York. In that era, her brother, a protégé of Teddy Roosevelt, was chairman of the Republican Party of New York County and the representative to Congress from the east side of Manhattan, the so-called Silk-Stocking District. With Protestant passion he fought the myriad forms of political corruption in New York politics, especially Tammany. Melioristically, he never for a moment doubted that organized effort by persons of good will could bring ever more nectar into the lives of every New Yorker, from those on the bottom rung of the socioeconomic ladder to those on the top rung where he and his family had for so many generations perched. Although he felt powerfully the presence of sin in America— and in himself—I doubt that he ever felt "ontological disconnectedness."

These personal stories bring me to the question I want to ask John about ontological disconnectedness and the American experience. Do you think, John, that the experience of ontological disconnectedness is so central to the American experience that someone who has never experienced ontological disconnectedness has not had a fully authentic American experience? I am myself inclined to believe that the experience of ontological disconnectedness is related to the American experience in a way analogous to the way mystical experience is related to religious experience. It is possible, indeed it is very common, to have had many fully authentic religious experiences without once having had a mystical experience. I ask this question because, though I applaud John's drawing our attention to the dark existentialist experiences that that are often neglected in philosophical discussions of American thought, I resist the idea that anyone who lacks such experience is somehow less authentically American in his or her experience.

Next I would like to ask John questions about his views on urban aesthetics that Rich Hart so helpfully discusses in his piece entitled "Landscape and Personscape in Urban Aesthetics." Before asking questions, let me say that I find McDermott's aesthetics of the ordinary utterly convincing. A Deweyan-Jamesian-Langerian aesthetics has never been more eloquently and concretely elaborated. What I find most appealing in John's aesthetics is his call for "making relations." I share his conviction that aesthetic values are found in fields of relations. My own lifelong identification of aesthetic value with relationality has so pervaded my thinking that the late Ed Madden, a dear friend of both John and me, enjoyed teasing me about it. "Peter," Ed would often joke as we sat in his study drinking Irish coffee, "you've never met two things that you weren't sure were internally related to one another." It was obvious to Ed that this powerful disposition of mine was as aesthetic and moral as it was metaphysical. Perhaps Ed also teased John about his obsession with relationality.

I also applaud John's sharp focus on urban personscapes of the ordinary in his aesthetic outlook. In that connection I would like to tell a story that I think illustrates how high culture can powerfully interact relationally with the quotidian.

My childhood in New York City was spent in a house of my modernist-architect father's design in the Turtle Bay Gardens section of the East Side of Manhattan. Turtle Bay Gardens, as those of you who are New Yorkers may know, was a full block between Forty-Eighth Street and Forty-Ninth Street and between Second and Third Avenue, cooperatively built by a group of affluent people in the arts. For example, Katherine Hepburn's house was a few doors down from ours on Forty-Ninth Street. Among the many notable features of this development was that all the houses in the entire block shared a huge well-tended backyard, called the Gardens, but the developed block also was nestled against an extremely ungarden-like feature of urban life, the Third Avenue elevated railroad. With boyish glee I could run from my bedroom window where I could see the trains in all their elevated glory to the other side of the house where I could look out on the vast Gardens. I'm sure that the relational and aesthetic tension between the industrially gritty Third Avenue El and the lush Gardens was part of what accounted for the choice of the site by these artists.

Some of my most nectar-filled memories as a small child are of lying in bed at night while hearing the clanging and screeching of a passing train and watching the play of light from the train on the ceiling of my room. Though I was much too young to distinguish consciously between aesthetic experience and nonaesthetic, in retrospect it is obvious to me that this was an aesthetic experience of the ordinary. But it was a childhood aesthetic experience of the ordinary through a prism of modernist art. Our modernist house was filled with modernist paintings, sculpture, and furniture. In my bedroom as well as throughout our home were many works by my painter godfather Clement Hurd, who some of you may know as an illustrator of children's books. Clem's most commercially successful children's books were *Goodnight Moon* and *Runaway Bunny* by Margaret Wise Brown. Anyway, my point is that my childhood aesthetic experience in the dead of night of the passing of the quotidian elevated train was an experience through the prism of modernist high art. I was experiencing the harsh noises and light patterns of the train as if they were a piece of modernist painting and music—an avant-garde opera, if you will. It was as if Clem and his pal, my modernist musician-poet Uncle Monty, had designed this artistic display for me to enjoy each night.

Now, the question I would like to ask John is this: In a culture like ours in which works of high art in millions and millions of reproductions saturate the culture at every level—in street and magazine advertisements, hotels, public buildings, not to mention the originals in museums open to the public—how should we understand the significance of our experiencing the ordinary through multiple prisms of high art? Although doubtless my own case is extreme, I believe that this situation is pervasive in our mass media culture. I wonder, John, in what sense and in what degree the ordinary is still accessible to us.

PART ONE

THE ETHICS OF BELIEF

The apparent freedom we have to choose our beliefs is a well-entrenched philosophical topic. Many prominent thinkers including Pascal, James, and Clifford have all expressed provocative views. It is a topic highly relevant to pragmatically based epistemologies, since our evidence for believing a proposition is frequently incomplete and inconclusive. In the essays selected, readers will be able to observe Hare's development on this topic. We have included two of his early essays, "The Right and Duty to Will to Believe" as well as "William James, Dickinson Miller, and C. J. Ducasse on the Ethics of Belief." Both nicely demonstrate Hare's historical grounding and technical ability. Along with these we have also included a more recent essay, "Problems and Prospects in the Ethics of Belief," where Hare argues for the relevance of so-called overbeliefs for modern views of epistemology.

Each essay is important for different reasons. The first thoughtfully yet forcefully evaluates cases made against the will to believe. The second connects Hare's well-known interests in James with the lesser-known

Miller and Ducasse, who were important to Hare's formative years as a thinker. In fact, Hare would go on to coauthor a book on Ducasse. In the final essay a mature Hare integrates forty years of philosophical wisdom with contemporary views in epistemology. The end result is a masterful work on philosophical naturalism.

ONE

THE RIGHT AND DUTY TO WILL TO BELIEVE

with Peter Kauber

R ights and duties to will to believe have too long been considered an embarrassing indulgence by philosophers who pride themselves on their methodological rigor. A fresh look at William James's work will show how a more robust, though no less analytically rigorous, ethics of belief is possible.

The history of James's ethics of belief is a stormy one, filled with mainly hostile criticisms on the part of others, with seminal suggestions, gropings, and retractions on the part of James himself. At various points in the development of this ethics of belief, one encounters such expressions as "duty to believe," "will to believe," and "right to believe," the last gaining prominence (and the others dropping out of sight) as James grew older. This has suggested to many commentators that the earlier expressions "duty to believe" and "will to believe" were rightly retracted by James, under the critical assault of his contemporaries. It is our point, first, to show that this is not so—that there are in fact good Jamesian arguments for the retention of the expressions "duty to believe" and "will to believe." Second, keeping the notions named by these expressions has interesting implications for the best-known aspect of the ethics of belief: namely, overbelief. Finally, we will suggest a terminology for use in future considerations both of James's ethics of belief and of the ethics of belief in general.

First, one preliminary. From a contemporary point of view, the very meaningfulness of the notion "ethics of belief" presents a problem, and James's somewhat uncareful terminology exacerbates the difficulty. The question is, simply, whether belief is enough like a voluntary act to warrant its subsumption under moral categories. The question is too complex to fully answer here, but it will become clear in what follows that, for James, belief *is* subject to the will and, thus, an ethics of belief is not, as is sometimes supposed, a total absurdity. Contemporary analyses of the problem tend to reinforce the Jamesian view, and we can utilize the conclusions of that study as follows: To the extent that James means to talk of belief as assenting, there is some sense to be made of voluntary belief (or disbelief, or suspension of belief); to the extent that he means by belief the disposition to act, we must interpret "ethics of belief" as elliptical for "ethics of trying to believe" (disbelieve, or withhold belief).[1] In short, one conception of belief leads directly to the meaningfulness of the notion "ethics of belief," while the other places the "ethics" in the context of so-called "enabling" phenomena, these enabling acts being those which tend to *lead* to belief, disbelief, or suspension of belief.

I

As early in his career as 1875, in a review for the *Nation*, James spoke of the duty to believe.[2] Though it was already typical of James to claim that the acquisition of truth, at least in some instances, required a prior act of faith or trust—in short, belief—he now felt compelled to add: "furthermore . . . any one *to whom it makes a practical difference* (whether of motive to action or of mental peace) is in duty bound to make it. If 'scientific' scruples withhold him from making it, this proves his intellect to have been simply sicklied o'er and paralyzed by scientific pursuits."[3] Thus, in addition to the well-known *right* to believe, a stronger *duty* to believe was here being advocated.

This pronouncement was scarcely off the press before it was assaulted, in this case by none other than Chauncey Wright. Wright, in private discussion, forced James to retract the word "duty." Not one to stand up easily to the older and dialectically superior Wright, James softened (unnecessarily) his position as follows: "All that he [James] meant to say was that it is foolish not to believe, or try to believe, if one is happier for believing."[4] This appears to be the first occurrence of James's use of "unfortunate" terminology with regard to the ethics of belief issue. The fact is, the remainder of James's philosophy virtually *dictates* the use of such expressions. He should have stuck to his guns! We will attempt to show this, first with regard to the expression "duty to believe."

One must recall the importance with which James viewed the moral project. His famous discussions of religion, free will, and pluralism are grounded in the overarching need for ethical behavior. The preeminence of this endeavor for James, along with the nature of the theoretical position he maintained here, has immediate implications for the ethics of belief.

The essence of James's moral view is contained in his sole systematic discussion of the topic, "The Moral Philosopher and the Moral Life."[5] For our purposes, it is the nature of the single "categorical imperative," maintained by James, that requires consideration. After discovering that "*the essence of good is simply to satisfy demand,*"[6] James says that "there is but one unconditional commandment, which is that we should seek incessantly, with fear and trembling, so to vote and to act as to bring about the very largest total universe of good which we can see."[7] Thus each of us is *obliged* to act so as to satisfy as many human demands as is possible.

Once we have understood this, we must reexamine the connection between action and belief. This becomes interesting indeed, for it is obvious that James views the relation as a rather tight one, leading us to suspect that, for him, if there are any duties *at all*—and we have noted that there surely are—then there will be duties to believe. That there are such duties to believe can in fact be shown.

At many points, James practically *identifies* belief with action: To believe a proposition is to act as if it is true, while on the other hand, action is significant of belief.[8] However implausible such an account may seem, the implications are that *all* duties (involving actions) require duties of belief. At other times, James appears (more plausibly) to identify belief with the *disposition* to act; here, belief yields action under the appropriate circumstances, while the fact of action signifies belief only upon certain conditions having been met.[9] Beliefs, from which actions *tend* to follow, are themselves enabling phenomena, prods to action. To the extent to which we are obliged to act in such and such fashion, we are similarly obliged to generate, if possible, the conditions which will enable or reinforce the primary morally required act. Under the dispositional analysis, then, we are obliged, we have a duty, to try to believe those propositions which will enable, or reinforce, us in our moral responsibilities.

The point here is that, given James's views on morality in general, coupled with his views on the relationship between belief and action, it follows that we have *duties* to believe. For, either beliefs mean acts, in which case when we have ordinary duties to act, we have duties to believe; or beliefs are dispositions to act, in which case when we have ordinary duties to act, we have duties to try to acquire dispositions. Thus James's philosophy as a whole warrants the reintroduction of the expression "duty to believe."

In 1896, James published his most famous essay, "The Will to Believe."[10] Criticism was immediate and forceful. James was accused of advocating a "will to deceive" or a "will to make-believe." A careful reading of the essay might have dispelled such an idea, though it should be remarked that certain philosophical discussions of the times reinforced such misinterpretation.[11] While James of course recognized the unfairness of much of this criticism, he himself came to question the tactical validity of the title (which he had borrowed from Renouvier): "I once wrote an essay on our right to believe, which I unluckily called the *Will* to Believe. All the critics, neglecting the essay, pounced upon the title."[12] James suggests here and elsewhere that the title is unfortunate rather than incorrect; others, however, have taken this to indicate a retraction of the expression. In any event, "will to believe" is a legitimate expression for a legitimate undertaking (given that certain conditions are met), on Jamesian grounds.

The focus of the essay "The Will to Believe" is a defense of our right to believe, in the absence of sufficient evidence for or against the belief—utilizing as the most convincing examples cases where beliefs are self-fulfilling—as well as an explication of the claim that under certain conditions we are forced to believe, again in the absence of adequate evidence—in short, that in some cases suspension of belief is impossible.

While we must say more about these concerns, it is sufficient to point out now that possessing the *right* to believe is not the same thing as *actually believing*, and thus the most straightforward sense of "willing" to believe is simply the exercising of the right to believe in cases where the belief in question is not already held. Now, *if* the right to believe is legitimate, under the conditions set out by James, then, it would appear, so is the willing. On this interpretation, those who wish to attack the legitimacy of willing to believe seem required to deny that of the right to believe. Yet the fact of the matter is, many philosophers have come to accept the right while remaining adamantly opposed to acquiescing in the will. We hope to shed some light here.

Our general intent is not that of defending the right to believe; it is rather to show that, on Jamesian grounds, there is justification for the retention of the expression "will to believe," once the acceptability of the right to believe has been established. To this end, we must examine the conditions under which the will is operative, and legitimately so, in the acquisition of belief. But there is one sense in which the will to believe functions in *defense* of the right to believe, and an initial brief look at this defense is in order.

James argues, in "The Will to Believe," that when an issue cannot be settled on intellectual grounds, then, of the hypotheses comprising the option in question, we have a right to believe whichever hypothesis *tempts our will.* In short, the "will" to believe is one of the conditions governing the right to believe; it is always live hypotheses, never dead ones, to which the right to believe is applicable. True, James sometimes distinguishes between "wish" and "will";[13] it would be more appropriate in that case to speak of the wish to believe as lying back of the right to believe. On the other hand, James more often characterizes the will simply as our active nature in general, and this of course would encompass desires, wishes, interests, etc.[14] In this latter, broader sense, then, the right to believe is dependent upon the will.

The defense of this view follows immediately from James's moral theory. In "The Moral Philosopher and the Moral Life," James argues persuasively that *every* demand made by a living being ought, prima facie, to be honored: "Take any demand, however slight, which any creature, however weak, may make. Ought it not, for its own sole sake, to be satisfied?

If not, prove why not."[15] But our wishes, wants, desires—our willings—are demands and should, in the absence of arguments to the contrary, be fulfilled. And it is precisely the point of "The Will to Believe" to show that some such arguments to the contrary are inadequate.

So much for the straightforward sense in which the right to believe is dependent upon the will. The more involved cases concern the function of the generating beliefs, the right to which has *already* been established. For James, there are two respects in which the will functions toward effecting belief: in the act of assent, and in the acquisition of dispositional belief.

It must be emphasized that many—perhaps most—of our beliefs are acquired through means independent of the will. First, there is the fact of "primitive credulity," the view that anything experienced (sensed, thought of) will be believed unless (or until) contradicted by something else experienced (sensed, thought of, already believed). Belief then is primary and in this sense, not really a function of the will at all. We are captive audiences with respect to the passing mental scene: "The sense that anything we think of is unreal can only come, then, when that thing is contradicted by some other things of which we think. *Any object which remains uncontradicted is ipso facto believed and posited as absolute reality.*"[16]

Not only does primitive credulity fix belief in realms where no incompatibilities arise, but, further, an enormous part of our thinking is simply intellectually coerced, by logic and experience in the form of evidence. As James puts it, speaking of our scientific and common-sense knowledge, "free-will and simple wishing do seem, in the matter of our credences, to be only fifth wheels to the coach."[17] Here, within science (in its "small" hypotheses at least), James rides with the Huxleys and the Cliffords. But he hastens to add:

> Yet if any one should thereupon assume that intellectual insight is what remains after wish and will and sentimental preference have taken wing, or that pure reason is what then settles our opinions, he would fly quite as directly in the teeth of the facts.[18]

We must examine the ways in which the will functions in effecting belief.

For our purposes, James's analysis of assent begins with the theory of primitive credulity, and what we must consider is the situation under which primitive credulity breaks down. Assent, in the sense of will, occurs only when experiences are incompatible.[19] For James, the "object" of consciousness can never be self-contradictory, and any perceived incompatibility must result in a choice, on the part of consciousness, to adhere to one or another consistent way of thinking. It is this "choosing" which way of thinking to adhere to (believe) which constitutes our first category of "willing to believe." For James, it is not that *all* belief is assent in the sense of decision, but rather that any incompatibility in beliefs which tempt our will must issue in such a decision. Thus is required a *will* to believe.

We might imagine James's method of assent functioning adequately in situations involving epistemic stalemate, issues concerning which evidence is balanced, pro and con (including, of course, cases in which there is *no* evidence either way). Even here, however, the forces of tradition, inertia, habit, though nonevidential, might serve to hinder the free determination of belief by the will. Further, James's mature ethics of belief in no way restricts the right to believe to conditions of epistemic stalemate. It is rather the existence or inexistence of "sufficient" evidence which functions as the major determinant for deciding on the legitimacy of the right to believe. And in such cases, where evidence is neither balanced nor sufficient to determine the issue on intellectual grounds, we cannot simply assume the adequacy of mere willing for effecting belief. It is for these reasons that James must address himself to the problem of the acquisition of dispositions.

To the extent that belief is a *disposition to act*—and this is one of the views on belief maintained by James—then the acquisition of a belief will in effect be the acquisition of a disposition or habit, and anything which promotes the latter likewise generates the former. It can be understood why the acquisition of dispositions becomes problematic once we have understood the limitations of assent. After James has shown the necessity of belief's resting upon an act of will, whenever incompatible conceptions of the same object are entertained, his discussion takes a pessimistic turn, as he now questions whether indeed "will" is up to the task of generating belief: "If belief consists in an emotional reaction of the entire man on an object, how *can* we believe at will? We cannot control our emotions. Truly enough, a man cannot believe at will abruptly."[20] But one *can* gradually and deliberately come to believe, one *can* acquire those dispositions to act which signify belief.[21]

Now in a sense there is nothing new here at all. Such techniques are at least as old as Aristotle, and James himself cites a literature dealing with the subject of acquiring dispositions.[22] The importance of the view derives from James's acceptance of the dispositional analysis of belief; the *will* to believe is now the deliberate acting-as-if which, carried through persistently enough, leads ultimately to belief itself, to *habits* of action. It simultaneously raises anew the fact of the ambiguities present in James's theory of belief since he here distinguishes sharply between deliberate actings and habits of action, dispositions to act: Once this distinction is drawn, no simple *identity* of action and belief is tenable.

Finally, on several occasions James lays out the mental correlate of the behavioral procedures outlined above. He refers to the "faith-ladder" by means of which the mind is carried from the mere *wish* to believe to the actual willing:

(1) There is nothing absurd in a certain view of the world being true, nothing self-contradictory.
(2) It *might* have been true under certain conditions;
(3) It *may* be true, even now;
(4) It is *fit* to be true;
(5) It *ought* to be true;
(6) It *must* be true;
(7) It *shall* be true; at any rate true for me.[23]

As for the logic of the progression: "Obviously this is no intellectual chain of inferences, like the *sorites* of the logic books. Yet it is a slope of good-will on which in the larger questions of life men habitually live."[24] Indeed, if the faith-ladder were a *sorites*, there would be no need whatever to pronounce upon the will to believe, nor to defend the right.

We have distinguished a right to believe from actual believings. James limits the former to cases in which intellectual evidence fails of being coercive or even sufficient, and in such a realm the will is, at least in some instances, to tip the scales of belief. And once again, we must emphasize that, while James often spoke in terms of forced options and self-fulfilling beliefs, the right to believe is *not* limited by James to these two categories.

We are forced to deal with a full-blown will to believe. James's psychology provides for two kinds of will to believe: the decisions of assent (where ways of thinking are contradictory) and the acquisition of dispositions. But we must ask, finally, if any cases of willing to believe are also cases to which the right to believe is legitimately applied. For, should it turn out that every case of the will to believe is illegitimate from the point of view of the conditions governing the right to believe, then there would be little reason for the retention of the will to believe within James's ethics of belief.

The least controversial application of the right to believe might well be to a joint case of epistemic stalemate and forced option. If the will to assent is *ever* to be effective, it should be so in cases of epistemic stalemate. It is precisely here, where incompatible hypotheses balance evidentially, that the additional force of assent, no matter how small, could tip the scales. And surely in some cases, where evidence alone is weighed by the mind (rare as these might be), the will would, on James's analysis, determine belief, particularly in a case of forced option where, by definition, "leaving the field" is precluded. It is because evidence is so seldom the sole determining factor that we must look beyond mere assent. Thus, confronted with a forced option, the individual is compelled to believe and, while the *evidence* may balance, tradition, social pressure, and other forms of inertia may line up behind one hypothesis while our desires may favor the (an) alternative. It is here that the long, deliberate march to the acquisition of a disposition (i.e., acquiring the belief we desire to hold) is most relevant. Thus we find that the regions of right and will to believe are not mutually exclusive, and further conclude that the "will to believe" is indeed a legitimate expression for a legitimate undertaking, once the right to believe is granted.

It has so far been the point of these remarks to argue for the retention within James's ethics of belief of the expressions "duty to believe," "will to believe." It has been noted, first, that James's ethical theory implies a duty to believe. Further, once the distinction is recognized between the right to believe and the exercising of that right in cases of beliefs not already held, then the will to believe—precisely this sort of exercise of the right, not the will to deceive, to make-believe—becomes problematic, while James's psychology provides the concepts of will required. Clearly there *is* a will to believe, and clearly *some* cases of its application are justifiable. It remains for us to consider somewhat more carefully the conditions of its legitimacy. In short, we intend to determine some of the implications for the ethics of belief of the retention of both of these conceptions.

II

By 1895 James's ethics of belief comprised at least the following elements:

(1)   We have a duty to attend to all accessible evidence. This we call the *duty of attention*.[25] We take this to include the duty to seek out the evidence, as opposed to merely attending to that which is conveniently available.

(2)   When "sufficient" intellectual (i.e., logical and observational) evidence is accessible, we have a duty to believe in accordance with that evidence. This we call the *duty of accord*.

(3)   When sufficient intellectual evidence is lacking, we have certain rights of belief; we have the right to believe, at our own risk, any hypothesis which tempts our will. This "right" is clarified as follows:

    (a)   In cases where we are confronted by a forced option, composed of two hypotheses, we have the right to believe either one and disbelieve the other, but are not free to suspend belief concerning either of them—in short, forced options preclude suspension of belief, logically. This we will call the *necessity to believe*.

    (b)   In cases where we are not confronted with a forced option, we are free to believe, disbelieve, or *withhold belief from* the various hypotheses involved. This we will call the *right to believe*.

Often James's right to believe is interpreted as being applicable only to genuine (forced, live, and momentous) options and, possibly, to self-fulfilling beliefs. That examples of each were utilized by James to make plausible the right which he was defending is not at issue. The plain fact is, he did not restrict his right to believe to these two categories.

On the basis of our remarks so far, we find the following elements must be included:

(4)   We have a right to will to believe; the initial limitation here is to confine the will to believe to those propositions which we do not now

believe but to which we have the right. Despite James's despair over the expression "will to believe," it appears that he continued to accept the enterprise of willing to believe.

(5) There are cases in which we have duties to believe. When we have ordinary duties, the doing of which could be assisted or effected through believing a hypothesis or hypotheses, then we have a *duty to believe* or try to believe such hypotheses. There is no evidence which convinces us that James continued to explicitly maintain the existence of this duty past 1875, but we have endeavored to show that his philosophy as a whole entails such a duty.

Within the context of this roughed-out sketch of the ethics of belief, our task now is to scout the interrelations between the will to believe and the right and duties of belief. The adequacy of attempts to admit the right while rejecting the will to believe is questioned, while a Jamesian limitation on the will to believe is developed. We shall urge that a *duty* to will to believe is implied by James's philosophy as a whole; thus, those who would reject out of hand any deliberate attempt to acquire beliefs not firmly based on evidence must be sorely pressed.

In considering the various criticisms directed at James's "Will to Believe" essay, both by his contemporaries and by ours, we are faced with the fact that many of James's readers, while sympathetic to the right to believe, nonetheless have coupled this with a profound reluctance to abide any will to believe. Yet if there is a right to believe, then this suggests the prima facie legitimacy of deliberately effecting assent precisely in the cases of propositions not now held but belief in which has been found permissible. Further, it is not clear how the right to believe *can* be sustained without at the same time countenancing a right to will to believe. An examination of even the least controversial cases of the right—namely, the forced option and the self-fulfilling belief—is illustrative.

As suggested earlier, the most acceptable cases of a right to believe are found in connection with the forced option-epistemic stalemate combination; in fact, some have misjudged the extent of James's right to believe, and have incorrectly limited that right to precisely these cases. Yet such a move seemingly fails to rescue one from the need to deal with a legitimate willing to believe. For, the *necessity to believe* which is generated by the forced nature of the option leaves open the question *which* hypothesis is to be believed. The fact of epistemic stalemate removes from that determination any possibility for settlement on intellectual grounds. Our "passional" or willing nature *must* decide the issue, and the issue *must* be decided—such is the logic of the case. It is difficult to see how those who would reject the will to believe while accepting the right are to gain solace from a limitation of the latter to cases of forced option and balanced evidence.

Others might be inclined to admit a right to believe in cases of self-fulfilling belief. Or, as is more likely, they might allow cases of self-fulfilling belief *and* cases of forced option within the pale—but no others. The "self-fulfilling" character of a belief fails, however, to alter one whit the fact of the distinction between a person's right to believe and his actually believing that to which he has a right. If one has a right to believe x because belief in x is self-fulfilling and because x is desirable, but at the same time one does not now believe x, then what is one to do? He cannot *acquire* the belief in x, if he has it not, without *willing* to believe it (we are assuming neither coercive nor sufficient evidence for x is available, of course).

There is a means of extrication here: namely, to limit the legitimate class of beliefs inadequately grounded in evidence to *beliefs now held*. One has a right to certain propositions but only if one believes them already. When one is confronted with a forced option, then, which hypothesis one has a right to believe is determined strictly by what he believed prior to his being confronted—the alternative, even if its evidential status be identical with that of the hypothesis already believed, is ruled out of bounds. What one is to do in cases of forced options where neither (none) of the hypotheses is held in advance becomes baffling indeed. In cases of self-fulfilling beliefs, again assuming inadequate evidence, one would be entitled only to those self-fulfilling beliefs which one maintained already. The "right" to believe is now conditioned not only by the self-fulfilling nature of the belief and the desirability of its object, but also by the fact that one now possesses that belief.

This is indeed a curious state of affairs. Such arbitrariness would be attributed by a Humean to "carelessness and inattention"; would be blasted by a Cartesian via his methodological skepticism. Closer to home, James's own view that beliefs held are innocent until proven guilty serves here only if one conveniently forgets that *desires, demands, impulses,* and *needs* are, on James's theory, similarly innocent until shown otherwise (if even they *can* be shown otherwise)[26]—and it is precisely such interests which open the door to the will to believe.

Given the foregoing discussion, one suspects that the willful acquisition of belief is taken to be so fraught with danger that any temptation to acquiesce in such a doctrine is to be strenuously resisted, regardless of the cogency of any arguments in favor of the less awesome right to believe. As it happens, there are good Jamesian grounds, too, for resisting the adoption of any *unrestrained* will to believe, while at the same time James refused to knuckle under to the pathological fears of his more squeamish (or perhaps less honest) contemporaries and thus abandon the will to believe altogether. In short, the will to believe can conflict with a more fundamental element of the ethics of belief, namely, the duty of attention; and, as the latter is—one might say—the "cardinal principle" in James's ethics of belief, the former must be restricted accordingly.

Our claim that the will to believe is capable of conflicting with the duty to attend to evidence is not new. James's will to believe was vigorously criticized in his own time, and one of those criticisms involved precisely this issue. Peirce, reading "The Will to Believe" and fearing that he was witnessing a resurgence of the method of tenacity, cautioned James: "'Faith,' and the sense that one will adhere consistently to a given line of conduct, is highly necessary in affairs. But if it means you are not going to be alert for indications that the moment has come to change your tactics, I think it ruinous in practice."[27] That such liabilities are involved in "trust" or the "faith-attitude" motivates us to prod our imaginations further.

One of James's most famous applications of the right to believe is to the issue of faith in God. It is unnecessary, for our purposes, to discuss the question whether or not this issue presents a forced option. The point is, it is a question concerning which evidence is insufficient and, should believing in God tempt the will, and it is tempting for many, then we have a clear-cut case of a right to believe in God.

Let us assume that we have in the past taken a negative or at least skeptical attitude toward this assertion of God's existence and that we find ourselves, epistemic inadequacy notwithstanding, unable to simply *assent* to the proposition that God exists, much as we might wish to. Our past attitudes and behavior have become habitual, and these nonevidential factors are preventing our simple assent. We therefore undertake to will to believe, in that more deliberate sense of James's: That is, we undertake some course of action, in a very painstaking way, which, we hope, will issue ultimately in belief. What courses of action are open to us?

We might ingest a drug whose effects are well known to include simulated (or perhaps actual) mystical experiences. If, after taking the drug once, we do experience these effects, we might initiate a regular program of ingestion. On the other hand, we might arrange to have an electrode implanted in the "pleasure center" of the brain: Each time the word "God" occurs to us, or is read or heard by us, the brain is to receive electrical stimulation so that eventually the notion of God becomes strongly associated with extreme pleasure. We might initiate a plan of selective attention, focusing on purchasing Bibles, going to church, reading religious news and articles, associating with religious people, praying, meditating, etc. Or we might employ someone to establish an advertising campaign to bombard us with the latest religious gimmickry, guaranteed to sell us on religion. The problem here is simply that actions and programs have effects *other* than (or beyond) those intended. We might indeed come to believe in God. But what other beliefs, attitudes, and values might we come to hold as a result? In particular, do any of these means involve the potential undermining of our capacity or desire to attend to evidence? Should this occur, the will to believe—or rather our particular implementation of it—conflicts with our *duty* to attend to the evidence.

It might be pointed out that the real possibility of this conflict occurring is a function of the method employed, the implementation chosen, and that *James's* particular means, namely, the deliberate acting-as-if (going to church, saying prayers, etc.) appears less harmful, threatening, or risky than drug-taking, brain-surgery, or self-deception through the arts of selling. It is our point only to call attention, once again, to the dangers involved in willing to believe, even when the right to believe is granted. Whether or not a particular method *has in fact* undesirable side effects is a matter for empirical investigation.

The foregoing considerations lead us to suggest that a metaprinciple be included in the ethics of belief, to indicate the order of priority in the event of a conflict between the will to believe and the duty of attention:

(6) No technique is allowable which, when employed to facilitate or implement the will to believe, has (appears to have, or tends to have) the added consequences of seriously rendering the subject incapable either of desiring to apprehend or of in fact apprehending further evidence, either on the issue in question or on any other issue.

While it is correct to say that James showed inadequate concern over this problem of the possible conflict between (1) and (4), and thus never explicitly stated a principle equivalent to (6), we are clearly true to James's intentions in adding such a principle. In many cases James justified over-belief (belief transcending the evidence) on the grounds that such beliefs could either produce the conditions under which additional evidence might be had, or produce the evidence itself. And, on James's view, since not all cases of overbelief are cases of self-fulfilling belief, we must assume that such newly discovered evidence could be positive *or* negative—in fact, he occasionally states this explicitly. In short, James's views virtually imply such a principle as ours.[28]

We have attempted to examine the reluctance with which thinkers have responded to the will to believe by considering, first, the interrelatedness of the right and will to believe; and second, the constraints upon the will to believe which James's own views seem to dictate. Nevertheless, nothing in that discussion must necessarily dislodge a staunch refusal to admit as legitimate the deliberate acquisition of belief even on the part of those who continue to sympathize with the right to believe. On the other hand, it seems to us that the implications of the *duty* to believe must surely undermine even this extreme of tenacity. James's philosophy provides us both with the duty to believe itself and with examples in which that duty might well be invoked.

It has been urged that James's moral theory implies a duty to believe. Since beliefs either are themselves actions or generate actions under the appropriate conditions, when we are ordinarily obliged to act, we are also obliged to believe or try to believe those propositions which will effect or aid in effecting such an act. For beliefs are, at the very least, enabling phenomena. If we call acts which must be done in order to do one's duty "secondary" or "enabling" duties, then primary duties generate enabling duties, and "trying to believe" is precisely such a secondary or enabling duty, in any case where that belief leads to the initial, morally required act. If the propositions we are obliged to believe are not now held by us, then we have a duty to try to believe them—we have, in short, a duty to will to believe.

Granted that James's writings offer us virtually no cases of explicit duties to believe—the sole exception being the *Nation* article of 1875—are there not examples of beliefs which, *on Jamesian principles*, ought to be held? That is, are there not Jamesian primary duties which generate enabling duties to believe? If so, what beliefs become obligatory? We will suggest that meliorism—a doctrine central to James's philosophy—is precisely such a belief. Our task will be to make plausible the claim that belief (or trying to believe) in meliorism is morally required, this duty being generated by that primary moral duty consisting of James's single categorical imperative.

Certainly James's pluralism militates against legislative pronouncements. An early note reads: "[Man's desires] exist by mere self-affirmation; and, appealing for legitimation to no principle back of them, are the lowest terms to which man can be reduced."[29] While this radical subjectivism may at times appear softened, there is throughout James's writings a respect for individual differences which simply rules out the proliferation of moral imperatives. James's single "categorical" imperative—that we must act to maximize the amount of good in the universe—is itself conditional upon the adoption of the moral endeavor itself. Should an individual be born and develop minus the sentiments grounding the ethical project, no amount of legislating would suffice, nor would it be really appropriate, in James's eyes. But surely one can, even within James's framework of tolerance, criticize and evaluate beliefs, philosophical and otherwise. There are, after all, questions of consistency (and this despite James's subjectivity); beginning with such and such motives or interests, this or that belief is warranted; should one or more points of departure be accepted, other points become causally related, logically presupposed, or morally obligatory. This understood, what can we say concerning the relationship between James's moral imperative and the philosophical position called meliorism?

Assuming that the moral project itself has been acknowledged—and without this assumption our talk of the ethics of belief is somewhat pointless—James's imperative becomes operative, and the question is, simply: What secondary duties, if any, are generated by our primary moral duty, so to act that the maximum of human demands are met? Our move is to consider what conditions should be fulfilled in order to secure the doing of our duty. Seemingly the best means of carrying out this primary duty is to maximize the energy available for (and expended in) the moral endeavor. In short, the strenuous moral attitude, so often emphasized by James, is to be reinforced to the fullest extent possible—"moral holidays," though legitimate, are not to proliferate. Any belief which might generate or aid in generating the strenuous moral life is thus called for; in fact, that set of beliefs *most* capable is morally required. Up to this point, then, the argument is simply this: The maximization of good requires those active attitudes characterizing the strenuous moral life, and, in turn, any beliefs seen to underlie those attitudes are themselves morally obligatory. Such beliefs are simply the enabling beliefs spoken of earlier.

Our claim is that one of the enabling beliefs called for is meliorism. This view asserts that the world is neither wholly good nor wholly evil; that the relative amounts of good and evil are alterable—in particular, that the relative mount of good can be increased—and that human agents, through moral effort, can be effective in increasing the relative amount of good in the world. The Jamesian analysis might proceed as follows. First, the issue is one in which scientific evidence is insufficient. After all, pessimists will claim that evil lurks everywhere in reality, all phenomenal appearances to the contrary notwithstanding. Optimists will claim some version of the reverse. How is phenomenal science to deal with such claims? Second, it appears that the belief in question alone generates the conditions for stimulating the strenuous moral attitude, granted that our beliefs and attitudes are to be consistent. Consider the alternatives. If the world is really irrevocably evil, then we are powerless to change it; if it is irrevocably good, then our activity is superfluous. If the qualities of good and evil are fixed, then again our efforts are fruitless. Believing any of these would lead, logically, to a moral slouch. Finally, if it is not *we* who are efficacious in controlling, at least to some extent, the relative mounts of good and bad, then our active life is irrelevant to these relative amounts. In short, the strenuous moral attitude presupposes some such view as meliorism, and logical consistency requires that if the former be obligatory, so too the latter. The categorical imperative, then, generates as a secondary duty the acquisition of the strenuous moral attitude which, in turn, generates the duty to try to believe the melioristic position to be true. There is a duty to believe in meliorism, and for those not possessing such a belief, there is in addition a *duty to will* to believe in meliorism.

Why then does James seemingly back off from the duty to will to believe, or even from the duty to believe itself? We have pointed earlier to the reluctance with which a pluralist must approach moral legislation. Perhaps James, despite his moral imperative and its implications, found himself constitutionally incapable of cramming philosophical views—or, for that matter, *any* views—down anyone's throat. Yet the obligations and legislations seem clear enough. We must conclude that James's philosophy as a whole implies a duty to will to believe.

Hence:

(7) When ordinary moral duties generate secondary or enabling duties to believe, then we have the duty to will to believe precisely those propositions not presently believed but to which we have this duty to assent.

III

One consequence of the foregoing analysis is our realization of the complexity of the entire ethics-of-belief theme. The failure of many commentators to distinguish the right to believe as it operates in cases of forced options from that right as it functions in less restrictive contexts is unfortunate, while some, recognizing the distinction, nevertheless employ terminology which appears to us to be misleading. Our reintroduction of the duty to believe complicates the issue further. Hence we are proposing that certain expressions be employed to mark the distinctions we have found it necessary to draw, hoping that future discussions both of James's ethics of belief and of the ethics of belief in general will aim at mapping the territory we have barely scouted. We have already introduced most of these expressions in the course of our remarks. In more systematic form, our proposed terminology is as follows:

First, there are the *epistemic duties*: there are two of these, namely, the *duty of attention* (including the duty of inquiry) and the *duty of accord*.

The former states simply that we have a duty at all times to seek out and attend to the evidence; the latter states that, whenever evidence is sufficient, we have a duty to believe in accordance with that evidence.

Second, there is the *duty to believe*. This asserts that whenever we have ordinary moral duties, the doing of which could be assisted or effected through believing a hypothesis, then we have a duty to believe or try to believe such hypotheses.

Third, there are the *rights of belief*. There are again two of these: the *necessity to believe* and the *right to believe*. The former applies to forced options. It asserts that, in such cases (and where evidence is insufficient), we have a right to believe any one of the hypotheses comprising the option (one which "tempts the will") and to disbelieve the other(s), but that suspension of belief concerning any of these hypotheses is precluded. Thus the necessity to believe is in fact the preclusion of doubt; it does *not* state that belief in some particular hypothesis is necessitated. The *right to believe* is to apply to the Jamesian class of cases where the option is *not* forced. In such a case, and again in the absence of sufficient evidence, we have the right to believe, disbelieve, or withhold belief from (i.e., doubt) a hypothesis.

Finally, there is the *will to believe*. This is simply the exercising of the rights and duties of belief in cases where a legitimate belief is not now held. When one has the moral right to exercise these rights of belief, then we say that one has the *right to will to believe*, on condition that (6) is respected; and when one has a moral duty to effect belief, then we say that one has a *duty to will to believe*.

TWO

WILLIAM JAMES, DICKINSON MILLER, AND C. J. DUCASSE ON THE ETHICS OF BELIEF

with Edward H. Madden

I

In American philosophy, few papers have generated as much discussion as William James's essay "The Will to Believe." James is America's most provocative philosopher, and this is one of his most controversial papers. According to R. B. Perry, "the most important of the discussions stimulated by *The Will to Believe* was that in which the leader was Dickinson S. Miller, one of the closest of James's personal friends, and on other issues a powerful ally."[1]

After reading the title essay of *The Will to Believe* as separately published in 1896, Miller engaged in extensive correspondence with James. In one of these letters James, with his customary charm, refers to Miller as his "most penetrating critic and intimate enemy."[2] The ideas Miller developed in this correspondence he brought together in an 1899 paper published in *Ethics*.[3] So critical was this paper that, we learn from the unpublished Ducasse-Miller correspondence, it "strained [their] friendship."[4]

Although Miller said that "there has been no human being of whom I should like so much to be a disciple as William James,"[5] he continued to develop his criticism of the Jamesian doctrine of the will to believe for more than half a century. That Miller's interest in this topic never lessened is evident in his publication of another criticism[6] of the doctrine in 1942 and also in his lengthy correspondence with C. J. Ducasse in the 1940s and 1950s, when Miller was in his seventies and eighties. This correspondence was started when Miller sent Ducasse an offprint of his 1942 article. In reply, Ducasse said that he agreed with almost all of Miller's criticisms of James, but that there was one significant point left untouched.[7] Miller, as we shall see, unwilling as ever to yield ground on this topic, replied that even that remaining point must fall before his critical assault.[8]

A few years later Ducasse sent Miller the typescript of *A Philosophical Scrutiny of Religion*, inviting him to write a foreword. Although Miller expressed great admiration for the scholarship of the book, he declined because he said he would feel conscience bound to criticize both Ducasse's defense of the right to believe and his favorable appraisal of the results of psychical research.[9] Ducasse's insistence that he shared Miller's reservations about the will to believe[10] led to further correspondence in which they continued to clarify their respective positions.

As this correspondence will demonstrate, Miller and Ducasse are extraordinarily acute in philosophical analysis, and consequently, by discussing these letters on the will to believe, we hope to clarify an issue which sorely needs clarification.

II

Ducasse initiated the correspondence with the following:

January 18, 1943

Dr. Dickinson S. Miller
95 Pinckney St.
Boston, Mass.

Dear Professor Miller,

Thank you for the reprint of your paper on James' "Right to Believe." I had intended to read it when I saw it in the *Philosophical Review*, but was diverted from my purpose by some one or other of the numerous things demanding immediate attention when one is teaching.

Permit me to say that your discussion seems to me admirably sound, penetrating, and clear throughout—much more so than any other that has come to my notice. This is what I expected, for in the days, about 1908, when I began to study philosophy, my teacher, Savery, often had occasion to point to the keenness of various articles from your pen.

The one important and sound point in James' essay—which, however, has nothing to do with volition to believe, or with a right to will to believe—seems to me to be that there are options which are "forced" not only in the sense that there are only two alternatives, Yes and No, but in the sense that the situation is one in which we cannot suspend decision between Yes and No (as Descartes mistakenly asserted was always possible), because to refuse to decide is then automatically to be deciding; *and* that there are cases of this sort in which evidence as to the probability of truth of a decision on one side or the other is wholly lacking to us or is equally balanced. To illustrate this to my students, I usually ask them to suppose themselves on a street car going down a hill when suddenly the brakes fail. There are then two possible things for a passenger to do: to jump off, or to stay on. But he does not known which of the two is more likely to save him from injury, and he cannot put off deciding which to do until he has consulted records of other accidents. In such a case decision is and has to be non-rational in the sense of being instinctive, impulsive, temperamental, instead of based on in your words "a rational gauging of the exigency." It might be denied that there ever is a case where we have an exact balance of evidence pro and contra, or no evidence at all pro and contra. But if it is true (as I think it is) that there are such cases, then I do not see how it can be denied that in those cases the decision has to be—not indeed irrational, but—non-rational in the sense just stated.

This is, I think, the one sound point in James' essay; but of course it affords no basis whatever for choice one way rather than the other; for claiming, for instance, as I think James was temperamentally disposed to do, that the instinct of affirmation is sounder, wiser, more likely to pick on the truth, than the instinct of negation. It means only that there are cases in human affairs where decision has to be pure gamble.

But although pure gamble is, by definition, non-rational in the sense that the alternative one chooses to bet on is not known to be more probably true than the other; yet pure gamble may be rational in another sense, viz., that, irrespective of whether one loses or wins one's bet, some immediate reward is known to be attached to *the act itself of betting* on a given side, whereas no such reward, or a lesser one, is attached to the act of betting on the other side.

Let us suppose, for instance, that a person—perhaps as a result of childhood suggestion—finds himself believing that there is a God, and that, after careful scrutiny, he comes to the conclusion (a) that the conception of God which he holds is free from internal inconsistencies; (b) that there is no empirical evidence either for or against the existence of the sort of God he believes in; and (c) that his belief in that God is to him a source of comfort, courage, and strength, and an inspiration to beneficence, in his daily living; and, so far as he can see, has no bad consequences. Let us suppose, further, that this person knows that although beliefs cannot be relinquished or acquired by the mere volition, yet there are various psychological devices, to which one can, if one wills, have recourse, which in many cases are effective in inducing or destroying beliefs not based on a preponderance of evidence.

Then the question is: Ought such a person in such a case to try, through the use of these psychological devices, to destroy the belief he has in his God? Or ought he, by means of them, try to strengthen it? So far as I can see, the latter would be the rational thing to do; but it would be rational, not in the sense that there is a preponderance of evidence for the truth of the proposition he believes and that his belief of it is determined by this, but in the sense that although he has no evidence for or against the truth of that proposition, belief itself of that proposition has the effect of making him a happier, more courageous, more beneficent person than would disbelief of it.

I wonder whether this is not perhaps the, as it seems to me, sound idea which, in spite of all confusions and errors in James' essay, people somehow get out of it, and which vindicates something that might be not inaptly described as (in cases of the kind supposed) a right to believe.

Sincerely yours,
[C. J. Ducasse]

To this Miller replied:

20 January, 1943

Dear Professor Ducasse:
    . . . As to the street-car, yes, there surely might be a case where one would see no data for a conclusion and would go solely by impulse. It

would seem however possible, as you describe the case, to think in a flash of how the land lies at the foot of the hill, just what are the chances of a smash-up, and to make a hasty comparison of the danger of jumping off at once. Our most rational effort of the moment might not be rational in the eyes of careful subsequent reflection but it would be none the less our best effort of reason.

Your final question as to the legitimacy of choosing to strengthen a religious belief for which there is no evidence happens to be identical with one I have been putting to myself since the article appeared. My best answer is this. Choices are right or wrong according as they produce or tend to produce good or harm, satisfactory life or the reverse, for all those concerned. Now the great deficiency of our morals, it seems to me, lies in the absence of any emphasis on the conscience of the mind, on the duty of being as intelligent as we can. It is a central duty because unintelligence bears more fruit of misery, wretchedness, and frustration than any other human weakness or sin. From the point of view of life at large it seems of primary importance to think with our best intelligence and clearest realism on every subject. And particularly in religion the ill consequences of baseless faith are enormous. I could not therefore think that such a faith would be an inspiration to genuine beneficence in daily living; not as much beneficence as clear-sighted intelligence on the subject would bring. . . .

Yours very truly,
Dickinson S. Miller

In this exchange Miller's reaction to Ducasse's presentation of the right to believe is similar to the reaction to James which he expressed in 1899 and again in 1942. In horror, Miller had said in 1899 that " 'The Will to Believe' is the will to deceive—to deceive one's self; and the deception, which begins at home, may be expected in due course to pass on to others."[11] It is not surprising to find Ducasse as puzzled by this reaction as James had been. Ducasse, like James, had taken pains to stress that he was speaking only about situations in which there is no preponderance of evidence. He is not recommending that anyone fail to attend to evidence. To be sure, if he were asking that we ignore evidence, Ducasse could understand the charge that we are being asked to deceive ourselves and to abandon our intelligence.

There seem to be two possible grounds for Miller's prophecy of doom. First, he may fear that if we acquire or strengthen belief by the "psychological devices" Ducasse mentions, our belief will be of a dogmatic sort which will discourage further inquiry and prevent us from recognizing a preponderance of counterevidence should it appear in the future. This fear, however, appears to be unjustified because the belief which James and Ducasse are speaking of has no special immunity to criticism in the future should no evidence appear. Miller, like W. K. Clifford, wishes at all costs to avoid error and thinks that any belief not supported by a preponderance of evidence is an open invitation to error. James and Ducasse, however, have never suggested that we invite error by failure to attend to evidence. They understand intelligence to be attendance to whatever evidence can be found; intelligence for them, however, is not something which paralyzes persons when there is no preponderance of evidence.

Not only do James and Ducasse insist on the duty to attend to the evidence, but they also limit the right to believe to the situations in which an option is "living," "forced," and "momentous." Miller's worry is unjustified both because the number of situations in which the right to believe applies is small and because even in those cases constant attention to new evidence minimizes risk of serious error.

The second possible ground for Miller's prophecy of doom appears to be his anticipation of the spreading of the right to believe into areas in which there is a preponderance of counterevidence or in which the option is neither "forced" nor "momentous." Belief without a preponderance of supporting evidence is, for Miller, a malignancy which will spread throughout our whole body of beliefs. This fear appears to be greatly exaggerated if we once understand that James and Ducasse insist on the duty to attend to evidence. In fact, James expressed fear of the opposite sort of spreading. He feared that this skeptical condemnation of belief where there is no preponderance of evidence might spread to areas where there is a supporting preponderance in the form of a probability. If we accept Miller's views, we may eventually find ourselves and others insisting on near certainty and unwilling to act on probabilities. One kind of spreading is as dangerous as the other.

III

In his book *A Philosophical Scrutiny of Religion*, which appeared about ten years after this exchange of letters, Ducasse used almost exactly the same example of a "living," "forced," and "momentous" option.[12] The only difference was caused by the passing of the streetcar from the New England scene, and it became an automobile which one must decide whether to jump out of. He went on to say that for many persons, religious belief is "genuine in the very sense specified, and . . . cannot be decided by them rationally for lack of the knowledge which would be necessary for this. *For such persons*, then, and, *in the absence of possession by them of such knowledge, wishful decision* as to whether to believe or not believe any particular such religious doctrine *is not merely legitimate but unavoidable*."[13] Ducasse makes it clear that this right to believe is not merely something to which the uneducated and unsophisticated can resort.

> No matter how intelligent, educated, vigorous, powerful and resourceful a man may be, there is always some limit to what he can do to safeguard his values. Hurricanes, earthquakes . . . threaten at times . . . either himself or the things or persons he holds most dear, in spite of his best efforts to safeguard them.[14]

Such a man, Ducasse claims, is justified in accepting a "hypothesis which, if true, would offer a way, more or less probably effective, of safeguarding those values, or if not, of anesthetizing himself more or less to their loss."[15] In short, for Ducasse a "fool's paradise" is preferable to a "fool's hell."[16] Again Ducasse is insisting that we have a right to believe anything which we think will be a "source of comfort, courage, and strength," and an "inspiration to beneficence" *provided that* it is not in conflict with our duty to attend to evidence, and it cannot be in conflict with that duty if there is no preponderance of evidence. Intelligent and well-educated men are equally justified in taking advantage of this right because there are always areas in which no investigators have been able to establish a preponderance of evidence.

However, when Ducasse sent the typescript of the book to Miller and invited him to write a foreword, Miller while deeply pleased, was no happier with Ducasse's remarks in the book than he had been about what he had said in the letter some nine years before.

186 Marlborough Street
Boston 16 10 Sept. '52

Dear Professor Ducasse:
... My difference of conviction as to will to believe happens to be profound, bound up with the principle that ethics calls upon us to be as intelligent as we can for the sake of results in life. I wrote two articles against W. to B. the first being during James's life, and it strained our friendship. ...

Yours cordially,
D. S. Miller

In his reply Ducasse tries to explain that the right to believe, as he conceives it, is in no way incompatible with being "as intelligent as we can."

September 11, 1952

Dear Dr. Miller:
... As to the "will-to-believe," it seems to me that I agree heartily with what you say about it. I don't have any use for any *will* to believe. I hold that one ought indeed to be as intelligent as possible, and always to abide by such evidence as one has or can get. Only, there are cases where one has none and can get none, or where the probabilities are equal pro and contra, and yet where one cannot put off choosing because putting it off is equivalent to choosing a particular one of the alternatives. In such cases, the choice—or, if one cannot properly call it "choice," then the "behavior" or "action" or "belief"—cannot, *ex hypothesi*, be based on the greater probability, but has to be a psychological instead of a logical matter. Whether James meant more than this by his unfortunate expression "will to believe," I am not sure. But, to me, his pointing out that situations of this peculiar kind sometimes occur is the real contribution of his essay. ...

Cordially yours,
C. J. Ducasse

Miller in his next letter is more passionate than ever in his rejection of the view that it is ever justifiable to believe anything without adequate evidence.

186 Marlborough St.
Boston 16
[no date]

Dear Professor Ducasse:

... I am flatly and insuperably debarred from doing what I want
to do, namely acting upon your suggestion that I write a Forward,—
which is, I think, the highest philosophical honour I have ever received.
And this because I *couldn't* honestly write it; some of the chief points
of Tendency in the book (I have given you frankly my estimate of its
scholarship, breadth, intellectual grasp and style of exposition) are in
conflict with convictions as deeply rooted and (critics might say)
fanatically held as any in my life.

... I hold that a religion should be true and verifiable and that in-
dulging a belief—not doing everything to dispel it in one's own mind—
which is unsupported by evidence is in deadly enmity with human
progress. I hold that none of James's arguments are sound—e.g. that
suspension of judgment is practically equivalent to disbelief. Above
all, I do not accept the view that theism (for example) is a subject in
which one has no evidence and can get none; I believe that there is
decisive evidence against one conclusion and in favour of another. I am
persuaded that human progress is bound up with the will to believe
the evidence—and the will (it often requires a good deal) to suspend
judgment where there is none. . . .

Yours cordially,
Dickinson S. Miller

Once again Miller expresses his conviction that the right to believe is
incompatible with the intelligence necessary for human progress; he fails
to recognize that intelligence, as we have pointed out, does not demand
suspension of belief but demands only attention to evidence. Miller argues for the absolute prohibition of belief without supporting evidence
on the grounds that if any such belief is permitted it will spread and the
ability to suspend judgment will be destroyed; the prohibition must be
maintained at any cost.

Miller's fears are similar to the fears of those who urge an absolute prohibition of lying on the grounds that if a few lies are permitted they will
lead to more and more lies until it is impossible to trust anyone. However, it is clear that there are special circumstances in which lying is justified. Few wish to condemn someone for using a lie to save a human life,

and few expect that lying under such special circumstances will spread to ordinary circumstances. Similarly, it seems unreasonable to suppose that belief without supporting evidence in the special circumstances of "living," "forced," and "momentous" options will spread and destroy the ability to suspend judgment in ordinary circumstances.

Miller also challenges in this letter the notion that the right to believe argument applies to theism. He does not believe that, as far as theism is concerned, the evidence is in balance. It may well be that he thinks the evidence is in favor of theism, or conceivably against it; but in either case, on Ducasse's view, then, the right to believe argument does not apply. Ducasse himself, for that matter, does not believe that his argument applies to theism. He is quite convinced that the evidence of gratuitous evil shows conclusively that theism is false. Ducasse, however, does have certain nontheistic beliefs for which he does not have adequate evidence, which he would like to believe, and which therefore he insists has the right to believe.

IV

Ducasse in his next letter takes a somewhat different tack.

September 24, 1952

Dear Dr. Miller:

. . . It seems to me that you do not give sufficient weight to the fact that the regimen of strict reason, which is suitable and practicable for you, and pretty well for me too, is not so for the vast masses of mankind that have neither the intelligence, nor the education, nor the time to think things out, and yet have to act from moment to moment. For suspense of judgment—or I should rather say of opinion, since I would define "judgment" as opinion based on the weighing of evidence—furnishes no basis for decisions, and yet the inaction which such suspense motivates has consequences just the same; and these (as my example of the car running down hill, I believe, definitely shows) sometimes are the same as would be those of deciding in favor of one of the alternatives. Of course, you might say that although, in this example, the person concerned is confronted by a "forced" and "genuine" option, yet there are none such in religious matters. I am not sure that is so even for me; but I think that for many persons, being what, *psychologically*, they are at the moment—irrational, uninformed, and yet equipped with some beliefs which *they* rank as definite and certain knowledge—there are in religious matters some options that are "forced" and also "genuine" in the other two respects. True, these options would not be "genuine" for you or for me. But the persons I have in view are not you or me; they just don't have, and cannot get at the time or at all, the intellectual equipment possession of which makes those options not genuine. And yet they are alive (after a fashion!) and (*qua* human beings rather than mere animals) they have to have *some* set of beliefs by which to act. But here I go again! So I'll quit before this becomes another book.

> As ever, cordially,
> C. J. Ducasse

In order to avoid the complicated question of whether for the most intelligent and educated persons there is a preponderance of evidence and a "genuine" option in religious matters, Ducasse in this letter limits himself to the more modest claim that the right to believe should at least apply to "the vast masses of mankind" who are neither so intelligent nor so well educated. He asks Miller whether he wishes educated persons to try to persuade the less educated to suffer the serious consequences which suspension of judgment may have for them.

186 Marlborough St.
Boston 16 26 Sept. '52

Dear Professor Ducasse:
... I decidedly would not disturb the faith of anyone to whom it gave consolation and moral motive, if he was not . . . of a rational type; such disturbance would upset, do harm, cause unhappiness to no good end. Few people are rational helmsmen of their minds.

But I would not *advocate* the indulgence of any belief without sufficient reason.

I would not in a particular case disturb beliefs ready-formed, but would not advocate forming such beliefs. . . .

Moral life, i.e. life guarding and increasing happy life, does not depend on unevidenced doubtful beliefs, though to an unenlightened person it may be promoted by them.

Cannot agree that suspension of opinion (taken with whole situation) furnishes no basis for decision. The decision to investigate, the

decision to wait and see, the decision to *try* an action though igno-
rant of how it will turn out, are possible. Etc. We may *try* because attractive, not on any probability—and without belief. . . .

Ever cordially yours,
Dickinson S. Miller

In great haste—

Miller concedes that we should not disturb the unsupported beliefs of
those not "of a rational type." He appears to make this concession on the
civil libertarian grounds that we should allow someone to perform whatever immoral act (that is, a belief without evidence) he wishes so long as
the act does not adversely affect the welfare of others.

Miller asks only of James and Ducasse that they "not *advocate* the indulgence of any belief without sufficient reason." But it is doubtful that
James and Ducasse ever intended such advocacy. On the contrary, their
concern is to persuade Clifford, Miller, and others to stop advocating suspension of judgment as a duty. They would agree that advocating belief
without evidence as a duty is unjustified, but they insist that advocating
suspension of judgment as a duty where there is no preponderance of evidence is equally unjustified. The doctrine of the right to believe is an attempt to discredit both duties and to uphold only the duty to attend to
the evidence.[17] This doctrine does not discredit Miller's wish to himself
suspend belief in cases where there is no preponderance of evidence. The
right to believe is a defense of belief where there is a "genuine" option and
no preponderance of evidence, but it is also a defense of the right to suspend judgment under those circumstances. James (unlike Ducasse) may
personally prefer a more affirmative attitude but he does not wish to argue that Miller is abandoning his duty by suspending judgment. The right
to believe is the right, in circumstances where there is a genuine option
and no preponderance of evidence, to take any attitude our "passional nature" dictates. James and Ducasse are not disturbed by the fact that Miller's passional nature dictates suspension of judgment; they are disturbed
only by his attempt to impose his inclinations on everyone else; they are
disturbed by his attempt to show that it is everyone's *duty* to suspend judgment under those circumstances regardless of what their passional natures may demand.

Consequently, Ducasse can agree with much of what Miller says in this letter (the last which deals with the ethics of belief) without altering in the least the right to believe. Ducasse can agree that "moral life . . . does not depend on unevidenced, doubtful beliefs" and can agree that suspension of judgment for some people can furnish a basis for decision. He can agree on these points because he never intended to *exclude* suspension of belief as one of the attitudes which the passional natures of some people require and have every right to take. He intended only to include as equally legitimate (that is, equally compatible with the duty to attend to evidence) the attitudes of those with different passional natures.

THREE

PROBLEMS AND PROSPECTS
IN THE ETHICS OF BELIEF

Prospects have never been brighter for an ethics of belief in the tradition of William James. But the development of such an ethics of belief will require collaboration between diverse philosophical traditions and between philosophy and science, collaboration that we have not seen hitherto. Accordingly, I want to use this occasion to make a plea for cooperative effort. I urge cooperation between those working in the tradition of pragmatist metaphysics, those working in analytic epistemology, and those working in cognitive science. Let me briefly describe the relevant aspects of the current philosophical scene in a way that makes clear the need for such cooperation.[1]

Many philosophers trained in the analytic tradition have come to recognize that the epistemic cannot be understood in abstraction from the nonepistemic. They have further come to believe that knowledge cannot be understood in abstraction from the processes that produce it and the consequences that flow from it. They have also come to recognize that knowledge from the internal perspective of the knower cannot be understood in abstraction from knowledge by standards external to the knower—and conversely. Finally, they have recognized that personal knowledge can be understood only in the context of social knowledge. In short, they have come to reject dualisms that pragmatist metaphysicians long ago rejected.

We can best begin to appreciate these current developments by contrasting so-called "reliabilist" and "responsibilist" epistemologies. The reliabilist judges the epistemic merit of a belief on the basis of the reliability of the mechanisms which produced it. If those mechanisms can be shown to be of a sort that produce true beliefs reliably, then the belief in question is epistemically justified. This can be determined, the reliabilist supposes, without consideration of what the believer does or does not have access to; it can be done on a basis *external* to the consciousness of the agent who has the belief. The responsibilist, on the other hand, thinks that reliably produced belief is an ideal only and cannot be a requirement of epistemic justification; epistemic justification, the responsibilist says, is instead a question of whether the agent acted responsibly in the context of what was accessible to her.

This audience does not need to be told that responsibilist epistemology is part of a long history in this country of the evaluation of belief in ethical terms. William James proposed an ethics of belief, and C. I. Lewis also developed such a theory. Dickinson Miller and C. J. Ducasse carried on this work, and Roderick Chisholm, a student of both Ducasse and Lewis, is the most influential current proponent of such a view. Today an increasing number of philosophers are contributing to the systematic elaboration of an epistemology that relies on analogies with moral reasoning and rejects the dualisms I have mentioned. Lorraine Code, for example, urges that we reject a preoccupation with the "end-states of cognition" and concentrate instead on the processes used to achieve those end-states.[2] With that focus we come to recognize, she says, that "epistemic and moral considerations are so interwoven they cannot be absolutely separated."[3] She argues that we should judge the epistemic justification of a belief not on the basis of traits of the end-states of cognition but rather on the basis of whether the person came to the belief by way of a *responsible process*. A similar view is conceived in terms of "epistemic virtues" which the agent must manifest in prior actions if the resultant belief is to qualify as epistemically justified. James Montmarquet, who goes a good way toward making clear the notion of epistemic virtue, considers inadequate the view that an agent is epistemically virtuous if she is trying her best to arrive at the truth. "For just as a moral fanatic may qualify as conscientious without being, on balance, very virtuous at all (except to . . . co-fanatics), we can easily imagine an 'epistemic fanatic' who is not epistemically very virtuous at all—for example, an extreme dogmatist, absolutely convinced of his possession of the truth, absolutely convinced that his methods of study of some sacred text are everyday bringing in powerful new truths."[4]

Montmarquet suggests that a "balanced intellectual personality" will include virtues of two classes: impartiality and intellectual courage. The virtues of impartiality include "openness to the ideas of others, the willingness to exchange ideas with and learn from them, the lack of jealousy and personal bias directed at their ideas and the lively sense of one's own fallibility."[5] The virtues of intellectual courage include "the willingness to conceive and examine alternatives to popularly held beliefs, perseverance in the face of opposition from others (until one is convinced one is mistaken), and the Popperian willingness to examine, and even actively seek out, evidence that would refute one's own hypotheses."[6] The two classes of virtue are complementary sides of a balanced intellectual personality: the first, "the 'other-directed' virtues which are necessary to sustain an intellectual *community*," and the second, "the 'inner-directed' virtues of a person of high intellectual integrity."[7] These epistemic virtues, he holds, "are forms by which [epistemic conscientiousness] may be *regulated*. Unregulated by these, bare conscientiousness . . . may degenerate into some form of intellectual dogmatism, cowardice, or related evil."[8] Interestingly, Montmarquet notes that these are virtues only in our present epistemic situation with the world appearing to us as it does. *Other* worlds can be conceived in which they would not be virtues.

The social nature of knowledge has not been overlooked by contemporary analytic epistemologists, who have recently developed what is called "social epistemology." The attribution of knowledge to a person is considered partly dependent on intersubjective standards of evidentness, and intersubjective evidentness is partly a function of what evidence a normal inquirer has in a given epistemic community. Any standard of evidentness is thus sensitive to social context.[9]

Members of a society are often disposed to adopt the beliefs of others unselfconsciously. Although in traditional epistemology such suggestibility is considered an epistemic vice, recent social epistemologists have argued to the contrary. "If nine people report seeing a situation one way and I seem to see it another, this is surely very strong prima facie evidence of my error. It is possible, of course, that there is collusion among the nine, but by and large a tendency to take on the opinion of a unanimous majority in this kind of situation would serve me quite well."[10]

Belief perseverance is another epistemic tendency that is viewed differently today from what it was in traditional epistemology. We have a tendency to go on believing what we already believe. "This tendency will not outweigh the tendency to take on the opinions [of others] when the others constitute a large group. . . . Nevertheless, when the disagreement is with a single individual . . . [agents] will tend to persevere in their beliefs."[11] Although in the past this tendency has been assumed to be an epistemic vice, its usefulness has recently been pointed out. "Without a mechanism like belief perseverance, an agent would be faced with a choice between keeping track of the number of people who agree with each of his beliefs and those who disagree, or, alternatively, simply giving up beliefs for which evidence cannot be remembered whenever disagreement is discovered. Neither of these prospects is cognitively acceptable. The first requires extraordinary investment of cognitive time and effort; the latter results in large-scale dumping of beliefs in light of the frequency of disagreement."[12]

Other aspects of social epistemology are worth mentioning. For example, although epistemologists have traditionally assumed that for an inference to be reliable at all it must be reliable in all possible environments, recent social epistemologists have stressed that the same inference can serve well in one sort of environment and poorly in another sort of environment.[13]

Other social epistemologists have shown that a division of cognitive labor among subjects plays a major role in satisfying epistemic goals. One person's epistemic justification depends on the epistemic justification of others. Individuals in isolation would have a paucity of beliefs. Furthermore, the satisfaction of epistemic goals is well served by not having the same epistemic standard for everyone in a society. Different people usefully play different cognitive roles and epistemic virtue is relative to context. The demands of epistemic justification and virtue are relativized to roles and contexts. Epistemic rationality consists partly in forms of social interchange.[14]

Despite its important implications, this research in analytic epistemology with the help of cognitive science has received little attention from philosophers working in the pragmatic tradition. Although Peirce, James, Dewey, and Mead all took careful account of the empirical science of their day, today's pragmatists seem to believe that they can safely ignore recent work in cognitive science.

Perhaps the single most important development in recent epistemology concerns the relation between the epistemic and the nonepistemic. The epistemic is no longer considered to be a self-contained realm. As Morton White points out, this viewpoint is a natural development of William James's views.

White makes explicit and elaborates what he calls James's "epistemological corporatism" in an account of how we arrive at new opinions. "The individual has a 'stock of opinions already,' but he meets a new experience that puts them to a strain.' The result is 'inward trouble' for the inquirer. He tries to escape from this trouble by modifying his previous stock of opinions but . . . the inquirer saves as much of the stock as he can, thereby revealing the extreme conservatism affecting all inquirers."[15] In other words, James "thought that we test organically unified stocks of opinions rather than isolated opinions."[16] But, White argues, James includes not only opinions and experiences of a sensory sort. "One of the straining experiences can be a newly arisen desire that the opinions cease to satisfy . . . the affective or emotional part of our lives may have a bearing on what descriptive beliefs we are entitled to hold . . . ; a believer may change a descriptive belief, not because he is faced with a recalcitrant fact or sensory experience, but because he is faced with a recalcitrant emotion."[17] Let me give you White's example of this process. A mother has taken the life of a fetus that she has been carrying and she is confronted by a moral critic who presents the following argument.

(1) Whoever takes the life of a human being does something that ought not to be done.
(2) The mother took the life of a fetus in her womb.
(3) Every living fetus in the womb of a human being is a human being. Therefore,
(4) The mother took the life of a human being.

Therefore,

(5)   The mother did something that ought not to be done.

The premises of this argument form a stock of opinions which may be strained by an emotion or feeling that prompts the denial of that conclusion. The denial of that conclusion might be justified by arguing that a normal human being would *not* feel obligated *not* to take the life of the fetus. In that case, the whole mixed stock of opinions or premises may be denied and then altered.[18]

The mother has a choice among ways of altering the stock of descriptive and normative beliefs. She may reject the descriptive statement that a live fetus is a human being or she may reject a moral principle in her effort to organize her mixed flux of sensory experience and feeling.

Among the numerous other philosophers who recently have had interesting things to say about the relations between the epistemic and the nonepistemic, Richard Foley is one of the most noteworthy. Having worked out a theory of what he calls "epistemic rationality," Foley questions the tenability of "evidentialism," that is, the view that "epistemic reasons for believing something by their very nature are . . . superior to nonepistemic reasons for believing."[19] He thinks that it is clear that in the extreme case, for example, where the survival of the earth depends on a person believing proposition p that he has good epistemic reason to believe is false, it is rational for that person to believe p. He goes on to discuss the devices by which a person might acquire such a nonepistemically justified belief. He cautions that "given the holistic nature of beliefs, such a project frequently will involve [a person] not just in changing his attitudes toward p but also in changing his attitudes toward an enormous number of other propositions. For ordinarily, beliefs cannot be altered in a piecemeal fashion. . . . For example, if in order to win a million dollars, [a person] must come to believe that the earth is flat, he also is going to have to come to believe a whole range of other propositions that arc now epistemically irrational for him. Indeed, he presumably will have to come to believe that there is an enormous worldwide conspiracy to make it appear as if the earth is round when in fact it is flat."[20] Although Foley stresses that the effects of adopting epistemically irrational beliefs are not *always* far-reaching, the project of getting oneself to believe what is epistemically irrational is not "to be undertaken lightly."[21] He also makes the valuable point that there are normally good *non*epistemic, "practical" reasons against allowing practical considerations to motivate one to try to worsen one's epistemic situation. For although by deliberately worsening one's epistemic situation one may get oneself to believe what one has a practical reason to believe, worsening one's epistemic situation ordinarily will affect adversely one's chances of achieving one's other practical goals. This is an excellent illustration of how the epistemic and the nonepistemic are interconnected. Such interconnection is also apparent in the fact that it is a question of *epistemic* rationality whether a particular project of worsening one's epistemic situation for nonepistemic reasons will produce massive error and consequently disastrous practical consequences. Often the epistemic rationality of *second-order* beliefs about the nonepistemic rationality of first-order beliefs is crucial to reaching a conclusion about rationality, all things considered. This means that there is no incoherence in believing for good epistemic reasons that worsening one's epistemic situation is rational.

Foley suggests that one reason for its being unlikely that worsening one's epistemic situation will be nonepistemically justified all things considered is that usually the propositions which there are important nonepistemic reasons to believe are central to how we live (e.g., propositions about our own abilities) and those "propositions are just the ones that are least likely to be relatively isolated from other propositions."[22] He reaches the general conclusion that "insofar as it is now epistemically rational for an individual to believe that a deliberate worsening of his epistemic situation is likely to result in his choosing less effective means to [his other] goals than he would otherwise, he has reasons not to worsen his epistemic situation."[23]

But Foley also observes that nonepistemic reasons usually justify limiting the time and effort one devotes to trying to *improve* one's epistemic situation. Seldom do nonepistemic considerations justify a person in trying as hard as she can to improve her epistemic situation. It may be epistemically rational for a person to believe that additional epistemic effort will not result in greater success in reaching goals. At some point increased epistemic effort means less time and effort available to devote to one's various nonepistemic goals. Foley judiciously concludes that it is "rational, all things considered, for a person to be neither slovenly nor fanatical in his search to believe truths and not to believe falsehoods."[24]

He has not, Foley emphasizes, worked out a full theory of rationality which would require, among other things, a sorting out of the various kinds of nonepistemic rationality and a general theory of goals. As it happens, Paul Moser has made some progress in that direction. Moser distinguishes three types of rationality: epistemic, moral, and prudential. He shows how many of the traditional puzzles about the ethics of belief are generated by failure to distinguish these types of rationality. Having made those distinctions, he tries to answer the natural question of how we can resolve conflicts between types of rationality so as to arrive at "all-things-considered" rationality. If all-things-considered rationality is to be a distinctive sort of rationality, it must "allow for the possibility of each less general sort of rationality being overridden in an instance of rational conflict [and] . . . must require the consideration of factors other than the particular rational obligations in conflict."[25] All-things-considered rational belief must be most conducive to satisfaction of one's preferences regardless of whether they are epistemic, moral, or prudential preferences. He goes on to outline a theory of "superior preferences" as related to desires, goals and means to goals. Like Foley, Moser stresses the many complex interconnections between the epistemic and the nonepistemic. For example, in his analysis, a person's superior preference cannot "depend for its existence on an epistemically unjustified belief" of a person.[26]

A valuable feature of Moser's account is that he makes explicit the context-dependence of rationality. Something can, he thinks, be all-things-considered rational for a person in one context but not in another, due perhaps to a change of superior preference or to the relevance of additional conflicting rational obligations. All-things-considered rationality is also a function of the total evidence that a particular person in particular circumstances has and of the person's ability to recognize, after reflecting on her total evidence, that doing whatever is in question is likely or unlikely to satisfy her superior preference.

In light of these developments, let us examine a number of objections which have been made to the view that nonepistemic reasons for belief can sometimes override epistemic reasons, objections to the view that we are sometimes justified in believing beyond the evidence. In what follows

I hope to show that James's approach to such overbelief is fundamentally sound.

It is often objected that, if psychological devices are used to produce belief where the evidence is balanced pro and con or there is little evidence on either side, overbelief may be considered to have beneficial consequences only if one fails to take account of effects on *other* beliefs. It is predicted that when such devices are employed, there will be spreading of overbelief to other beliefs including beliefs against which there is a preponderance of evidence. This objection, however, fails to note an equally legitimate concern, a concern characteristic of James. If an ethics of belief demands that we refuse to use devices to produce such a belief, that demand is likely to spread to other beliefs where the evidence is overwhelmingly favorable and to lead one to reject them out of a commitment to what might be called epistemic asceticism. Any worry we may have about the spreading of *over*belief must be balanced by a concern about the spreading of *under*belief. Underbelief can be just as disastrous as overbelief. Cases abound in which underbelief paralyzes action—the underbeliever refuses to act on probabilities. For example, many Germans during World War II had ample evidence that genocide was going on but refused to believe it on the basis of what they considered inadequate evidence. A demand for certain knowledge of consequences of action in practical situations can be just as harmful as wishful thinking about those consequences, and there is no reason to suppose that underbelief will be less likely to slip down a slope to the disastrous extreme of epistemic asceticism than overbelief will be to slip down a slope to a disastrous extreme of belief against conclusive evidence. Such armchair speculation about the long-term consequences of epistemic strategies cuts both ways. Moreover, such sinister tendencies in overbelief are not found in numerous empirical studies of overbelief. Emphatic rejection of overbelief on the grounds that the acquisition of one belief will inevitably affect a great many other beliefs that have some logical relation to the original belief reflects lack of familiarity with relevant empirical studies. Studies indicate that beliefs are acquired by processes "operating in a highly local manner" without involving "an agent's entire corpus of belief."[27]

As I have already noted, Foley worries that, "if in order to win a million dollars, [a person] must come to believe that the earth is flat, he also is going to have to come to believe a whole range of other propositions that are now epistemically irrational for him. Indeed, he presumably will have to come to believe that there is an enormous worldwide conspiracy to make it appear as if the earth is round when in fact it is flat." But again, armchair psychology is not good enough. Although doubtless there are situations in which the acquisition of one belief will cause changes in many other beliefs, it has been found by psychologists not to happen in many instances where we might a priori expect it to happen.

Hard as it is for some philosophers to accept, human beings in their intercourse with the world do very nicely despite having a formally inconsistent body of beliefs. There is good reason to suppose that certain fonts of epistemic inconsistency are adaptively advantageous.

Foley, you'll recall, also is concerned that the most important overbeliefs are usually about matters that are "central to how we live," such as beliefs about our own abilities, and those "propositions," he says, "are just the ones that are least likely to be relatively isolated from other propositions." Despite the common-sense plausibility of that worry, it is not supported by empirical studies, which have shown that people can have overbeliefs about their abilities without harmful ramifications in their other beliefs.

Philosophers inclined to speculation about the effects of overbeliefs would do well to study a recent book by Shelley Taylor.[28] Taylor, herself a psychological researcher, provides a summary of recent research on what she calls "positive illusions." Her picture of human cognitive powers is very different from what philosophers have traditionally presented. Human beings are found to be amazingly adept in using overbelief and inconsistency to their adaptive advantage. Genuinely adaptive rationality turns out to be akin to the concept of rationality James proposed.

Cognitive research has established that "the normal human mind distorts incoming information in a positive direction. In particular, people think of themselves, their future, and their ability to have an impact on what goes on around them in a more positive manner than reality can sustain. . . . At one level [the human mind] constructs beneficent interpretation of threatening events that raises self-esteem and promotes motivation; yet at another level it recognizes the threat or challenge that is posed by these events."[29]

For example, most people "believe that they drive [a car] better than others. . . . [I]n one survey, 90 percent of automobile drivers considered themselves to be better than average drivers [and] these beliefs sometimes show an unresponsiveness to feedback that reminds one of a very young child. When people whose driving had involved them in accidents serious enough to involve hospitalization were interviewed about their driving skills and compared with drivers who had not had accident histories, the two groups gave almost identical descriptions of their driving abilities . . . and this was true even when the drivers involved in accidents had been responsible for them."[30] Although we philosophers may lament such cognitive behavior, there is considerable evidence that overbeliefs of this sort, at least when mild, are often beneficial in their overall consequences. The truth is that the common-sense psychology that philosophers have always relied on is incapable of predicting the long-term on-balance consequences of such positive illusions. This is not to deny that overbelief can sometimes have disastrous consequences. It is to say that empirical research has shown that on-balance beneficial overbeliefs are much more common than has hitherto been supposed. We can no longer consider that overbeliefs in general have a presumption against them. The numerous empirical studies Taylor reports have shown that overbeliefs about certain basic matters have a presumption in their favor. The types of overbelief that have a presumption in their favor are those about: (a) self-worth, (b) ability to control the environment, and (c) favorable events in the future.

A few examples. When people have overbeliefs about their own abilities, they have more benign views of other people and are more likely to help people in need. People can tolerate extreme stress better if they have an overbelief in their ability to control that stress. If a person has an overbelief about the good things the future holds in store, present sacrifices may seem bearable steps on the way to a more promising future.

But the role of different types of overbelief is complex. Even in the course of a single project, different overbeliefs can be beneficial at different stages. "At the outset of the project, it may be very valuable to have a certain naive optimism that the goal will be accomplished. The ability to keep that final state in mind may provide motivation and persistence when otherwise one might be tempted to turn away from the task because the goal is so far off. However, as work toward the goal progresses and the goal comes into sight, [another kind of] optimism may be more functional. In the last stages of a project, as a goal is coming to fruition, what becomes important is the ability to see exactly what tasks remain to be accomplished and to put one's mind to doing them, rather than to keep an overly optimistic assessment of the future in mind."[31] The healthy human mind, it turns out, is adept at increasing or decreasing the degree of overbelief as the needs of the situation change.

Taylor summarizes the benefits of these three types of overbelief: "People who hold positive illusions about themselves, the world and the future may be better able to develop the skills and organization necessary to make their creative ideas and high level of motivation work effectively for them. They seem more able to engage in constructive thinking. They can tie their illusions concretely to the project at hand, developing a task-oriented optimism and sense of control that enable them to accomplish more ambitious goals. They are more likely to take certain risks that may enable them to bring their ventures to fruition. And they seem better able to choose appropriate tasks, gauge the effort involved, and make realistic estimates of their need to persevere. Moreover, by developing the ability to postpone gratification, they are able to commit themselves to a longer term task that may involve sacrifices and delayed rewards along the way."[32]

Taylor notes genuine risks in overbelief, risks that are especially obvious in matters of physical health. She gives this illustration. "A colleague was called in as a psychological consultant on a very difficult medical case involving a twenty-year-old graduate student with an inoperable brain tumor. The physicians knew that the patient was virtually certain to die within the next few weeks. Understandably, the young man resisted this prognosis and turned to an alternative treatment center for hope, inspiration, and help in curing himself. The counselor asked him to describe his life, in an apparent effort to determine what had brought on the tumor at such a young age. Most of the events of the man's life had progressed rather normally, except that his mother had died when he was sixteen. The counselor latched on to this as an explanation for the tumor, informing him that he had never successfully come to terms with the loss and adjusted to it. Only by doing so now would he be able to free himself of the cancer. The young man was given some mental exercises to perform that involved imagining the tumor gradually shrinking. He was also urged to come to terms with the loss, but not told exactly how to do so. Within days, the young man was seriously distressed, agitated over his apparent inability to manage the loss. He had always believed that he had done so successfully, but the counselor had persuaded him otherwise. He worked himself into near-frenzy."[33]

One important reason that positive illusions are so often on-balance adaptive is that human beings are able "to maintain self-aggrandizing views of themselves while simultaneously making adaptive use of negative information from the environment."[34] We can simultaneously process information in very different ways so that we get the benefits of *both* overbelief and epistemic rationality.

It is also interesting to note that, though the extreme overbelief of denial or repression is usually not adaptive, a healthy human mind can temporarily use denial adaptively. "If a child is hit by a car and killed, the mental response may be that the bodies were mixed up, that the child's friend, not one's own child, has died. Precisely because the dramatic and sudden news alters life so profoundly in so many ways, denial can serve a protective function while these changes are sorting themselves out. Thus, early on in adjustment to a life-threatening or shocking event, denial can be both normal and useful."[35]

Human beings are much more cognitively flexible than they are usually thought to be by philosophers. We can rapidly change cognitive strategies to adapt our cognitive powers to a changing situation. Our cognitive powers are also capable of simultaneously operating in diverse ways in a mix of strategies that allows us to use the most beneficial strategy for each aspect of our situation.

Much is known about the strategies we use to control negative information in such a way that we can maintain positive illusions and their benefits while simultaneously making adaptive use of that information. As Taylor points out, such cognitive flexibility has been recognized in literature as well as in cognitive psychology. George Orwell noted in the novel *1984*: "The secret of rulership is to combine a belief in one's own infallibility with the power to learn from past mistakes."[36]

Although philosophers have roundly condemned all forms of self-deception, there is much empirical evidence to support the view that "through the twin mechanisms of selective attention and selective memory, it is possible to self-deceive not only successfully but adaptively."[37]

There are adaptive limits to positive illusions. These can be seen most clearly in the manic period in the life of a manic-depressive. While manic, a person has greatly exaggerated positive illusions. While there are many historical examples of people being extraordinarily creative while manic, there can be no question of the overall harmful consequences of such a cognitive strategy. Contrary to the notions of rationality found traditionally in philosophy, there is no simple set of principles that will allow us to determine the best cognitive strategies. It is easy enough to point to examples of disastrous use of a strategy and also examples of successful use of a strategy. The trouble is that in much of our lives the cognitive situation does not admit of simple analysis. Consequently, I am not today recommending that we all set about systematically acquiring positive illusions of the sorts Shelley Taylor describes. Instead I am saying that overbeliefs have been so categorically rejected that philosophers have been blind to the adaptive flexibility of human cognitive powers. This failure was perhaps forgivable in the era of William James when empirical psychology was in its infancy. But cognitive science has flourished for some decades now and deserves more philosophical attention than it has hitherto received.

To be sure, contemporary epistemologists have often made use of the results of cognitive science. But such epistemologists are working in the analytic tradition and consequently have a seriously inadequate metaphysics, and in particular, inadequate conceptions of nature and experience. Philosophers working in the pragmatic tradition can do much to contribute a needed metaphysical framework. Let me give some examples.

(1) As you'll recall, Moser in his account of all-things-considered rationality relies on the notion of a "superior preference." But nothing is said about how those preferences arise. He treats those preferences as antecedently given. However, as every student of Dewey knows, every end-in-view is itself the resolution of a problematic situation. Some of you will recall the discussion of this by Hilary and Ruth Anna Putnam at the SAAP meeting last December in Atlanta (1989). In their illustration a graduate student in philosophy begins to wonder whether philosophy is what she wants to do. She ends up opting for a life of social service rather than a life in a philosophy department. Philosophers without the resources of pragma-

tist metaphysics ask what is the higher ranked end for which philosophy was given up. The Putnams point out there was no such end antecedently given in terms of which the student could decide what to do. "She had to discover the origin of her malaise and to institute the problem: namely, 'What end-in-view shall I now pursue?' The formulation of the new end-in-view of social service was itself the resolution of that problematic situation."[38]

(2) Although, as we have seen, analytic epistemologists such as Foley and Moser have come to recognize that the epistemic cannot be understood in abstraction from the nonepistemic, they lack a metaphysical framework within which to make sense of the natural dependence between the epistemic and the nonepistemic. The account of the cognitive in Dewey's *Logic* and *Experience and Nature* is set within an appropriate metaphysics, I believe.

(3) Both reliabilists and responsibilists in analytic epistemology recognize that knowledge cannot be understood in abstraction from the processes that produce it and the consequences that flow from it, but they offer no metaphysical analysis of the epistemic comparable to Dewey's account of value in his essay "The Construction of the Good."

(4) Contemporary epistemologists recognize that knowledge possessed by an individual can be understood only in the context of social knowledge but they lack a metaphysics which illuminates the complex relationships between the individual and society.

(5) Recent theorists of knowledge have been wrestling with the conflict between so-called "internalist" and "externalist" theories, and most have concluded that a sound epistemology must somehow combine crucial features of both types of epistemology. Surely they could make more sense of this combination if they could bring to bear the pragmatist view of how experience and nature are interrelated.

What is needed then is cooperative effort by cognitive scientists, analytic epistemologists, and pragmatist metaphysicians. The problems of the ethics of belief are formidable. Although it is clear that the role of over-beliefs has been badly misunderstood by epistemologists because they have not appreciated the adaptive flexibility of our cognitive powers, it is not clear what an ethics of belief that took full account of that flexibility would look like.

James appears to suppose that, if both our epistemic and nonepistemic demands are taken fairly into account, our beliefs on crucial issues will typically be optimistic. However, my colleague Newton Garver has taken James to task for this doxastic optimism. Garver uses the example of police reform to illustrate his objection to James's optimism. In Garver's account it is admitted that a belief that police reform is possible or impossible can play the legitimate role of an enabling belief, a belief that enables one to meet one's primary obligation to make our society more just and humane. He also admits that one has a right to either of the two beliefs since the evidence does not allow one to resolve the conflict between the two beliefs epistemically. However, Garver rejects the argument that "we need hope in order to act—and hope can survive only when there is a prospect for improvement and for the elimination of brutal excesses and aberrations of the police role,"[39] an argument he thinks is Jamesian. He argues that there is another "posture for a humane and compassionate person to adopt."[40] Does this mean that Garver thinks we have a duty to believe that police reform is impossible? Not quite. Despite his statement that "for an honest person, there is no real possibility of sitting on the fence," he describes his view as "the cynicism of [a] hard-headed epistemology, reminiscent of Clifford against James, which refuses to justify basic beliefs by their pragmatic necessity rather than their demonstrable truth."[41] According to Clifford, our duty is to *suspend judgment* anywhere and everywhere there is insufficient evidence. So, despite the fact that Garver's initial characterization of the problem suggests that we must choose between adopting an overbelief in the possibility of police reform and an overbelief in the impossibility of police reform, he ends up saying we are obliged to suspend judgment in the manner of Clifford.

It is important to note that Garver does not advise us to suspend judgment for the reasons Clifford would have us do so. Garver seems not to have categorically rejected obligations to have overbeliefs. He simply argues that in "a matter of public policy" an overbelief in the possibility of reform is likely to do more harm than good. "If [this approach] is," he says, "less adventurous than Jamesian optimism, it is also less pretentious and less dangerous. Perhaps a sense of adventure is appropriate in the matter of personal faith to which James addressed himself . . . but in the matter of public policy where the consequences may be that fellow citizens are bloodied, harassed, and imprisoned, caution would seem preferable to adventure."[42]

Although I agree that James is inclined to adopt *indiscriminately* belief in the possibility of reform, what I find troublesome in Garver's basically Jamesian position is that he concludes that suspension of judgment is morally required in all matters of public policy. I would urge instead a more flexible Jamesian view which, depending on the circumstances surrounding a particular social problem, advocates sometimes a pessimistic view, and sometimes an optimistic view. An indiscriminately pessimistic view such as Garver advocates may be as unfortunate in its consequences as James's indiscriminate optimism.

It is an open question whether Garver is correct in his suggestion that optimistic overbeliefs are generally more appropriate on personal matters than on social concerns. Surely this is another question in which armchair philosophy is not enough. Empirical studies are needed. Social psychologists might examine, for example, the role of pessimism and optimism in fostering or thwarting Soviet perestroika. My personal impression is that traditional Russian pessimism on matters of social reform is a formidable obstacle in the way of Gorbachev's economic reforms, but here as elsewhere in the development of an ethics of belief, philosophy should collaborate with cognitive science.

Another puzzle concerns the voluntariness of belief as a crucial presupposition of any ethics of belief. William James and all subsequent writers have recognized that only if belief is voluntary can persons be considered responsible for belief. There is now an extensive literature on what is called "doxastic voluntarism." Many have concluded that *direct* control of one's belief is impossible, but it is generally conceded that our indirect control is sufficient to justify often holding a person responsible for his or her beliefs. Although it is a complicated question for another occasion, in my view the voluntariness of belief is more comparable to the voluntariness of ordinary action than is usually supposed. Philosophers have tended to hold belief to a more demanding standard of voluntariness than they hold ordinary action to, and consequently have exaggerated the voluntariness of action and the involuntariness of belief.

Be that as it may, there is an interesting aspect of this problem that has been overlooked in the debates about doxastic voluntarism. It has not been

noted that overbelief about voluntariness of belief is beneficial epistemically and nonepistemically. A person who has positive illusions about her
control of belief is likely to be more strongly motivated to expend time
and effort in inquiry intended to modify belief. It is partly because a scientist presumes that he can make choices among beliefs that he develops
a program of empirical research. Similarly, a philosopher takes the trouble
to examine arguments on the assumption that she can choose beliefs
in light of the merits of those arguments. Even if it were true, as I think it
is not, that direct control over one's belief is never possible, *belief* in one's
direct control is, I suggest, of great importance to human inquiry. In other
words, overbelief in the voluntariness of belief has *extrinsic* or *instrumen-*
tal epistemic merit—it makes possible inquiry at the end of which there
is knowledge not otherwise available. Epistemic rationality demands
belief in the voluntariness of belief.

Interesting questions have also been raised about the consequences of
applying *moral* terms to belief as opposed to terms of *prudence* only. H. H.
Price, for example, argues that "the consequences of this doctrine that there
is sometimes a moral obligation to believe are of course pretty horrifying. The religious wars of the sixteenth and seventeenth centuries were," he
says, "based on such a theory."[43] In my view an otherwise laudable commitment to freedom of thought is partly responsible for philosophers such as
Price being appalled by the prospect of having duties to believe. Imprisonment, torture, or worse are imagined as the sanctions that would be imposed on persons morally irresponsible in belief. Surely it is possible to
distinguish between the sanctions appropriate for misbelief that causes
harm or prevents good being done and sanctions appropriate for overt
action that has those effects. Don't we distinguish between sanctions to
be imposed on people whose *characters* are morally objectionable and
sanctions to be imposed on those whose *overt acts* are objectionable? The
sanctions imposed for bad character may be only such things as social os-
tracism or denying them the respect they would otherwise receive. Execution, imprisonment, or fine are hardly called for. Analogously, lesser
sanctions can be imposed for misbeliefs; sanctions which, while not jeopar-
dizing freedom of thought, take seriously the moral consequences of belief.

Admittedly, this is a rather casual dismissal of the important problem
of determining the moral consequences of widespread adoption of the view

that persons are morally responsible for their beliefs. We don't have to look to the sixteenth or seventeenth centuries to appreciate the magnitude of this problem. Consider the late Henry Luce, head of Time Life, whose possession of enormous power to control the beliefs of citizens is vividly described by David Halberstam in *The Powers That Be*. Luce seems to have been convinced that people were morally irresponsible in believing that Senator Robert Taft would be a good president of the United States. So convinced, Luce deliberately manipulated the "truth" in his publications so as to make people believe in accordance with what he took to be their moral responsibilities.[44] This *is* "pretty horrifying."

Jonathan Harrison has raised another intriguing question about allowing moral reasons to override epistemic reasons for belief. He asks under what conditions it would be right or wrong to believe that whites are on average more intelligent than blacks. "It is an odd thing," he points out, "that the people who think it wrong for whites to believe that whites are more intelligent than blacks, do not usually believe it wrong for whites to believe that blacks are more intelligent than whites . . . [though from] this it would follow . . . that there are some true propositions that some, but not others, ought not to believe."[45]

This is yet another indication that the development of an ethics of belief is fraught with problems. However, as I suggested at the outset, a rapprochement between pragmatism, analytic epistemology, and cognitive science promises significant success in addressing those problems. Let me conclude, then, by repeating the plea for cooperative effort with which I began. In our day of philosophical pluralism, tolerance of other traditions too often leads to scattered effort and consequent lack of philosophical progress. In my view, if we are not to succumb to the cynicism of deconstruction, we have no choice but to foster a cooperative spirit.

PART TWO

REFLECTIONS ON CLASSICAL PRAGMATISM

B ecause Hare was best known as a pragmatist, it is important and appropriate to dedicate a section to this subject. We include here several of his essays dealing with classical pragmatism. Hare's essays on James have been the subject of significant debate. Scholars such as John McDermott and Charlene Haddock Seigfried have commented on Hare's work both at conferences and in print. The second essay on Frederic Harold Young is required reading for any serious scholar of pragmatism. Those who are unfamiliar with it will find the story of the Peirce Society's early days both compelling and edifying. Finally, we have included a short unpublished piece in which a forward-thinking Hare addresses the relationship between pragmatism and naturalism. Both stylistically and in terms of content, readers who knew Hare will find that this section represents him well. For those who are only beginning to appreciate his work, we believe that these pieces paint a vivid portrait.

FOUR

A CRITICAL APPRAISAL OF JAMES'S VIEW OF CAUSALITY

with Edward H. Madden

We are convinced that James saw the issues of causality in the proper light and correctly estimated the direction in which their solutions lie. He was right in arguing that potentiality and counterfactuality are irreducible ontological concepts and that the Humean is unable to make sense of them. Moreover, both his earlier and later efforts to supply the needed alternative analysis, though inadequate by themselves, provide genuine insights into a more adequate view. In his discussions of causality and objective reference James, as elsewhere in his writings, makes useful reading for the contemporary philosopher.

I

As early as the 1870s James held that properties and events are not always logically and physically independent of each other and that the British empiricists were wrong in thinking they always are. If connections are always de facto as Hume claimed, then the concepts of potentiality and possibility become metaphysical phantoms. Yet common-sense statements about physical objects and scientific laws both entail something about what could, would, or might happen. James is on the side of common sense and science.

James's commitment to the nonindependence view and to the categories of potentiality and possibility is everywhere evident in his early piece called "Against Nihilism": "The British School say that laws are nil—*nominis umbra*," whereas in fact they "are as real as the phenomena which they unite";[1] the "thing operates, or is in some way effective or recognized, where it does not actually and plenarily exist";[2] the positivist "thinks that there is no *nature* in things," while "we say that things behave so and so because of their nature or properties";[3] "nihilism [positivism] denies continuity" but common sense is right in holding a thing "to exist potentially or in substance where its antecedent is . . .";[4] and "dynamic connection with other existences becomes the test of substantial reality; or, in other words, a thing only has being at all as it enters in some way into the being of other things, or constitutes parts of a universe or organism."[5] James hastens to clarify his concept of a substance. Insofar as being continuous "is what people mean when they affirm a substance, substance must be held to exist."[6] But frequently philosophers mean by substance "a primordial *thing* on a plane behind that of phenomena, and numerically additional to them."[7] James rejects this concept.

James never developed this embryonic analysis of causality in terms of "the nature of a particular" and "substance," where these concepts are empirically conceived, and it is useful to see what kept him from developing them. James seemed to think that the concept of the "nature" of a particular meant "essential nature," and he became increasingly unwilling to believe that particulars have any essential nature. He eventually formulated his teleological analysis of "essential" characteristic, the classical formulation of which appears in the chapter on reasoning in *The Principles of Psychology*, according to which any property taken as essential simply reflects the interests or intent of a person on that occasion and hence that there are as many essential properties as there are human interests and occasions for acting toward a thing with any given property as a "handle."[8] It seems unfortunate to us that James's teleological analysis of "essence" led him away from an empirically conceived and a posteriori grounded concept of the nature of a particular that was equally promising.[9]

At an equally early date, James, encouraged by the work of such philosophers as Renouvier and Hodgson,[10] held that spatial and temporal relations are an irreducible part of "the given" and saw this view as reinforcing the nonindependence claim. "If each representation is totally independent," James asks, "how does it ever come into collision with any other, how can it be synthesized with another?" James answers, "Space and time, at least . . . they have in common."[11] James realized that spatial and temporal relations are not enough to yield the required counterfactuality, but thought they helped: "And although these are not dynamic or substantial bonds of union, yet they in some sense unite the heterogeneous into a universe period."[12]

To achieve the full goal, James eventually added causal connections as an irreducible element to "the given."[13] Like the experience of spatial and temporal relations, the experience of the causal relations cannot be conceptually decomposed. According to James, the volitional context is the place to look for the causal experience. For example, I directly experience my seeking to remember a forgotten name and my remembering it as causally related. The perception of such causal relations "is clear to anyone who has lived through the experience, but to no one else; just as 'loud,' 'red,' 'sweet' mean something only to beings with ears, eyes, and tongue."[14] Just as spatial and temporal relations are basic and unanalysable, so are the experiences of causal relatedness irreducible to anything else.

If the meaning of direct experience of causality is as clear to those who have lived through it as the meaning of "red," why, one might ask, don't we have names to denote such experiences? James replied that to ask for separate names is to presuppose separate facts, which is precisely the assumption that *radical* empiricism challenges. "The conceptualist rule," James says, "is to suppose that where there is a separate name there ought to be a fact as separate; and Hume, following this rule, and finding no such fact corresponding to the word 'power' concludes that the word is meaningless."[15] But, James objects, "By this rule, every conjunction and preposition in human speech is meaningless—*in, on, of, with, but, and, if* are as meaningless as *for* and *because*. The truth is that neither the elements of fact nor the meanings of our words are separable as the words are."[16]

James frequently warns against the tendency to reify causal connections, to set them apart from what they are experienced to be. James writes,

"If there is anything hiding in the background, it ought not to be called causal agency, but should get itself another name."[17] In his usual colorful way he advises us that "the healthy thing for philosophy is to leave off grubbing underground for what effects effectuation, or what makes action act, and try to solve the concrete questions of where effectuation in this world is located, of which things are the true causal agents there, and of what the more remote effects consist."[18]

However, the direct-experience-of-causality view still does not yield the required sense of counterfactuality. As long as the experience of causal connection is restricted to volitional contexts, we do not have the nonindependence of properties and events in the physical world that we need to turn the laws of science into something more than summaries of actual events. The causal connection experienced between my striving to remember a name and my remembering it does not help in the least to get causal connections between such things as x's being unsupported and x's falling, or between the atmospheric pressure and water going up a pump. Since James discusses the experience of causality only in volitional contexts, he is apparently committed to the notion that one must *infer* its existence between physical events.[19] An example supposedly would be this: We experience an exertion of power when we bend a young tree, and when we feel the wind blow and see the trees bend, we infer the exertion of such power on the part of the wind. We have got to the physical world at last and hopefully the causal relation there secures ontologically the concepts of potentiality, possibility, and counterfactuality!

II

In order to understand and appreciate James's view of causality, we need to see how it fits with other major themes of his mature philosophy.

(i) James is everywhere a staunch empiricist where this means that all nonlogical truths are known a posteriori. He unequivocally rejects the rationalist notion that there can be a priori knowledge of matters of fact. It is clear that his view of causality qualifies on this score. Since knowledge of causal relations is a matter of immediate acquaintance, it is wholly a posteriori. James, however—and this point is important—equally rejects the Humean contention that there is a material equivalence between "p is a posteriori" and "p is contingent" on the one hand, and between "p is a priori" and "p is necessary" on the other. James crosses the lines in his analysis of the causal relation: Causal relations are dynamic nonlogical connections but they are known in no other than a posteriori ways.

(ii) James is committed to the concept of a plural, open, ambiguous future, and his view of causality, not being a version of the determinist thesis, fits this commitment admirably. Causal connections exist wherever they are experienced—there is that much nonindependence of properties and events in the world. In many contexts of deliberation, however, there is no such experience and hence no ground for ascribing a causal connection. There is, then, an admirable escape from the concept of a "block universe." Let us examine this point more closely.

Say that p at t_1 is choosing between a and b, and that if he chooses a, consequence x will follow at t_n, while if he chooses b, consequence b will follow at t_n. Now if at t_0 God or anyone else knows that x will occur at t_n—or even if the proposition at t_0 "x occurs at t_n" is in fact true whether anyone knows it or not—then it would follow that at t_1, p must "choose" a—it is the only possibility open to him since x in fact is what will be. However, since deliberation does make a difference in the future, the future in certain respects must be conceived as open, plural, and ambiguous.

On the ontological level, then, James can best be understood as steering a middle course between the completely loose universe of the positivist and the block universe of the determinist. There must be enough connection in the world to account for the potentiality and counterfactuality but not so much connection in the world that it is impossible to say of anything that it could have been otherwise. Either too little or too much connection loses some precious aspect of that metaphysically profound concept of possibility. James's middle way may best be stated in the following way: He believed both in the partial dependence of various properties and events (not all conjunctions are coincidental) and in the partial plurality of the future (not all propositional truth values are antecedently determined).

(iii) James's middle way, in turn, is supported by his theory of truth. At least part of the meaning of "p is true" is that p leads us prosperously from one part of our experience to another and that it coheres with the great body of propositions that have already qualified on this count. This p, then, can be said to "become true" as it grows in this way. A proposition, then, is not antecedently true or false; truth or falsity is something that happens to propositions. Hence James is able to say in the case of propositions about future events like x and y dependent upon deliberation that they are not at t_0 either true or false because what is needed to make them either one or the other has not yet been determined and will not be until the person decides at t_1. An ambiguous or open future requires the present indeterminacy of the truth values of certain propositions, and James's view of truth provides the ground—though not the only ground—for such indeterminacy.

III

In spite of the way James's view of causality fits other aspects of his mature philosophy, and so receives support via the coherence route, it remained unsatisfactory in its own right—and we are not referring here simply to its lack of development. The lack of development follows rather from intrinsic difficulties with the view itself, one of which James himself keenly realized. Not knowing how to meet this difficulty, he never developed his view, though he never doubted he was on the right track and was at work on causality when he died. The major difficulties with James's analysis of "causality" are these:

(1) It is not clear that the causal concept is even applicable in volitional contexts. The supposition that a motive is always the cause of a person doing whatever he intentionally does has come under vigorous attack in recent years. The model offered instead of "x caused y to do" is "y decided to do z," where "y" refers to a self that initiates causal sequences but is not causally activated itself. This notion of a self with effective powers might still provide the original of "making x occur" that is the model followed by the panpsychists. But the important point is that however one construes intentional acts, whether along the motive model or the self model, the notion of cause involved in these contexts is invariably characterized as a subspecies of "cause" significantly different from the subspecies that includes physical objects and events.

(2) The inference claim is highly doubtful. It is contrary to appearances to claim that we only infer causal connections in the physical world. No one is aware of inferences like "me-bending tree, wind-bending tree." The reply to such a criticism is that one is unaware of the inference because it

is automatic, telescoped, and nondiscursive. To an eye unprejudiced by previous commitments, this reply seems equivalent to saying they aren't inferences at all.

(3) The inference claim is highly doubtful in yet another way. In James's view all causal powers of a physical sort supposedly have to be inferred. One is no more directly aware of the force of the hurricane bending the trees than one is directly aware of the pressure of the atmosphere pushing the water up the pump. Such a view seems prima facie absurd, however, since we do ordinarily usefully distinguish between inferred and experienced physical powers. If one adopts James's way of talking, he has the difficult problem in his new way of speaking of making this useful distinction.

(4) The extrapolation from volitional contexts to the physical world entails the disastrous consequence of panpsychism. We will not argue that panpsychism is a disaster but will simply assume it to be so. It is this difficulty of which James was aware and about which he worried.[20] James in fact was not wholly unsympathetic to panpsychism and was occasionally on the brink of accepting it, but he was never willing to make the required jump into this sort of metaphysics.[21] Not seeing how to reject the premise that we experience causality only in volitional contexts, worried about supposing a full analogy with physical power, and unable to develop a limited analogy, James was unable to advance any further in anchoring the concepts of possibility and counterfactuality in the physical world.

(5) James's premise that we are directly aware of causality only in volitional contexts seems in fact false. Not only are we not confined to volitional contexts for our experiences of causal power, we discover them less easily and quickly there than in physical contexts. According to Sterling Lamprecht, "instead of going from the physical facts of volition to the physical thrusts of things (so that belief in causality would be a kind of lingering animistic interpretation of the material world), we begin with the experience of causality in bodily thrusts and only later extend the notion to our own mental life (and the degree to which such extension is legitimate is still to some philosophers an open question)."[22] Indeed, the idea of causality first arises not even from an awareness of things bumping, banging, and pushing on the child, but from his awareness of things banging, bumping, and clashing among themselves. Only gradually does he

learn to isolate his own body for special attention, learn its prowess and various kinds of skill, and eventually arrive at an understanding of his own mental powers and the efficacy of his will.

Such a theory of the external origin of the notion of causal power receives strong support from the experimental findings of the Belgian psychologist A. Michotte.[23] We need not describe his experimental apparatus and procedures here, but simply note that they are highly ingenious and well worth close study. What is significant for our purposes is his finding that the experience of purely mechanical causality (i.e., causation in which one moving object causes another object to move) external to the perceiver is primary. Moreover, he shows, contrary to Hume, that habit and expectation are not necessary conditions for the perception of mechanical causation.

The upshot of our criticism is this: James was wrong in limiting causality in the physical world to what is known inferentially. He was right in being worried about panpsychistic notions of causality but he cannot avoid them if he keeps his premise that we are aware of causal connections only in volitional contexts. James in principle is correct in claiming that causal connections are an irreducible part of the immediately given.[24] He simply identified or located the irreducible causal relation incorrectly or too parochially. We join Lamprecht and Michotte in claiming that the experience of objective causal connection is an irreducible aspect of the immediately given. In this way, then, we would emend and extend James's view of causality.

IV

The immediate response of the Humean is not hard to guess. He may well agree that the emendation of James's view is all to the good but would argue that ultimately any claim about the ontological irreducibility of causal connections is doomed to failure. The Humean tradition claims to show that the direct perception of causal power is *in principle* impossible. The argument for this conclusion is very simple: One cannot perceive what is not there; "causal power" entails "necessary connection"; there are no necessary connections between matters of fact; therefore one cannot perceive causal power. The heart of this argument, and the backbone of the

Humean tradition, is that there are no necessary connections between matters of fact. This contention is supported by the familiar Humean dialectic: If there were a necessary connection of any kind between C and E, then the conjunction of C · ~ E would be self-contradictory; but such a conjunction is not self-inconsistent since it is always logically possible that nature may change its course. Moreover, the Humeans do not deny that we have a phenomenologically irreducible experience of causal power; what they deny is that this sort of experience corresponds to any irreducible physical reality. The second part of the Humean argument, then, is to show why one mistakenly thinks his irreducible experience points to physical reality, and it is to this end that Hume introduces his associationistic explanation in terms of custom and its projection onto objects and events. Contemporary Humeans add other projective explanations.

The immediate response is that the second part of the Humean argument is without doubt wholly inadequate. This second claim is not a philosophical one but a factual one, psychological in nature, which common-sense observation and the experiments of Michotte tend to show to be false. Michotte's findings effectively show not only that the Humean associationistic explanations are likely factually false but also that the panpsychist's genetic explanations of inferential causal knowledge are also. We have argued elsewhere that contemporary Humean projective explanations are no more successful than Hume's or the panpsychists, and we will not repeat ourselves here.[25] The upshot, then, is that the Humean's system is not without difficulty. However, unless the in-principle argument is countered, neither is James's nor any Humean analysis adequate. The crucial point, then, is whether the Humean in-principle argument is valid or not.

What sort of reply to this argument is possible, by James or anyone else? The following reply is our own but is certainly in the spirit of James and the main outline is no doubt implicit in much of his writing. As we shall see, even some of the details are there.

The crucial point of our reply is that Hume's in-principle argument is really superfluous in the context of his own ontology. The argument supposedly establishes the independence of events by showing that there are no necessary connections between matters of fact. In fact, however, the very concept of an event in the Humean ontology is identical with the concept of the independence of events, properties, and predicates. It is generally supposed that the in-principle argument of the Humean is not ontology-bound, that is, is relevant to all ontologies. In fact the independence of properties, etc., and hence the in-principle argument, is simply a consequence of a particular ontology which there seems little reason to hold. Hume's argument, in short, is ontologically bound in a damaging way. To document these claims, of course, we need to examine the concept of an "event."

In the ordinary and scientific view "event" is construed in terms of an ontology of enduring things, while on the Humean view enduring things are conceived to be constructions out of "events." An event in the Humean sense must be seen as a temporal cross-section of what we would ordinarily call a physical object: "x is red at t_1"; "x is round at t_1"; "x is sweet at t_1"; etc. would each be an event in this sense. The only connection this sense of "event" has with the ordinary one is that all Humean events are momentary "happenings" in consciousness, the immediate awareness of the moment. A physical object, then, is construed as a construction out of such events; it is a collection of such events bound together by temporal continuity and identity, or continuous change of place. For the Humean, in short, all events are logically and physically independent of each other.

There seems little reason nowadays to hold such an ontology. Humeans begin with an epistemic atomism and think it entails an ontological atomism; but Dretske and Joske have shown that the former does not entail the latter at all.[26] And we have seen how James effectively attacks the epistemic atomism of the Humean. Moreover, the efforts to construct physical object sentences from sentences about events in the Humean sense are notorious failures. The trouble with such "constructions" is that they ignore the fact that what we sense depends upon the state of the observer and the conditions of observation as well as other factors, some reference to which is required *before* one can construct physical object sentences. Hence such constructed physical object sentences presuppose the very thing they are trying to eliminate. Finally, the antimetaphysical bias of the Humean is already violated in his effort to interpret physical objects as collections of events in his sense bound together by temporal continuity or continuous change of place. This effort requires the assumption of both the density and continuity of time, neither of which are empirical concepts. James, then, was on sounder ground than even he supposed when he claimed that communality in space and time alone, even without causal considerations, goes a long way toward making the concept of a physical object unconstruable out of atomic impressions, and thus essentially presenting the ontology of enduring things as required for securing the required concepts of potentiality, possibility, and counterfactuality.

V

There is good evidence that James *intended* to meet the Humean thrust by avoiding a phenomenalistic ontology in which the independence of events is simply a corollary, and by defending instead an ontology of enduring physical objects in which some properties are bound together and in which changes, or events, consequently are sometimes connected. We must be careful on this issue, however, since James is sometimes interpreted as a phenomenalist, A. J. Ayer being a recent example.[27] That this interpretation is false is suggested by taking seriously James's own explicit declarations.

First, James unambiguously announces his aversion to phenomenalism as a satisfactory way of understanding the nature of physical objects. In his notes for a "Seminary" on "Philosophical Problems of Psychology" given at Harvard in 1897–98, he writes: "The great difference between the phenomenalist and the common-sense view is that the latter gives *stable* elements whilst the former is affected by a restlessness which is painful to the mind. In it one never gets out of the conception of flux, or process; although it might well seem that all the *actual* found its place in the flux."[28] Thus James both early and late tied together phenomenalism, Humeanism, and actualism, on the one hand, and common-sense enduring objects and potentiality, on the other, and always maintained allegiance to the latter. Second, James on numerous occasions referred to himself straightforwardly as a natural realist and a defender of common-sense ontology. These statements of allegiance come to the fore forcefully in the discussions in those parts of his *Essays in Radical Empiricism* devoted to the concept of pure experience. "Radical empiricism has, in fact, more affinities with natural realism than with the views of Berkeley or of Mill, and this can be easily shown."[29]

We need to examine this issue in detail, however, since it is not enough to know only what James said but what he meant and what he was committed to. We want to get to the center of James's vision and not simply string together quotations from him that fit our thesis. Moreover, in order to make headway in analysis we need to say precisely what *we* mean by key terms, so that whatever others may mean by them, the *issues* involved are clear and all of us avoid misunderstandings and disguised arguments about what some terms *really* mean.

The naive or presentational realist believes that we are directly aware of physical objects and their properties, a view which seemingly founders on the issues of false appearances and the mediation of stimuli. The traditional epistemic alternative has been that the only things we are directly aware of are our own sensations, either actual or possible, or sense data, or whatever else we choose to call the particulars of direct acquaintance. Three issues immediately arise on this alternative:

(1)   Are the particulars of direct awareness public or private?
(2)   What level of complexity are the particulars—red patches, etc., or apples?
(3)   Is there any objective reference from such particulars to physical objects?

There are numerous historical permutations of answers to these questions, but for our purposes only one permutation is important:

(1)   The particulars of direct awareness are private (held by some phenomenalists and sense data theorists but by no means all);
(2)   such particulars are "atomistic" and physical objects must be construed as "constructions" out of them (held in one version or another by all phenomenalists); and
(3)   such particulars have no "objective reference" to physical objects in addition to whatever "construction" is involved (again common to all forms of phenomenalism).

James can be understood best as accepting (1) and firmly rejecting (2) and (3). That he accepted (1) is clear from the fact that he believed no two observers can have numerically the same percept. The particular you are directly aware of when you look at Memorial Hall from angle x is numerically distinct from the particular I am directly aware of from angle y. That he rejected (2) is apparent from his constant rejection of epistemic atomism in all forms and the absence of any "constructions" out of sense data in his radical empiricism essays. That he rejected (3) is clear from his repeated claims that the different percepts different people have of the same object are in identically the same place in public space. James's natural realism, then, is his effort—whether successful or not—to introduce objective reference into a private data scheme and hence make room for the enduring objects of science and ordinary life for the sake of accounting for potentiality and counterfacuality—something that phenomenalism, positivism, actualism, and Humeanism are unable to do.

While James's objective, in our view, is a worthy one, he was not, it seems, wholly successful in his efforts; the task of reconciling private data with public, enduring objects is a difficult one indeed. James is committed to the view that the different particulars different people are aware of are in identically the same place in public space. The jarring consequence of this view, however, is that numerically distinct contents can occupy the same place—a consequence most philosophers would like to avoid. E.g., G. E. Moore shared James's commitment to private data but not being able to accept the jarring consequence concluded that space as well as data must be in some way private.[30] That way out was of no help to James, however, since public space was the only way he could see to achieve objective reference and hence an adequate analysis of potentiality. On our view, the best way out for James would be to reject (1)—deny the private premise—and substitute in its place the more adequate presentational view already present in Reid and developed more fully in the recent writings of C. J. Ducasse and Roderick M. Chisholm—namely, the adverbial view of sensing and the dispositional analysis of properties.[31] There are, of course, other epistemic possibilities, including perspectival realism, but whatever alternative one might choose to help James avoid the jarring consequence, it should be abundantly clear that James was serious about natural realism and object reference and was serious about these views because he was deeply concerned throughout his philosophical career to make sense of potentiality and counterfactuality and saw these commitments as necessary to that end.

FIVE

IN MEMORIAM: FREDERIC HAROLD YOUNG (1905–2003) AND THE FOUNDING OF THE PEIRCE SOCIETY

On October 15, 1945, while he was the minister of St. Stephen's Episcopal Church in Newark, New Jersey, and a Wyman Fellow in Philosophy at Princeton University, the Reverend Frederic Harold Young[1] delivered to the Pike County Historical Society in Milford, Pennsylvania, an address entitled "Charles Sanders Peirce: America's Greatest Logician and Most Original Philosopher." While revealing much of Young's own approach to Peirce, the address also tells us about the attitudes toward Peirce of several eminent philosophers of that day, philosophers Young had enlisted in support of his campaign to memorialize Peirce and promote the study of his writings. The paper is important enough to the background of the establishment of the Peirce Society to be worth reproducing in full.

Young's Address

I

In this community where he spent the last twenty-seven years of his life, or more than a third of his lifetime, and where he composed so many of those papers which, since his death, have increasingly brought him world-recognition as a logician and philosopher, we are met under the auspices of the Pike County Historical Society to honor Charles Sanders Peirce. We are to honor him, not only on and for this occasion, but to inspire a consideration of the best means whereby to establish a worthy memorial to him who was not only one of Milford's most distinguished citizens but who was also the greatest logician and the most original philosopher in our nation's history. In attempting to achieve an adequate understanding of this remarkable man, our subject inevitably divides itself into two main parts: the one biographical; the other critical—that is to say, a statement and estimate of his achievements. We shall consider first the biographical, and then the critical and interpretative aspect of our theme.

Charles Sanders Peirce—he did not acquire the additional name of "Santiago" until middle life—was born in Cambridge, Massachusetts, on the tenth of September, 1839, the second son of Benjamin and Sarah Peirce. His father, professor of mathematics at Harvard, was recognized as the foremost mathematician of his time in America, and he took all pains to see that his son was given an incomparable training in the theory and application of physical science, mathematics, and philosophy. His method was to give the boy problems to work, and leave him to induct the general principle from the problems. Most of us experienced sufficient difficulty in working problems with the general formulae given in advance. What would have been our consciousness of incapacity had we been asked to work our way to the formulae for ourselves! He also drilled Charles in chess and other games that required and developed logical ability. Sometimes he played double dummy with his son from ten in the evening until sunrise. The lad was reading Whatley's *Logic* at thirteen. Entering Harvard at sixteen and graduating at twenty, he read widely in philosophy. So profoundly conversant was he with German philosophy that in a few years he was to tell the Metaphysical Club, which included such figures as Chauncey Wright, William James, Oliver Wendell Holmes Jr., and a number of other notable minds, that the whole of German philosophy was only a "suggestion" of what true philosophy might be! This was unmitigated heresy to a generation that had based its ethical theory on Kant. But they had to listen to him because of his mastery of Kantian thought.

He once remarked that soon after he was twenty he was able to recite the *Critique of Pure Reason* almost word for word.

Two years after graduation from college he went into the United States Coast and Geodetic Survey, in which activity he remained for thirty years and during a period of which he was Acting Chief of the Survey at Washington. He found time, however, to give lectures at Harvard in the Philosophy of Science when he was thirty. It is interesting to note that he was one of a group of special lecturers which included Ralph Waldo Emerson, James E. Cabot, and John Fiske. In 1877 he was elected a Fellow of the American Academy of Arts and Sciences, before which body he delivered addresses on various occasions.

Although eager to pursue an academic career, he taught only eight years in his life—including logic at Johns Hopkins for five years, and lecturing intermittently at Harvard for three years. His unhappy first marriage is regarded as one factor in preventing him from securing a university chair. At twenty-three, in 1862, he had married Harriet M. Fay, afterward noted in Cambridge as a writer and organizer. He divorced her in 1883 and shortly afterward married Mademoiselle Juliette Frissy of Nancy, France. The other negative factor seems to have been his own eccentric personality. In the article on Peirce in the *Dictionary of American Biography*, his biographer speaks of him as "emotional, easily duped, forgetful of appointments, and careless of appearance in later years." In connection with these remarks, I wish I possessed the advantage enjoyed by some members of this Society in being able to compare these impressions of Peirce with first-hand impressions of one's own.

At the age of forty-eight, in 1887, he retired to this community in Pike County which he regarded as "the wildest county in the northern states." Here he bought the home known to you all, three miles from this spot on the road to Port Jervis, and now known as "Philwood." In that house he wrote some of his greatest papers.[2] He began his literary activities in Milford with writing definitions for *The Century Dictionary*, and with book reviews for *The Nation*. He was always extravagant financially, and he came to financial grief. It is recorded that he had a ladder leading to his attic, which ladder, after he ascended it, was pulled up, thus enabling him to evade creditors when they happened to appear at the door.[3] By 1906 he was penniless. He applied to the Carnegie Fund to enable him to execute a project he long had contemplated, of producing a twelve-volume work in philosophy. It was to have been his "magnum opus." But the Fund refused a grant on the grounds that they were bound by the terms of the foundation to extend assistance only for work in a "natural science," and logic was not precisely a "natural science." It was during this pathetic period that William James and a few of Peirce's former students secured aid for him through an appeal. It was in recognition of his profound esteem for his dear friend William James, that Peirce added "Santiago" to his name which is, of course, the Spanish for "St. James."

By 1909 he was a man of seventy, suffering from incipient cancer and using morphine regularly to alleviate the pain. However, he stuck to his writing, many times composing until sunrise, as he had so many years before played double dummy with his father the whole night through. Despite the imperial strength of his mind, his body grew weaker and the end grew near. On the nineteenth of April, 1914, he died of cancer in Milford at the age of seventy-five. To quote his biographer's tersely eloquent words: "he died . . . a frustrated, isolated man, still working on his logic, without a publisher, with scarcely a disciple, unknown to the public at large."

In such few and simple words is conveyed, hauntingly enough to transfix the sensitive imagination, a tragic vision of the last years and days of Charles Peirce's earthly pilgrimage. Of all that he wrote, later to fill six large volumes and four others projected, one book only was published during his life. Let us hope that, in the natural beauty of this region, in companionship with his devoted wife, and in the creative outpourings of his magnificent intellect, he found, amid the world's unheeding ways, a joy and peace which the world could neither give nor take away.

II

The second part of our task opens before us. We are now to attempt an appreciation of Peirce's attainments in logic and philosophy. Observe that I say appreciation rather than evaluation, since evaluation is possible only to men competent to judge. There are two chief authorities on Peirce— Doctors Weiss and Hartshorne—who jointly edited Peirce's papers after his death. An intelligent appreciation of Peirce must rest primarily, then, upon the judgment of these editors. Although I myself have read rather widely in Peirce's writings, there is a marked difference between a student and an authority.

Peirce's manuscripts, after his death, were bought from his wife by the Philosophy Department of Harvard University. What with leaves missing, pages unnumbered, dates omitted, and no sequence apparent on the surface; it was a vast undertaking to edit the hundreds of papers thus acquired. But it was done with consummate ability by the editors and issued in six volumes by the Harvard University Press from 1931 to 1935. The editors have given us to expect four more volumes at some future date. The titles of the published volumes are indicative of the range of Peirce's speculations:

Volume I: Principles of Philosophy
Volume II: Elements of Logic
Volume III: Exact Logic
Volume IV: Simplest Mathematics
Volume V: Pragmatism and Pragmaticism
Volume VI: Scientific Metaphysics

Besides the published works, which included material drawn chiefly from the fields of logic, mathematics, pragmatism, and metaphysics, there was a corpus of data in such diverse subject-matters as geodesy, religion, chemistry, astronomy, investigations in English and classical Greek pronunciation, criminology, psychical research, the history of science, Egyptology, ancient history, Napoleon, a thesaurus and editor's manual, and translations from Latin and German. We shall confine our attention to two areas in which Peirce attained preeminence: logic and pragmatism.

Although he was, as he once said, practically brought up in a laboratory, Peirce regarded himself primarily as a logician. The self-estimate appears to be perfectly accurate, since it is now generally recognized by authorities that he is one of the five or six creative intellects in logic since Aristotle wrote the *Organon* over twenty-three centuries ago. Bacon talked much about a *Novum Organum*, but Peirce created one. The Peircian canon is itself a monument to one of the most powerful intellects in western thought. Little wonder that William James called him "the most original mind of his generation." He might have added: "and for many generations."

In connection with Peirce's specific accomplishments in logic, I quote at length from Weiss's admirable article in the *Dictionary of American Biography*:

> In 1847, George Boole, the founder of modern logic, published *The Mathematical Analysis of Logic*, followed in 1854 by his definitive work, *An Investigation of the Laws of Thought*. These works, destined to revolutionize the entire science of logic and free it from the thrall of the Aristotelian syllogism were practically unnoticed in America until Peirce . . . referred to Boole's work, and made a number of vital and permanent improvements in the Boolean system. . . . (Peirce's) technical papers of 1867–1885 established him as the greatest formal logician of his time, and the most important single force in the period from Boole to Schroeder. These papers are difficult, inaccessible, scattered, and fragmentary, and their value might never have been known if it had not been that Schroeder based a large portion of his *Vorlesungen über die Algebra der Logik* on them. . . . Peirce radically modified, extended, and transformed the Boolean algebra, making it applicable to propositions, relations, probability, and arithmetic. Practically singlehanded since De Morgan, Peirce laid the foundations of the logic of relations, the instrument for the logical analysis of mathematics. He invented the copula of inclusion, the most important symbol in the logic of classes, two new logical algebras, two new systems of logical graphs, discovered the link between the logic of classes and the logic of propositions, was the first to give the fundamental principle for the logical development of mathematics, and made exceedingly important contributions to probability theory, induction, and the logic of scientific methodology. . . . Many of his more important writings on logic, among which are his detailed papers on his new science of semiotics, he never published, and the final appreciation of his full strength and importance as a logician awaits the assimilation of the posthumous papers.

And in reference to Peirce's mathematical powers, Weiss says:

> In 1867 in his paper *Upon the Logic of Mathematics*, he clearly anticipated the method for the derivation and definition of a number employed in the epochal *Principia Mathematica* of A. N. Whitehead and Bertrand Russell, published in three volumes in 1910–1913. . . . Had all his mathematical papers been published during his lifetime . . . he would have been a more important factor in the history of

mathematics than he is today. His work on the logical and philosophical problems of mathematics remains, however, among the foremost in the field.

So much for Peirce's eminence as a logician.

In the *Popular Science Monthly* for January 1878, appeared an article by Peirce entitled: "How to Make Our Ideas Clear." In this particular article was the statement which afterwards became famous as the "pragmatic maxim" and which led to his reputation as the founder of that philosophical movement in America known during the past fifty years as Pragmatism.

Pragmatism, in layman's language, is that philosophy particularly concerned with judging the meaning of any thought or experience in terms of its effects and results. Ruggiero, an Italian philosopher, says: "Pragmatism was born in America, the country of business, and is, par excellence, the philosophy of the business man."

But this is a provincial view for a historian of philosophy to take. Just as idealism, realism, empiricism, and skepticism are permanently recurring tendencies in philosophic thought, so is pragmatism with its appeal to practical judgment. That is why William James called Pragmatism "a new name for old ways of thinking." Immanuel Kant and Fichte, in the eighteenth and nineteenth centuries, had, among other viewpoints, given stress to the "practical reason," and to the profound element of decision-for-action in the human ego. Kant occasionally used the word "pragmatic."

Returning to Peirce, I quote the maxim itself:

> Consider what effects which might conceivably have practical bearings, we conceive the object of our conception to have. Then, our conception of these effects is the whole of our conception of the object.

It is Peirce's exclusive emphasis upon "effects" as giving us "the whole of our conception of an object" which made him the founder of Pragmatism as a movement in America. Peirce was perfectly clear as to the nature, value, and limitations of this principle. In countering criticism of the maxim he stressed the fact that it was concerned with concepts rather than things, and that it was to be employed as a "principle of method" rather than as a proposition in metaphysics.

Considering the maxim again, observe that the frame of reference is strictly to our conceptions, and not [an] appeal to action or decision such as James later developed. Peirce coined the word "pragmaticism" to distinguish his position from that of James's "pragmatism," with its relatively greater emphasis on the will over the intellect. Peirce's maxim, as conceived and used by him, is a guiding principle of investigation within such fields as semantics, logic, and the epistemology of conception. But it has been applied by James, Dewey, and others to such subject-matter as ethics, sociology, education, and psychology. Watson's doctrine of behaviorism in psychology is an illustration in point of the method of interpreting by "effects" as applied to a specific science; in this case, a reading of the human organism exclusively in terms of its visible, or measurable, responses rather than the emphasis on stimuli as in the older psychology. In a letter from Professor W. T. Stace of the Philosophy Department at Princeton University, it is pointed out that this maxim has been used also by the Logical Positivists in their "verifiability principle of meaning."

Whatever the later applications by Pragmatists and Positivists, Peirce, because of his metaphysical and speculative bent, remained severely intellectualistic in his theory and use of the maxim.

The mention of his speculative bent brings us to a recognition of his metaphysical power. He is perhaps the second mind since Aristotle—the first being Leibniz—to have gone so far in the construction of a completely scientific metaphysics. This point requires no further amplification here, since it is essentially contained in letters that I have received from present-day philosophers, whose estimate of our Philosopher I will shortly read to you.

To indulge in a rapid summary: Peirce was preeminent as a mathematician (greater than his father who was the greatest in America), scientist, logician, and metaphysician. He was the rarest of combinations in any domain of human thought—a man of immense erudition and equally a man of immense originality. In fact, he is a philosopher's philosopher, and that role has belonged to only a few such as Aristotle, Leibniz, Kant, and Hegel.

Our foremost creative thinkers in American history may be counted with less than our ten fingers. In the eighteenth century we produced Jonathan Edwards, Count Rumford (who spent most of his life in exile),

Benjamin Franklin, and Thomas Jefferson. In the nineteenth and twentieth centuries we produced Willard Gibbs, Thorstein Veblen, Henry Adams, and Charles Peirce. These eight minds: Edwards in theology and philosophy, Rumford in physics, Franklin in science and statecraft, Jefferson in political science and education, Gibbs in physics, Veblen in economics and anthropology, Adams in social and historico-literary criticism, and Peirce in logic and metaphysics, were intellects of the first rate; and among these eight, Peirce is surpassed by none in sheer intellectual power. Weiss concludes his article on Peirce with this estimate: "This much is now certain: he is the most original and versatile of America's philosophers, and America's greatest logician."

I am extremely happy on this occasion to present opinions of Peirce from several outstanding thinkers of the nation and the world, but before I quote from them, it will heighten, with a pathetic irony, the contrast of inappreciation in his own day and the profound appreciation of these days, if Charles Peirce be allowed to speak to us in his own words, taken from the preface to volume I of his *Collected Papers*:

> I am a man of whom critics have never found anything good to say. When they could see no opportunity to injure me, they have held their peace. The little laudation I have had has come from such sources, that the only satisfaction I have derived from it, has been such slices of bread and butter as it might waft my way. Only once, as far as I remember, in all my lifetime have I experienced the pleasure of praise—not for what it might bring but in itself. That pleasure was beatific; and the praise that conferred it was meant for blame. It was that a critic said of me that I did not seem to be absolutely sure of my conclusions. Never, if I can help it, shall that critic's eye ever rest on what I am now writing; for I owe a great pleasure to him; for such was his evident animus, that should he find out, I fear the fires of hell would be fed with new fuel in his breast.

He then proceeds:

> My book is meant for people who want to find out; and people who want philosophy ladled out to them can go elsewhere. There are philosophical soup shops at every corner, thank God! . . . The first step toward finding out is to acknowledge you do not satisfactorily know already; so that no blight can so surely arrest all intellectual growth

as the blight of cocksureness; and ninety-nine out of every hundred good heads are reduced to impotence by that malady—of whose inroads they are most strangely unaware!

Now let us attend to the tributes from some of our nationally known philosophers who, upon my solicitations, sent them especially for this occasion. The first quotation is from Sidney Hook, Professor of Philosophy at New York University. By him I was introduced to a study of Peirce:

> More than any one man in the history of human thought, Charles Peirce pointed the way to bridging the age-old dualism between things and human thought. This he did in his epoch-making conception of man as a sign-using animal, and his interpretation of the life of mind as the life inherent in symbols. It is by the use of symbols that man as a piece of nature becomes human; and it is through man's activity directed by symbols that nature becomes meaningful and reasonable. The rich implications of Peirce's fundamental insight are yet to be explored. Today he is just as much the philosopher's philosopher, just as much the pioneer of a second Copernican revolution in thought (one more genuine than Kant's) as he was when his meteoric genius first flashed across American skies.

From Charles Hartshorne, of the Department of Philosophy, the University of Chicago, and coeditor with Paul Weiss of Peirce's papers:

> Besides being a great logician, Peirce was a great mathematician—according to a foremost English authority who was at Johns Hopkins with him, a "much greater" mathematician than his father, Benjamin Peirce, who had been the leading mathematician of his day.
>
> In general philosophy, beyond logic, Peirce wrote brilliantly in several fields. And here, too, his views were revolutionary for his own day, and such as fifty years later came to be widely seen as important. The most ambitious and complete philosophy of our day, that of Whitehead, is more fully anticipated by Peirce, probably, than by anyone of his time, unless, perhaps, William James is an exception. . . . Other important doctrines are his classification of signs, his theory of the three categories, his synecism and tychism (the first and in some respects still the best efforts to do justice to the ideals of continuity and chance in philosophy), and his evolutionary "agapism." . . . Peirce, so far as I can find, combined more knowledge of exact science and the history of ideas with more inventive genius in philosophy than any man of

his time. . . . It was the first time since Leibniz that there had been such a phenomenon, a mathematician who was a logician and a physicist and a chemist and a metaphysician. He even did work in experimental psychology.

From Professor F. C. S. Northrop, of the Department of Philosophy, Yale University:

Charles Santiago [*sic*] Peirce ranks with Willard Gibbs as one of the greatest systematic theoretical and creative minds this country has ever produced. Not only did he formulate certain basic ideas in technical, mathematical, and symbolic logic, but also he laid the technical foundations of the philosophical movement known as pragmatism. . . . For all their technical precision and originality, these doctrines of Peirce's grew out of a thorough understanding of the works of the past, especially those of Immanuel Kant. In the field of empirical logic and scientific method similarly he combined a thorough understanding of the formal mathematical and deductive side of scientific and philosophical procedure with an informed emphasis upon its empirical inductive and pragmatic aspects. When one compares him with previous minds in the history of western thought, one thinks of Aristotle and Leibniz.

From John Dewey, lately retired from the Philosophy Department of Columbia University, and generally regarded as the Dean of American philosophers today:

C. S. Peirce was ahead of his times intellectually by more than a generation. Psychology and Philosophy are even now only slowly catching up, beginning to understand what he wrote. I note the following points: (1) What is called the "external world" is not primarily a matter of knowledge but of that "two-sided" direct interaction of organism and environmental conditions that occurs in "effort-resistance," the effort side being called "action," while the influence of the resisting conditions determines the "perceptual" side. Peirce never separates "motor" and "sensory"; neither is primary, though we may distinguish phases in which one or the other is dominant. Contemporary psychology is just beginning to take account of the full force of this position. (2) What is called thought is a matter of that form of signs that constitutes languages. Thought is language, and language is thought, not an expression or clothing for it. Since language is a mode of communication, "logic is rooted in the social principles"—Peirce's own words. (3) Language elevates habit, otherwise physical and physiological, to the plain of acknowledged continuity, generality, or reasonableness. (4) There is no fixity nor finality in the process. Its nature is growth, indefinite and continuous. The continuity of growth is our chief ground of hope with respect to the future of man.

From Dr. Alfred North Whitehead, formerly of the Philosophy Department of Harvard University, and a man who is recognizedly one of the very greatest philosophical intellects living among men today:

> Peirce was a very great man, with a variety of interests in each of which he made original contributions. The essence of his thought was originality in every subject he taught. For this reason none of the conventional labels apply to him. He conceived every topic in his own original way.

Lastly, from Paul Weiss of the Department of Philosophy of Bryn Mawr College, and coeditor with Hartshorne of Peirce's *Collected Papers*. I quote first from a paper delivered by him, in 1939 on the hundredth anniversary of Peirce's birth, before the American Philosophical Association at Columbia University, and then from a personal letter with a memorandum for this particular occasion.

> I am not concerned with praising Peirce—that would be impertinent—but in doing honor to him on this hundredth anniversary of his birth. . . . Peirce was a metaphysician as well as a logician, a realist as well as a semiotician, a speculative thinker as well as an experimental scientist, an idealist as well as a naturalist, and a pragmatist who had a theory of ethics which acknowledged a fixed and universal ideal. These were not for him, and they ought not be for us, inconsistent positions. Truth is rich and complex enough to accommodate both the abstract and the concrete, the temporal and the eternal, the general and the specific, the absolute and the relative, the probable and the certain. Peirce was a philosopher precisely because he saw that these different factors were facets of one encompassing truth and reality, and that philosophy was not a point of view but a study of that which embraces all points of view.

I conclude this series of tributes with a paragraph from Dr. Weiss's letter for this occasion:

Charles S. Peirce is one of the greatest minds of the 19th century. He is one of the most unusual, original, and erudite men born in America. He is the founder of pragmatism—America's great contribution to philosophy; he is the founder of the modern theory of signs; he is one of the founders of modern logic; he was one of the very few in the history of thought who was at home equally in the laboratory and the library, in ancient and modern thought, in English and German culture. He influenced Royce, James, Dewey, Cohen, his editors, and a host of other thinkers in this century. Almost entirely ignored in his day, he is now becoming better and better known as one of America's great contributions to civilization.

III

In contemplating and executing a worthy memorial to Charles Sanders Peirce in this community you are honoring not only him, but yourselves, and ultimately, the nation. It is the happy destiny of this village to have vouchsafed habitation to this man who lived quietly in your midst not so many years gone. You could hardly have understood that a titan of intellectual glory was living among you. Even university circles were strangely negligent and cruelly inappreciative, with far less excuse. Now that we better understand what manner of mind he was, it is time to pay our respects in a tangible and lasting form.

In addressing you as members of the Pike County Historical Society, I would remind you that your Society, in contemplating this project, is acting not merely as a custodian of the past, but as trustees of the future, since the influence of this man grows with each passing year. Consequently, it behooves you to think of memorials that will themselves grow with the coming years.[4] Obviously you will want to purchase the six volumes of his *Collected Papers*, along with three books on him, namely: *Chance, Love, and Logic*, edited by Morris Cohen; *The Philosophy of Peirce*, by Justus Buchler; also, *Peirce's Empiricism* by Buchler. But I am thinking even more of the raising of funds for establishing a Charles S. Peirce Scholarship, the income from which to be given annually to that boy or girl graduating from the local academy who ranks highest in science and mathematics, thus enabling him or her to attend college. Perhaps the finest possibility of all for you to consider is the following suggestion from Dr. Weiss. I was excited by the thought and I think you will be. He writes:

> It is good that Milford acknowledges him in this public way. In fact, it would be very nice if these ideas of yours could be supplemented by a yearly lectureship on some phase of Peirce. I think it would be necessary to put up no more than the fare and a modest stipend in order to get a distinguished scholar to lecture at Milford each year on the anniversary of Peirce's birth.[—which is the tenth of September.]

Do you not have a vision of what that would mean to Milford? You already have your summer theater. The execution of this project would still further distinguish Milford as a community of culture, through the honoring of its great citizen and the bringing of distinguished scholars to its people.

Though not a completely native Milfordite like your Gifford Pinchot who, as I understand, knew Mr. Peirce in the flesh; yet, philosopher and citizen Peirce must have loved this town and countryside where he gave up his years to great thoughts. Milford, through the medium of this Historical Society, has a large trust to perform. Keeping alive the value of a very great man is not the kind of privilege and responsibility that falls to every town. The world of letters and scholarship is concerned with your action beyond this present occasion. Milford will not fail to do the generous and significant thing for herself, for the larger community of human culture, and for her immortal son.

Commentary

Before he sent his address to the Historical Society to be printed, Young added this:

> NOTE: Three weeks after the delivery of the present paper, the author sent, to the chief philosophical journals of Britain and America, a notice in which he announced his intention of founding at Milford a Charles S. Peirce Society. Doctors Weiss and Hartshorne have consented to act as advisers. Membership will be open on a local, national, and international basis. Such a Society would consider and manage such projects as have been mentioned in the above paper, as well as others that may well be conceived and executed. For

example: Peirce's remains are at preset resting in a neglected plot, with only this inscription on the plainest and smallest of headstones: CHARLES S. PEIRCE; and then, below his name: Juliette Peirce, 1934. A fitting monument is one of the first considerations for a Peirce Society.

In his cover letter to the Historical Society, Young explained that he would be "addressing the American Philosophical Association soon after February 10th, and so I'm counting utterly on you to have them ready for me by then (of course you couldn't hurt my feelings if you happened to have them ready earlier!)."[5] It was in conjunction with that APA meeting that the Peirce Society was founded and had its first meeting as announced subsequently in *Philosophy and Phenomenological Research* (vol. 4, no. 4 [June 1946], 657–58):

> The meeting was called by Rev'd Frederic H. Young of Princeton University for the founding of a Peirce Society was held on the 22nd of February 1946, Sarah Lawrence College, Bronxville, New York, after the tea for the American Philosophical Association which was on its second day in annual session, with the following result:
>
> Those present were: Paul Weiss—who acted as Chairman; Sidney Hook, Philip Wiener, Frederic H. Young, Albert Abarbanell, James K. Feibleman, A. P. Ushenko, Daniel Bronstein, S. J. Kahn, M. Wertz, A. W. Burks, J. Buchler, Joseph Ratner, Max Black, H. S. Leonard, A. J. Benson, G. V. Edwards Jr., David Savan, Howard M. Wiedemann, Roderick M. Chisholm, W. H. Hay, Lenore D. Bloom, Otis Lee, J. E. Smith, and Martin Lyons.
>
> These gentlemen organized themselves, after considerable discussion of the purposes of a Peirce Society, into the Charles S. Peirce Society, and proceeded to elect temporary officers whose function was to draw up a statement of aims, and also to prepare a constitution and by-laws, to be submitted to each member present and to those who joined subsequently to this meeting. Mr. James Feibleman was assigned the task of preparing the data in the first instance, after which, subsequent to criticism of other officers, it was to be mailed to the members.
>
> These officers were elected: President, Dr. Paul Weiss; Secretary, Rev'd Frederic H. Young;[6] Treasurer, James K. Feibleman. Mr. Young gave $20.00 to the treasurer as a donation from St. Stephen's Episcopal

Church, Newark, N. J., and from the graduate students in philosophy at Princeton. The meeting opened at 5:15 p.m. and adjourned at 6:00 p.m.

Address communications to the Secretary, Graduate College, Princeton, N.J.

Frederic H. Young
Secretary, Charles S. Peirce Society

After completing his Wyman fellowship at Princeton, Young became a graduate student at Columbia University where he received a PhD in 1948 with a dissertation directed by Herbert W. Schneider.[7] His prefatory comments on his thesis suggest interests in some ways similar to those he had in the study of Peirce:

> The reader will find, in the accompanying exposition, a presentation of James's philosophy which, in its wholeness, constitutes a remarkably unified system; but this system in his thought-as-whole had to be discovered and articulated by the present writer. The task of exhibiting James's system as an interrelated totality was complicated by the fact that the literary unit of James's expression of his thought is not the sentence, nor the book-length, but rather the "essay" (or "letter"), as one who consults the full titles of his work will readily discover; moreover, there are no indexes in any of his books.
>
> James's philosophic vision is one of imposing vitality and possesses a kind of architectural grandeur. This vision is garmented in the sinewy yet graceful English of a prose master. It is hoped that James, Sr., long eclipsed in fame by his sons William and Henry, may come now into his own as a recognized brilliant thinker and author in the epic of American thought and literature.[8]

Near the end of the book, Young describes James Sr., Peirce, and Josiah Royce as representatives of the same basic trends:

> Another American thinker, Charles Sanders Peirce, was beginning to speculate on Chance ("Tychism") and Spontaneity before James died, but Peirce's "spontaneity" was weighted on the cosmological side as a theory of indeterminism, while James's was anthropological and sociological in reference. It would indeed be an attractive task to trace certain parallel *directions* of thought between James and Peirce: James's Spiritual Socialism and Peirce's "Unlimited Community," followed by Royce's "Beloved Community"; between James's Spontaneity and

Peirce's "Tychism," between James's stress on the Divine Love as the supreme essence of God and Peirce's "Evolutionary Agapism."

With different presuppositions and conclusions, thinkers in a given age are often paralleling each other in the great basic trends of their thought. Regardless of technical differences, there is a much greater similarity in their mutual emphasis on the *objective*, the *generalized*, the *socialized*, between the elder James and Peirce than there is between either one of them and the individualistic William James.[9]

Young's work on Henry James Sr. by no means ended his labors as secretary of the Peirce Society. When Arthur O. Lovejoy wrote him to suggest that the Society organize a "cooperative volume which would at once bring his whole scheme of ideas into clearer focus than he himself ever brought it, and present the most thorough critical examinations both into the validity of his reasonings and the consistency of his conclusions,"[10] Young accepted the challenge—with the aid of Philip P. Wiener.

In the foreword to the resulting volume they jointly edited, Wiener and Young proudly announced that "this volume is a first and significant step in attaining the aim of the Charles S. Peirce Society to encourage actively 'the study and development of Peirce's ideas.'" *Studies in the Philosophy of Charles Sanders Peirce*, published in 1952, immediately became, and remains today, a classic of Peirce scholarship. The short piece that Young contributed to the volume of which he was coeditor, "Charles Sanders Peirce: 1839–1914," recapitulates some of the points made in his address to the Pike County Historical Society seven years earlier.

From 1948 until 1968 Young taught philosophy and world literature at Montclair State University in New Jersey. During that period he also lectured abroad often. Perhaps most noteworthy was a 1958–59 Fulbright Lectureship in India. A few years later he was thrilled to deliver an address on June 16, 1964 ("Bloomsday") on the occasion of the unveiling of a plaque placed at James Joyce's birthplace in Dublin. The plaque was a gift to Dublin from his students at Montclair.

Having retired from full-time teaching in 1968, he taught courses in philosophy and religion for the World Campus Afloat program sponsored by Chapman College in Orange, California. Wanderlust still unsatisfied, he and his wife "took a year off for our own around-the-world trip (going to relatively out-of-the-way places such as Kashmir, Afghanistan, Iran, the Sudan, and Ethiopia)."[11] In 1970 they moved permanently to California where Young taught at both Chapman College and at the Leisure World senior citizen community. In 1990, when he decided to stop even part-time teaching, he wrote his dean: "My 18 years of teaching at Leisure World (7 under the auspices of Saddleback Central School District, and 11 for the Emeritus Institute of Saddleback College) have been the creative climax of all my years as a professor."[12] Teaching gave Young at least as much pleasure as travel, and, by all accounts, he was a gifted and much loved instructor. Among his most appreciative students was Lee A. DuBridge who had retired from the California Institute of Technology after serving twenty-three years as president of that institution. DuBridge wrote the Saddleback dean: "My wife and I have both attended his classes and we can assure you they were not only full of meaning for us but also a fascinating experience . . . Since we both spent our lives in educational work, I think we can both recognize a fine teacher when we see one."[13] Always eager to teach at least informally, Young created and for many years hosted "The Very Idea," a TV interview program broadcast from Leisure World.

In 1993, shortly after Joseph Brent's biography of Peirce was published,[14] Young, then eighty-eight years old, wrote Brent:

> What an intellectual delight, is your PEIRCE! Its knowledge, architectonic, and literary grace, are blended in a beautiful achievement. As you will note in perusing the enclosed material, I have had a special interest beginning in 1945. Therefore, you could not have a happier and more impressed reader of your book, than myself . . . From about 1955 I veered away from Peirce studies, to teach Comparative & Philosophy of Religion, Philosophy of History, and World Literature. But Peirce was resurrected for me by your book for which I am inexpressibly grateful.[15]

In 2001, at age 96, Young wrote a letter to Nathan Houser to thank him for a complimentary copy of volume I of *The Essential Peirce*:

> [The volume] recalled so vividly that day when, at Sarah Lawrence College, we formed the Peirce Society on Feb. 22 (I think it was 1947 or 8—my memory is failing so). I had mailed out 7 or 8 invitations to

the chief phi. Journals in USA and Britain, to form a Peirce Society, after discussing the idea with Paul Weiss.[16]

Gloria Tucker, Young's daughter by his first wife, reports that in the months before his death on February 28, 2003, at the age of 97, with a mind still clear and active, her father was reading Peirce and discussing his ideas with anyone he encountered.[17]

SIX

THE AMERICAN PHILOSOPHICAL
TRADITION AS PROGRESSIVELY
ENRICHED NATURALISM

C omments on Arnold Berleant's "Metapragmatism and the Future of American Philosophy" (Meeting of Society for the Advancement of American Philosophy, Bentley College, Waltham, Mass., March 1995)
Let me begin my comments by noting that, whatever disagreements with Arnold Berleant I express in what follows, he and I share a firm commitment to American pragmatic naturalism. Where we may perhaps differ, as you shall see, is in our views about what strategies to use in fostering future development of that tradition. However, before you can understand how my strategies may differ from Arnold's, you need to understand my conception of the entire sweep of American philosophy from colonial times to the present. In my view, the history of American philosophy can best be understood as the incorporative, progressive, and cumulative development of naturalism. In other words, this ever-evolving naturalism is the "spirit" of American philosophy. Obviously, in these brief comments I cannot present a convincing case for this conception of our philosophical history, but let me give a few examples of what I have in mind.

The Enlightenment naturalism found in Jefferson and others was enriched in the nineteenth century by German and British idealism—the concept of experience in American naturalism was much broadened by wrestling with idealism; the same sources contributed process logic to American naturalism. As is widely recognized, Darwinian biology also enriched American naturalism; to mention still another example, medieval logic enriched Peirce's naturalism. In the twentieth century, the close study of Aristotle's logic enriched Randall's naturalism. C. I. Lewis's naturalism was enriched by lifelong study of Kant. Marxism enriched the naturalisms of Roy Wood Sellars and Marvin Farber. Quine's naturalism has been enriched by Carnap's linguistic philosophy, Tarski's philosophy of logic, and Duhem's philosophy of science. And the naturalisms of those present at this meeting have been enriched by many sources. Among our most distinguished members I'd like to mention Abe Edel; his naturalism has been enriched by close study of Aristotle. Finally, let me mention the work of Murray Murphey. The version of naturalism found in his most recent book would not have been possible without detailed and painstaking examination of diverse types of recent analytic philosophy.

Where, you may ask, does pragmatism fit in this picture of ever-more-enriched naturalism as the spirit of American philosophy? I suggest that "pragmatism" is a helpful way of calling attention to various interconnected features that have supervened on American naturalism in its late nineteenth- and early twentieth-century development. But I believe that it is seriously misleading to suggest that pragmatism is the chief American claim to importance and distinctiveness in world philosophical history. Instead our claim should be to have developed over many generations the most enriched naturalism in world philosophical history—and what is usually called American pragmatism is a significant aspect of that enriched naturalism.

Now, if the conception of the American philosophical tradition that I have sketched is even roughly correct, it has important implications for how we should go about fostering further development of American naturalism. It implies, I suggest, that we should not get uptight about what appear to be alien types of philosophy in our midst. We should encourage the most thorough discussion of "foreign" ideas that for one reason or another attract the attention of our American colleagues. We should do this confident in our belief that the temper of American culture has always been such that immigrant ideas sooner or later enrich American naturalism. "Hang loose!" is my advice. Don't spend a lot of time fretting about the possible demise of American naturalism. I'm not suggesting that we not scrutinize imported ideas. The most significant enrichment emerges from dialogue between imported and domestic ideas.

I recognize that my advice will be difficult to accept for some naturalists, including the older members of this society. During the quarter century in which various forms of imported eliminativist analytic philosophy had much institutional power in American academe, many naturalists were unfairly treated in ways that members of this audience don't need to be reminded of. This unjust treatment caused understandable bitterness and resentment. Although these feelings are understandable, hypersensitivity to any philosophy deeply critical of American naturalism has unfortunate consequences. Year after year of intense preoccupation with Richard Rorty, for example, is—at the very least—distracting. Shortly after Rorty's *Philosophy and the Mirror of Nature* was published in 1979, it was quite adequately shown that Rorty's so-called "pragmatism" was radically inconsistent with the pragmatism of American naturalism and that his "pragmatism" was not a genuine threat to the American naturalist tradition. But today hypersensitive naturalists continue frantically refuting Rorty. Rorty, who enjoys cleverly baiting his critics, encourages this pointless activity. *Neglect* is what Rorty's philosophy now calls for, in my view. I urge that we take the "long view" of the Rorty phenomenon. I predict that fifty years from now when historians look back at this period in American philosophy they will consider that Rorty played a significant role only because the discussion of his charming prose stimulated useful clarification of the character of American naturalism. The American naturalist tradition is too resilient and resourceful to be seriously threatened by Rorty. In the long run, Rorty is enriching the naturalist tradition he is laboring to discredit.

Let me explore another possible reason for the breast-beating among American naturalists. Many American naturalists today seem deeply disappointed that we have no giants on the contemporary scene of the magnitude of Aristotle, Spinoza, Peirce, or Dewey. They take that lack to indicate that the tradition is in *crisis*—in danger of being superseded. It strikes me as especially ironic when Deweyan naturalists bemoan the lack of such giants. Recall that no one better explained the resources and promise of "social intelligence" than Dewey. Deweyans should recognize that since World War II major philosophical advances have usually been accomplished by legions of philosophers working more or less connectedly on a problem. What could be more appropriate for an American naturalist than to recognize that philosophy is a *social* product? Instead of decrying that absence of "great" philosophers, American naturalists should do everything they can to nurture lively exercise of "social intelligence" in the widest and most diverse intellectual community—confident that sooner or later the upshot will be further enrichment of naturalism. The "genius" of the American philosophical temper is, and always has been, its capacity to respond creatively to foreign influences so as to enrich naturalism. That naturalistic genius does not depend on philosophical superstars.

An important part of nurturing social intelligence in the philosophical community should be encouraging philosophers to explore any and all developments in the empirical sciences that seem of philosophical interest. For example, work in the cognitive sciences should be encouraged. Often American naturalists vehemently dismiss cognitive science, protesting that it is based on an erroneous metaphysics. To be sure, cognitive scientists often make idiotic metaphysical pronouncements, but that does not rob their empirical work of philosophical significance. Recall that Peirce, James, Dewey, and Mead eagerly explored all empirical inquiry going on in their day, however philosophically inadequate that scientific work was. Wouldn't they advise us not to be intimidated by legions of clever and well-funded scientists who enjoy from time to time jeering at professional philosophers while blithely propounding their own philosophical views disguised as empirical science?

So, like Professor Berleant, I urge that we follow Jefferson's example. But I want to stress that Jefferson didn't worry about the possibility of naturalist philosophy being overwhelmed by its fashionable critics. Instead he threw himself into study of the latest scientific investigations, confident that his studies would, sooner or later, strengthen his naturalism.

Let me conclude these comments by saying something about the proper role of historical work in the American tradition. Some of you may be having the unkind thought that my previous remarks are at odds with my quarter century of editorial work on a journal specializing in the history of American philosophy. I plead innocent to the charge of inconsistency. My view is that among the many sorts of activity needed to further the American naturalist tradition, *one* is the activity of critically preserving full use of past work in further enriching the tradition. Dick Robin and I have striven to make the *Transactions* serve that purpose, but we have never supposed that our efforts *alone*—even at their best—are *sufficient* to "advance" American philosophy. In the advancement of American philosophy, as in the advancement of much else that is worthwhile in this world, a division of labor is needed for success. Our aim has been only to help contribute one element needed in the social process—the socially intelligent process—that progressively enriches the American naturalist tradition.

PART THREE

NATURALISM, HOLISM, CONTEXTUALISM

Many of Hare's earliest influences as a student would stay with him throughout his career. At Columbia he would discover Deweyan pragmatic naturalism under philosophers such as John Herman Randall, Herbert Schneider, Joseph Blau, and Justus Buchler. This section highlights many of these influences while also showing that Hare had developed his own holistic and contextualized naturalism. In the first essay Hare discusses the metaphysical status of propositions, an important topic for modern perspectives on logic. His treatment of the topic is mediated through C. J. Ducasse's analysis and has recently received attention from the preeminent historian of logic John Corcoran. The second essay fleshes out many of Hare's early beliefs about pragmatic naturalism. In this piece he develops a so-called "thick" holism, where the deep continuities between our normative and descriptive beliefs are brought to bear. Readers will see from this section that Hare was not simply a historian of philosophical ideas. Rather, as a naturalist he contributed to a number of live epistemological and metaphysical debates.

SEVEN

PROPOSITIONS AND
ADVERBIAL METAPHYSICS

Not many philosophers are adept both in the use of modern techniques of philosophical analysis and in the construction of a comprehensive philosophical system—C. J. Ducasse is one of the few. I share Professor Santoni's estimate of the importance of Ducasse's philosophy and welcome his penetrating examination of an important and challenging part of Ducasse's epistemology. Although in one respect Santoni has perhaps not been entirely fair to Ducasse, he has done an admirable job of showing how Ducasse's analysis of the meaning of "proposition" is in conflict with his ordinary-language methodology, and of explaining Ducasse's difficulties with false propositions.

It is important to point out, however, that a number of Ducasse's doctrines besides his methodology are in conflict with his theory of propositions. Even more important to point out than additional conflicts is the fact that these other doctrines—namely, his adverbial theory of sense data, his analysis of signs and symbols, and his critical realism—provide a foundation for an alternative theory of propositions that not only fits better into Ducasse's system as a whole but seems a more satisfactory theory of propositions whatever its place in a philosophical system.

Santoni's Criticism of Ducasse's Theory of Propositions as Excluding Negative Verb-Forms

Santoni criticizes Ducasse's theory on the grounds that it depends on his mistaken contention that "not" cannot be a constituent of a proposition. Here I think Santoni is not entirely fair to Ducasse. To be sure, Ducasse makes a number of remarks which suggest that he insists upon excluding *every* sort of negative from a proposition, but in fairness to Ducasse it should be noted that he also (in one passage at least) indicates that he wishes to exclude only one kind of negative, and not to exclude another kind, namely, negatives which are *nonassertorial*. Ducasse is willing to include a "not" in a proposition provided that it is made clear that the "not" in the sentence symbolizing such a proposition does not symbolize disbelief. "I would accept," Ducasse says, " 'not short' as a negative term only if it is taken as synonymous with 'either tall or medium-sized.' "[1] "Not short" as synonymous with "either tall or medium-sized" is what I have called nonassertorial since it does not symbolize disbelief. In practice the distinction between assertorial and nonassertorial verb-forms is not easily made. Sentences are often ambiguous in this respect: Their syntax permits their verb-forms to be interpreted as either assertorial or nonassertorial. "God does not exist," for example, may be interpreted as expressing the speaker's disbelief in the proposition symbolized by "God existing" or it may be interpreted as symbolizing the proposition also symbolized by "nonexisting God." It is this ambiguity that has led some philosophers to symbolize a proposition by using a participial phrase (e.g., C. I. Lewis's "Mary making pies"). The syntax of a participial phrase makes it unlikely that negative or affirmative verb forms will be interpreted as symbolizing an epistemic attitude, or what others have called a "propositional attitude." I conclude that Ducasse's nonassertorial theory of propositions is not in the least threatened by his exclusion of "not" since he means to exclude only the *assertorial* sort of "not" from propositions. Santoni's remark that Ducasse takes for granted the "affirmativeness" of propositions seems to indicate that Santoni not only fails to appreciate Ducasse's nonassertorial use of "not" but also fails to take seriously the possibility of a completely nonassertorial theory of propositions. Ducasse's remarks about negative verb-forms can be fairly considered only in the context of such a nonassertorial theory, though admittedly such a theory is in conflict with much ordinary usage.

Ordinary Language and Ducasse's Theory of Propositions

Santoni accurately describes some of the discrepancies between Ducasse's ordinary-language methodology and his account of the meaning of "proposition."[2] Indeed, the venerable doctrine that a proposition is "the verbal expression of a judgment," unpopular as this view is among modern logicians, probably is more in accord with both man-in-the-street usage and the history of logic than Ducasse's account. However, I am less disturbed than Santoni by such discrepancies between Ducasse's philosophical method and his account of the meaning of "proposition."

Though I have not the space to do so here, I believe it can be shown that such discrepancies also exist in other parts of Ducasse's philosophy. In his definitions of "causation," "punishment," "religion," and "art" (to give only a few examples) he also fails to follow consistently his own methodological precepts; but in each case Ducasse's analysis of a key philosophical term is illuminating despite his inability to formulate a formal definition that captures usage. The distinctions he draws attention to have a significance for philosophy which is independent of the particular terminology and its merits that he adopts.

More important than the question of whether Ducasse's account of the meaning of "proposition" reflects ordinary usage as well as he thinks it does is the question of whether his definitions enable him to deal effectively with the many epistemological and metaphysical puzzles which arise when we ask questions about the nature and status of the entities which serve as the objects of believings, doubtings, etc. Ultimately, any theory of propositions stands or falls on its ability to answer these crucial philosophical questions, which arise regardless of the terminology we favor; and it is in dealing with these crucial issues that Ducasse's theory encounters genuinely fatal difficulties. Indeed, Ducasse's account of propositions, as we shall see, is in conflict with his own epistemological and metaphysical principles.

Propositions and Adverbial Metaphysics

Ducasse's unwillingness to identify a proposition with a linguistic entity is understandable. Clearly it is not a sentence itself but what a sentence is used to state that is true or false. However, it is not clear that the rejection of a linguistic theory must lead to the identification of a proposition with a state of affairs. While the identification of a proposition with a state of affairs admittedly has the advantage of avoiding the problem of the subsistence of *true* propositions, the remaining problem of the subsistence of *false* propositions should persuade us to explore other options. Another option is to suppose that a proposition is a species of mental activity *characterizing* a state of affairs that may, or may not, be actual.[3] Whatever objections to this opinion might be advanced, it appears to be an option much more consistent with the adverbial metaphysics Ducasse develops in opposition to G. E. Moore's theory of sense data.[4]

Moore supposes that sense data are entities whose existence is independent of the activity of sensing them, while Ducasse argues that sense data are species or modulations of consciousness.[5] When we see a blue patch, Ducasse says, there is before our mind no blue entity separate from both our mind and the material world—rather we are seeing bluely and patchily. He distinguishes between an "alien" accusative of an activity where the accusative may exist independently of occurrence of the activity (e.g., a fence is an alien accusative of the activity of jumping it) and a "connate" accusative where the accusative can exist only in the occurrence of the activity (e.g., a jump can exist only in the jumping of it). A sense datum is a connate, not an alien, accusative of jumping.

If Ducasse applied these adverbial principles to propositions, he might suppose that a proposition is a species of epistemic mental activity and hence a connate accusative that can exist only in the activity of believing, doubting, etc. The parallel between sense data and propositions can be extended by supposing that just as the activity of sensing may, or may not, have an *alien* accusative (i.e., a material object), so an epistemic mental activity may, or may not, have an alien accusative (i.e., a state of affairs as characterized). A widely accepted logical distinction can be incorporated in the theory by saying that a propositional expression *connotes* a proposition and *denotes* a state of affairs; furthermore, the expression can connote a proposition while having *zero*-denotation (i.e., the proposition expressed is false).

It may be protested that our need to speak of *the* proposition is not satisfied by an adverbial analysis that seems confined to specific occurrences of believing, doubting, etc. This need can, I believe, be satisfied within an adverbial framework by means of a device such as Wilfrid Sellars's notion of a "distributive singular term."[6] Using this technique we say that to speak of *the* proposition that snow is white is equivalent to speaking of all acts of saying or thinking that snow is white.[7]

This is obviously too complicated a matter to be discussed further here, but for our purposes it is sufficient to note that Ducasse does not explore the possibility of a theory of the objects of epistemic attitudes parallel to his theory of the objects of perception. Although Santoni clearly describes major difficulties in Ducasse's theory of propositions, he does not notice that Ducasse has at hand the metaphysical principles to deal with these problems.

Signs and Symbols

Ducasse's theory of propositions appears to be not in harmony with his philosophy of language as well as with his theory of perception. Signs and symbols he analyses in terms of "mental operations."[8] Although Ducasse shares with behaviorists a causal theory in which signs are understood in terms of dispositions to respond, he differs from behaviorists in holding that a response need not be public.[9] His theory of language is a phenomenological version of the stimulus-response theory in which responses may include private images, feelings, desires, and attitudes such as belief and disbelief.

Although Ducasse, in opposition to the behaviorists, insists on the privacy of responses, he is as enthusiastic as the behaviorists in the rejection of an ideational theory according to which meanings are "ideas" somehow existing independently of a tetradic relation between (a) the *interpreter* (the complex of mental habits, dispositions, etc., of the person concerned); (b) the *context of interpretation* (the kinds of things, whether subjective or objective, of which he is conscious at the time); (c) the *interpretand* (a change of some kind supervening in the context of interpretation and thus functioning as cause); and (d) the *interpretant* (a change of some other kind following it immediately and functioning as effect). While behaviorists avoid postulating such independently existing meanings by instead postulating minute neural and muscular changes, Ducasse wishes to avoid both the independently existing meanings of the ideationalists and the minute neural and muscular changes of the behaviorists. But why, if Ducasse considers plausible such an account of the meanings of signs and symbols in terms of mental activities, does he not consider equally plausible an account of propositions in terms of mental activities?

Critical Realism

Finally, it should be noted that Ducasse's theory of propositions implies a direct awareness of independently existing nonmental entities which is incompatible with the causal theory of perception contained in his critical realism. Ducasse says, for example, that " 'perception of physical pressure,' as distinguished from intuition of the kind called 'pressure' intuition, consists in *belief* (unformulated) that *an occurring pressure-intuition is being caused by an event which is* not *being intuited by us.*"[10] We are, he thinks, directly aware of intuitions (mental events) but we can have only an unformulated belief in, not a direct awareness of, the independently exiting entities causing these mental events. But if a proposition is, for Ducasse, an independently existing nonmental state of affairs, how can the principles of critical realism allow us to suppose that we are directly aware of propositions as we must suppose ourselves to be when we are engaged in epistemic mental activity having a proposition as its object? Other philosophers have supposed that because these entities are abstract and outside of the material as well as the mental realm, we can be directly aware of them as we cannot be aware of material objects whose existence we can only infer as the cause of our sensings. However, this platonizing strategy is not available to Ducasse since he has insisted that the constituents of propositions belong to the same realm as the objects of sense perception. In short, the combination of his critical realism and his theory of propositions forces Ducasse to apply two incompatible sets of epistemological principles to one and the same set of objects.

Perhaps if Ducasse had recognized this incompatibility between his theory of propositions and his critical realism as well as the conflicts with his theory of sense data and theory of language, he might have developed an adverbial theory of propositions both plausible in itself and an important contribution to the systematic unity of his philosophy.

EIGHT

THICKENING HOLISTIC PRAGMATISM

Since W. V. Quine propounded a thin holism in 1951 in "Two Dogmas of Empiricism," there has occurred a historical process in which investigators working more or less independently with widely different vocabularies in virtually every specialized area of philosophy and many other disciplines have thickened Quine's holistic web. Fierce critics of holism have often done as much to thicken holism as avid supporters. But we must not assume that increased thickness is to be identified with more extreme holism. Henry Jackman, for example, achieves greater thickness by moderating semantic holism. Pragmatists attribute a degree and type of holism in a specific context consonant with the thickest description available. Morton White finds Quine's holism unacceptable not because discontinuities cannot be found in experience but because Quine, in failing to appreciate the deep continuities between the normative and the descriptive, refuses to accept a thickening of our experience of the world.

I

When philosophers are asked about the status and future of their discipline, they seldom have encouraging news to offer about more than a few pockets of scholarship, usually areas in which they are personally involved. Although I recognize that there are reasons to be discouraged by current trends, in this paper I wish to suggest that in the second half of the twentieth century and the beginning of this century there has occurred a broad philosophical development that has gone unnoticed largely because it has cut across many disciplines in the humanities and sciences. Intellectual work has become so specialized and compartmentalized—each specialty with its own vocabulary and distinctive way of framing problems—that it is difficult for us to recognize a trend that is spread over a wide swath of disciplines. And we hesitate to identify a pervasive intellectual movement that lacks leaders identified by famous prizes or celebrated centers or institutes. Further, the longstanding trend of which I am speaking is obscured by the fact there is, and always has been, fierce debate among contributors to the movement who have myriad agendas that appear unrelated to the overall thrust of the trend. I shall call this encouraging trend "thickening holistic pragmatism." In what follows I shall present a sketch of this development by giving a number of examples.

Before going further I want to concede that I am inviting trouble in using the term "holistic pragmatism." Philosophers have bandied about the term "holism" for many decades—not to mention the freewheeling use of the term in medical contexts and in vernacular speech. The term "pragmatism" is only modestly less troublesome. Even those with only casual acquaintance with the last twenty years of Anglophone philosophy appreciate what a daunting variety of philosophers have been called pragmatists by someone. However, I hope to show by the end of this paper that the idiom I have chosen is helpful.

Perhaps I can best illustrate the dangers implicit in speaking of "holism" by relating some of the things that a logician friend and a philosopher of science have said to me on the subject. My logician friend is anxious to speak of holism only in a narrow, logical sense. In order to flag this narrow sense, he adds the letter "w" and speaks of "the principle of wholistic reference"—a principle he claims was first developed in George Boole's philosophy of logic. The principle goes something like this: Not only is each proposition about some entity or entities, but also about the universe of discourse itself. His choice of orthography is, he says, intended to discourage any suggestion of sympathy with so-called "holistic" philosophies that affirm such theses as that no particular experience could refute any particular belief, that no particular therapy could cure any particular illness, or that no one word has any meaning except in the context of a whole sentence. And the idea that the part depends for its "meaning" on the whole has nothing to do, he insists, with what he is talking about. To my protest that this principle in the philosophy of logic has *something* important in common with the holisms other philosophers have talked about, he reluctantly concedes that his principle has "strong holistic resonance."

My philosopher of science friend worries just as much about how holism might be understood or misunderstood in philosophy of physics. Max Wertheimer and Wolfgang Koehler have, he tells me, characterized Newtonian physics as the prime example of atomistic, nonholistic thinking; classical physics defines a whole as the sum of its parts. On the other hand, he notes, classical mechanics has also been cited as an example of Duhemian holism. On this view, the Newtonian concepts of force, mass, and momentum are all theoretical terms that have meaning only as a result of being part of a relationship. To resolve this oddity, he says, requires that we look at classical physics in some detail. After discoursing at some length on those details, he says that, while it is false that classical physics is a reductionist model of explanation, it is difficult to see why it should have influenced holistic pragmatists of the Quinean sort. Unlike modern field theory, the values of variables are not determined by the relationships in which they occur, he adds. Neither classical physics nor Duhemian philosophy of science supports the view that descriptive and logical statements are on a continuum. He is unpersuaded by the efforts to support the claim of continuity between descriptive and logical statements by appeal to the authority of science itself. According to this view, for example, quantum mechanics, with its concept of "no local entanglement of potentiality," supposedly has thrown doubt on at least one of the laws of logic. However, my friend refers to a recent commentator who, he thinks, has helpfully clarified the role of quantum mechanics in the discussion of holism. According to this commentator, because each related entity has some characteristics—mass, charge, spin—before its emergent properties are evoked, each can be reduced to some extent to atomistic parts, as in classical physics. To further complicate the situation, a quantum system may also vary between being more atomistic at some times and more holistic at others; the degrees of entanglement may vary.

To my knowledge, the most comprehensive critique of holism in its many guises appears in the 1992 book by J. Fodor and E. Lepore called *Holism: A Shopper's Guide.*[1] This is not the place even to attempt to discuss the hundreds of arguments presented by Fodor and Lepore. Fortunately, such a discussion is not necessary for me to make the points that I want to make about the thickening of holism. Just as I am not dismayed by the doubts expressed by my friends in logic and philosophy of science, because the lesson I draw from what they tell me is that much more work needs to be done to sort out the full range of forms of holism so that we can reliably distinguish between them and know where and how a particular form of holism obtains or fails to obtain, I am not bothered by the fact that Fodor and Lepore leave the philosophical battlefield littered with the dead forms of holism. Since I see no reason to assume that the logician's referential holism in relation to universes of discourse has an entailment relation with other forms of holism, I am not disturbed by the dismissive tone he adopts in mentioning other forms of holism. Similarly, since I do not assume that the fact that any particular form of holism that obtains in physics has an entailment relation with other forms of holism in physics, I am not discouraged by the philosopher of science's firm rejection of many forms of holism in physics.

Also, I cannot stress too strongly that I am not suggesting that there are tidy causal chains of historical influence between earlier forms of holism in one domain and later forms of holism in other domains. I know too much about the sociology of ideas and intellectual biography to be tempted by simple causal narratives of that sort. One of the many reasons why such narratives would be seriously misleading is that the thickening trend I am speaking about has often been quickened and deepened by holism's fiercest critics. For example, critics of Quine's holism may often have understood themselves as doing serious damage to the future prospects of holism when actually in the long term their critiques served to thicken and strengthen the forms of holism that survive those criticisms. Though it has never been his intention, it may ironically be that in the long run Fodor will turn out to be one of holism's most helpful friends. Sometimes, it seems, there is a philosophical analogue of Adam Smith's "invisible hand." Ambitious intellectuals in many fields try with all their might to score points in specialized battles with their opponents without any intention of making the contribution to the thickening trend that they are in fact making. Such are sometimes the benefits of the free market of ideas.

II

Some of Henry Jackman's work nicely illustrates how constructive responses can be made to the challenges holism faces. Jackman's approach has additional appeal for me because in other of his publications he has done much to develop the type of pragmatism found in William James, so I think that Jackman can be counted among holistic pragmatists, though he never uses that term, and his brand of holistic pragmatism is different from that found in the work of Morton White, a philosopher I will later discuss. Jackman ably defends what he calls "moderate" holism in the face of what he terms "the instability thesis." His argument goes as follows:

> Mental or semantic *holism* can be roughly characterized as the doctrine that the meanings of one's sentences or the contents of one's beliefs are a function of (and are determined by) their relations to all of one's other sentences and beliefs. Holistic theories of meaning and content are typically criticized for (among other things) leaving the ideas of translation, disagreement, and change of mind problematic. However, such criticisms are more properly directed at an "instability thesis" that, while often taken to be a consequence of holism, can be separated from it. A "moderate" holist need not be committed to the instability thesis, and can thus avoid many of the problems traditionally associated with holism.
>
> Holism has two alternatives: atomism (the doctrine that each of one's beliefs or sentences gets its content independently of its relation to one's other beliefs or sentences) and molecularism (the doctrine that each of one's beliefs or sentences gets its content of its relation to a corresponding subset of one's other beliefs or sentences). Atomistic and molecular theories face a number of well-known problems. Nevertheless, they are favored over holistic theories because holism seems to

demand that *any* differences in belief must result in differences in meaning and content. Among the most frequently cited reasons for not being a holist are the following consequences of this purported demand.

First, holism seems to make literal translation from one person's language into another's impossible. No two people have exactly the same beliefs, so by insisting that what one means by one's terms is a function of all one's beliefs, holism suggests that no two people mean quite the same thing by any of their terms. If what one meant by, say, "elephant" were determined by one's elephant beliefs, then someone who believed that "elephants are afraid of mice" would mean something different by "elephant" than someone who disbelieved it. . . . Unless two people share *all* their beliefs, they wouldn't share *any* of them. . . . Consequently, a translation from one of their languages into the other's couldn't be completely accurate, and their ascriptions of beliefs to each other would be, strictly speaking, false . . . [and] we would never fully grasp the content of anyone's words and thoughts. Worse still, the same phenomenon occurs with even our most recently past selves. Since our total set of beliefs is constantly changing, the holist seems committed to saying that the meanings of all of our terms and the contents of our beliefs are constantly changing as well. . . .

Similarly, holism seems to make disagreement over matters of fact impossible. Peter and Mary might have *seemed* to disagree over a matter of fact about elephants, but the holist can only treat their "disagreement" as being over whether or not to accept the sentence "elephants are afraid of mice." Since the two would mean different things by the sentence, their "disagreement" would just be a case of their talking past each other. . . . Holism also seems to make it impossible to disagree with one's own past self. . . . Such purported consequences of holism are extremely counterintuitive. . . .

Short of giving up holism in favor of atomism or molecularism, there are two popular responses to the problems raised above. One is to adopt a "two factor" theory in which a "narrow content" is determined holistically while a nonholistic "wide content" is comparatively invariant and shared. . . . The other response is to suggest that we replace talk of content identity and difference with talk of content similarity. Both of these responses, however, concede that the holist is committed to what will here be called the "instability thesis," namely:

Any change in one's attitude toward a sentence will change the meanings of the terms contained in it and the contents of the associated beliefs. Since the instability thesis requires that there be no changes of belief without changes of meaning, its truth would leave meaning and content tremendously unstable. . . . Nevertheless, holism's commitment to the instability thesis is assumed by its defenders as often as by its critics. Both of the responses mentioned above suggest ways for the holist to try to live with the instability thesis. The first admits the instability thesis to be true of one type of content, and then looks for a second nonholistic type of content for which it doesn't hold. The second suggests that we accommodate the instability thesis by realizing that we can replace talk of *sameness* of meaning or content with talk of *similarity* of meaning and content, and recognize that the thesis doesn't leave meaning *that* unstable. . . .

Fortunately, such attempts to make the instability thesis palatable may not be necessary because it isn't at all obvious that every holist must embrace instability. Holism only requires that the content of any one of one's beliefs *depend upon* or be a *function of* one's other beliefs, and *this* claim need not commit one to the instability thesis. After all, one can claim that *A* is a function of *B* without implying that any change in *B* will produce a change in *A*. Consider, for instance, the claim that one's final letter grade in a class is a function of (depends upon) the results of one's exams, quizzes, and homework. The truth of this claim certainly doesn't entail that no two people could have the same final grade unless they had precisely the same score on all of their homework, exams, and quizzes. Neither does it entail that any change to one of one's quiz scores will produce a change in one's final grade. Each result makes *some* contribution to one's final grade, but not every change among the contributors will produce a corresponding change in the ultimate outcome. The function from contributing scores to final grades is *many-to-one*, and thus allows a good deal of stability in the output in spite of the possibility of tremendous variation in the input. . . .

We can thus distinguish *moderate* versions of holism, which treat the function from belief to meaning as many-to-one (and thus allow variations in belief that fail to produce variations in meaning), from *radical* versions of holism, which treat the function as one-to-one (and thus require any change in belief to produce a corresponding change in meaning). It is only radical holism that entails the instability thesis.[2]

There is much more to Jackman's moderate holism, much more than I can discuss here, but I would like to highlight briefly the *contextualism* of this form of holism. He writes:

There are two traditional ways in which a word's semantic value can be context sensitive. The first is to be ambiguous. "Bank," for instance, has two entries in one's mental lexicon: one designating a financial institution, and another designating the edge of a river. The context-sensitivity of "bank" is thus explained in terms of the different lexical entries being assessed in different contexts. The second is for the word's semantic value to incorporate an "indexical" component, allowing the entry for the word in one's mental lexicon to make reference to various contextual features. The word "here," for instance, is context-sensitive because the entry for it in one's lexicon makes reference to its place of utterance. However, there are many cases where words seem to refer to different things in different contexts without being straightforwardly ambiguous or indexical, and such contextual variation is exactly what semantic holism predicts.

Semantic holism is here (very) roughly characterized as the doctrine that the semantic values of one's words is a function of all of one's explicit and implicit commitments that involve the words. . . .

Holistic theories of semantic value are thus typically accused of (among other things) entailing that no two people (or no person at two times) ever attach the same semantic value to any of their words.[3]

But Jackman suggests that we can solve this problem by using the same strategy that we used above. We can conceive of the function as a many-to-one relation and say that a moderate holist about semantic value

> can consistently claim that the semantic value of what one's words mean is a function of *all* of one's beliefs without suggesting that *any* change to these beliefs would produce a corresponding change in semantic value. . . . If the function from belief to semantic value allows some constancy of output through variations in input, then holism won't entail that semantic values are unstable.
>
> We can arrive at such a holistic account of semantic value by tying the semantic value of a speaker's terms to whatever object or set of objects maximizes the (weighted) total number of truths the speaker is committed to. Such an account of semantic value will undoubtedly be holistic: a term picks out the object it does because of the role that object plays in contributing, either directly or indirectly, to the truth of countless beliefs. Nevertheless, even if countless beliefs played some role in determining the term's reference, there is little reason to think that a change in one (or even a considerable number) of these beliefs will change what is referred to.[4]

Note that,

> the function which maximizes the number of truths believed by the speaker can account for these contextual features by looking to maximize not just the total number of true beliefs, but rather some *weighted* total of them. Some beliefs will be more important to the speaker than others, and preserving the truth of these beliefs will have a higher priority than preserving the truth of the beliefs assigned less weight.[5]

Thus, Jackman argues, the reference weighing will be contextually sensitive to the speaker's *interests* at the time of utterance.

What I have said so far has suggested how the philosophical understanding of holism has "thickened" since the middle of the last century. Gradually philosophers have come to be able to distinguish many types of holism and, most importantly, to explain why particular types obtain in some contexts and not in others. Once the analysis of holism becomes context-sensitive, it is possible for philosophers such as Jackman to formulate and convincingly defend "moderate" forms of holism in this or that particular context. I hasten to add, and I am sure Jackman would agree, that this encouraging thickening has not yielded in a general theory of holism. At best it can be said to yield a "research program."

III

How does pragmatism figure into all this? To be sure, most discussions of holism make no mention of pragmatism. I focus my attention on "holistic pragmatism" for two reasons. First, I want to highlight the role of *interests* in the contextual sensitivity found in thickened and moderate holisms such as that of Jackman described above. Relativity to interests is, of course, central to any pragmatism. I also wish to draw attention to a form of holism that links the descriptive and the normative *holistically*, a type of linkage more characteristic of the pragmatist tradition than of any other tradition.

Significantly, W. V. Quine, a philosopher usually considered in the pragmatist tradition, was responsible directly or indirectly for stimulating a vast literature on holism and related ideas. The critical discussion of Quine's brand of holism is daunting in its bulk. Fortunately, there is no need for me to attempt a summary of all the critiques of Quine on this subject that have been published. I shall limit my attention to criticism of Quine for not extending holism to the normative, in particular the criticism developed by Quine's longtime colleague and friend Morton White. I take the exchange between Quine and White to be an illuminating example of how holistic pragmatism can be thickened.

The best way to understand the beginnings of White's view is to see how he reacted to Quine's modification of Pierre Duhem's holism. Duhem held that science never tests a *single* belief but always a *body* of beliefs. As Quine famously expressed the doctrine: Our statements about the external world "face the tribunal of sense experience not individually but only as a corporate body."[6] But Quine proposed to extend Duhem's view so that not only scientific principles are involved but also logic and mathematics. Hence formal truths, for Quine, bear a relation to the external world not different in kind from the relation that empirical statements bear to the world of sense. What White urged was that the Duhemian doctrine be extended far beyond what Quine would allow. He argued that we should "broaden our linguistic structure so that it includes ethical statements, and broadens the other element in the situation beyond sensory experience to include feelings of approval, revulsion, loathing, etc., toward actions."[7] Starting in 1956, White has wished to break down not only the analytic-synthetic dichotomy but also the remaining dualism between logic-cum-empirical science and ethics. His aim has been to close "the epistemic gap between the normative and the descriptive."[8] He outlines the contrast between his view and Quine's as follows:

> In developing his version of Duhem's approach, Quine has sometimes distinguished (a) the descriptive scientific thinker, (b) the body of purely descriptive science that such a thinker uses as a tool for organizing or linking sensory experiences, and (c) those sensory experiences themselves. By analogy, when I deal with normative belief I distinguish (a') the normative thinker, (b') the body of descriptive *and* normative beliefs that a normative thinker uses as a tool for organizing

or linking sensory experiences with each other *and with emotions,* and (c') those experiences and emotions themselves.[9]

White's illustration of this holistic testing process is illuminating:

> I ask Quine to suppose that the following argument is presented by a critic of abortion, bearing in mind that it does not make explicit any assumed logical truth that might be added by the holist who wanted to dramatize the fact that such logical truths were also elements of the system of beliefs in question:
>
> (1) Whoever takes the life of a human being does something that ought not to be done.
> (2) The mother took the life of a fetus in her womb.
> (3) Every living fetus in the womb of a human being is a human being.
>
> Therefore,
>
> (4) The mother took the life of a human being.
>
> Therefore,
>
> (5) The mother did something that ought not to be done.[10]

Next White supposes that the mother lacks the feeling that she was obligated not to have done what she did. She might then, White suggests, be justified under certain conditions to deny (5) and in doing so would be doing what a scientist might be doing upon "failing to have a sensory experience that was predicted by some chunk of purely descriptive belief."[11] She would have a recalcitrant *feeling* compared to the recalcitrant *sensory experience* that famously figures crucially in Quine's view.

After denying (5) the mother may deny the conjunction that implies it, may amend or abandon a logical law that gets us from (2) and (3) to (4); an ethical principle such as (1); or a descriptive statement such as (2), (3), or (4). If she denies (3), she has a different conjunction of beliefs since she has replaced one descriptive belief with another, namely, with the belief that not every living fetus in the womb of a human being is a human being. According to White, altering one's logic in response to feelings about the act is analogous to altering one's logic in response to sensory experience. "If [White argues] a conjunction containing descriptive and moral statements logically implies a moral conclusion which is denied, we may alter the conjunction by surrendering *either* a moral or a descriptive statement."[12]

White stresses that he does not advocate giving up the distinction between normative and descriptive sentences. He does not wish to reduce "ought" sentences to "is" sentences. What he wants to give up is the epistemological distinction between the *testing* of the two types of sentences, that is, to give up a methodological dualism to which Quine is committed. This he thinks is comparable to what Quine does when he keeps a distinction between logical and empirical statements while rejecting a distinction between the *testing* of logical and nonlogical statements. By giving a holistic account of normative belief, he hopes to have persuaded Quine to "strike yet another blow for methodological monism,"[13] to have convinced Quine to abandon another "untenable dualism."

This is not the place to give a full account of the long-running exchange on this subject between White and Quine. Suffice it to say that Quine's acceptance of Carnap's version of what constitutes cognitive meaning (i.e., his positivism) prevents him from accepting White's holistic treatment of the normative.

But there is one important further lesson I wish to draw from the White-Quine exchange. Further thickening of holistic pragmatism demands, I suggest, a theory of epistemic value and virtue epistemology that is entirely foreign to Quine's philosophy and in no small part absent from White's work.

Quine explains his disagreement with White on the status of epistemic values by saying: "Naturalization of epistemology does not jettison the normative and settle for the indiscriminate description of ongoing procedures. For me normative epistemology is a branch of engineering. It is the technology of truth or prediction."[14] For Quine, epistemic practices can have only *extrinsic* value, as means to the *intrinsic* value of truth or prediction. He allows for the criticism of existing epistemic practices but only on the grounds that the "engineering" could be improved so that more truth or prediction is produced. When White cites Quine's remark about "the ultimate duty of language, science, and philosophy," Quine explains that he was using "duty" only as a way to refer to the *purpose* of language, science, and philosophy, what they are good *for*. White makes the same objection to this as he did to David Hume's and G. E. Moore's analyses of ethical concepts. Both Hume and Moore, White says, try "to tell us what we *mean* by saying that certain acts are moral crimes, namely, that they have causal consequences of a certain kind."[15] In Hume's case this is naturalistic reductionism, whereas Moore's reductionism is antinaturalistic, but both appeal to the mysterious notion of synonymy. However, White felt some hesitation in going after Quine's covert appeal to meanings here because at least in this passage Quine "explicitly rests his view on what he calls the *purpose* of science and not on what is *meant* by science."[16] So instead White points out that "the notion of purpose in this context may be as obscure as the notion of meaning."[17]

White also takes exception to Quine's remark about "epistemic values." He doubts that normally "we regard science's respect for older truths and for simplicity as *contributory* epistemic values."[18] Quoting William James at length, White urges that we acknowledge that there are independent epistemic values which "might be ordered differently or assigned different weights by different scientists and philosophers."[19]

Interestingly, the naturalized epistemologist Alvin Goldman has defended roughly the same view that White finds problematic in Quine. Goldman "makes a case for the unity of epistemic virtues in which the cardinal value, or underlying motif, is something like true, or accurate, belief. I call this view *veritism*."[20] Although Goldman's account is basically "externalist," he attempts to take account of our internalist intuitions by saying that "the core epistemic value is a high degree of truth-possession *on topics of interest*."[21] But feelings (e.g., of obligation) are clearly given derivative status by Goldman. He says, for example, "Subjective justifiedness is a secondary concept, derived in an obvious way from objective justifiedness."[22] He also tries to mollify the critics of veritism by saying that he does not "deny that moral values might sometimes trump epistemic values. . . . Although veritistic value is the fundamental benchmark of epistemic virtue, it is obviously not the *only value*. Nor is it the preeminent value for all purposes of life and action."[23] This sounds similar to something that Quine tells White. Quine admits that sometimes moral and epistemic norms are intertwined "but not inextricably. Falsification of an experiment is immoral, and also it is epistemologically inefficacious, however rewarding in respect to fame and fortune."[24] In other words, Quine thinks that from the fact that an act or belief can have both moral and epistemic properties it does not follow that there are any *epistemic* values independent of the value of true belief and prediction.

In contrast to Quine's and Goldman's veritism, normative epistemology, for White, is a heterogeneous conjunction of beliefs, practices, sensory experiences, and emotions. Though White vigorously defends a form of *methodological* monism, he is dubious about a monism of epistemic values.

Mention should be made of the book, *The Collapse of the Fact/Value Dichotomy and Other Essays*, published by White's former student Hilary Putnam.[25] Although Putnam's critique of the fact/value dichotomy is doubtless more fine-grained and informed by recent literature than White's, White's holistic pragmatism is, I suggest, stronger than Putnam's in at least two respects: (a) White's approach encourages an improved view of a key epistemic value, and (b) his form of holism has more to contribute to the virtue epistemology that thickened holistic pragmatism requires. Let me explain.

As I have noted, White is critical of Quine's view that the *only* intrinsic epistemic value is truth or prediction. Goldman has a much more elaborately worked out version of basically the same view. Quite apart from the fact that White holds that there are many other intrinsic epistemic values, his version of the temporal endpoint of inquiry is strikingly more consonant with the most recent work in the theory of epistemic justification than Quine's version. I cannot here review today's complex debates about epistemic justification. But there are, I think, powerful reasons to replace the goal of "true belief" with the goal of "understanding." Mark Bross provides a concise statement of what understanding is:

> Understanding is holistic, and by this I mean that when some content is understood, the subject is able to relate the content to other things so that the subject can use it for her purposes. An alternative way to put the same point is that when a subject understands a certain content X, she is able to see the interconnectedness between X and some other facts. Perceiving and awareness, on the other hand, are atomistic states such that a subject can perceive or be aware of X without seeing any connection between X and any other information. Second, the cognitive state of understanding is often an unconscious state whereas perceiving and being aware are usually considered conscious states. By "unconscious" here, I simply mean a subject is usually not consciously aware of understanding some content X and cannot tell by reflection or introspection that she understands X.[26]

The kinship should be clear between understanding so described and what White speaks of as trying "to work a manageable structure into a flux composed of both sensory experiences and feelings of moral obligation."[27] It should also be apparent that this way to conceive of this key epistemic value better captures *both* our internalist intuitions and our externalist intuitions than true belief or predictive power do; the latter shows a decided externalist bias.

The second notable strength of White's approach is that it can make a contribution to virtue epistemology. Linda Zagzebski, whose virtue epistemology is arguably more fully developed than any other, provides a long list of epistemic virtues and skills, and then argues in Aristotelian fashion that the virtue of *phronesis* is required if the whole conjunction of virtues and skills is to work. "The ability to mediate between and among the individual moral virtues must be itself a virtue. *Phronesis* is defined in part as the virtue that has this function."[28] I suggest that the holistic and pragmatic method that White recommends is, in effect, a version of the second-order virtue of *phronesis*. The ability and disposition to give manageable structure to one's heterogeneous flux of sensory experiences and feelings, surrendering a belief there, adding a feeling here, etc., is a second-order virtue without which all our first-order epistemic virtues are largely useless in our efforts to navigate a world of problems without shipwreck.

IV

Let me summarize the narrative I have given so far. I have suggested that, if one surveys the recent philosophical landscape, one can pull together materials from (a) discriminating and moderate holism, (b) Morton White's holistic pragmatism, (c) virtue epistemology, and (d) theories of epistemic value, to use in the development of a thicker form of holistic pragmatism. Where the materials I have already discussed are strongest lie in the *epistemological* and *linguistic* dimensions of holistic pragmatism. Recall that White is especially concerned to find a single method of *testing* both empirical claims and normative judgments. And Henry Jackman's work is illustrative of how *philosophy of language* can be developed in the direction of a thicker holistic pragmatism. Where the above materials are weakest is in the *ontological* dimensions of holistic pragmatism.

Let me now briefly discuss materials that are especially useful in filling out the ontological features. Joseph Rouse's book *How Scientific Practices Matter: Reclaiming Philosophical Naturalism*[29] contains an abundance of such materials. And it should be noted Rouse himself draws heavily on materials found in recent philosophers such as Sellars, Putnam, McDowell, Haugeland, and Brandom who are in some ways allied with his own naturalism. He also devotes extended sympathetic discussion to allies among feminist epistemologists such as Lynn Hankinson Nelson and Helen Logino. Though Rouse has in mind a genealogy different from mine, a genealogy that makes little reference to the pragmatist tradition and no reference at all to Morton White, there are striking similarities between his preferred form of naturalism and what I speak of as thickened holistic pragmatism. In my idiom, the natural necessities that are central to Rouse's philosophy are crucial elements in the holistic web. As it happens, Rom Harre and Edward H. Madden developed a similar theory of *natural necessity* more than thirty years ago without thinking of their theory as part of an overall project of naturalism of the sort Rouse favors or as part of some form of pragmatism.[30] Though Harre and Madden worked out their view, a view that includes the notion of a "powerful particular," in order to save problems in the ontology and epistemology of science, it is helpful in order to develop a broader philosophical theory. A moderate holism calls for the replacement of narrowly empiricist ontologies by an ontology that counts *modalities* as fully real elements of the natural world. Insofar as the web is constituted by relations of *causal* dependence, a naturalistic account of the causal powers of particulars is also required.

The normativity of practices that figures so prominently in Rouse's work is similarly important to the thickening I have in mind. "We should," Rouse says, "recognize . . . the normativity of nature, manifest in the possibilities expressible in part through scientific practices."[31] "Causality," he adds, "must be understood as always already normative, and normativity always already causally efficacious. . . . The *intra*twining of the normativity of understanding and action with the causal powers of things must actually be intelligibly articulated."[32] His account of intentionality is also based on mutual implication of a holistic and pragmatic sort. "Causal determinacy and intentional significance," he writes, "are mutually implicated rather than either being the independently intelligible ground for the explication of the other. . . . Only a being intra-actively situated in the world can engage in intentional interpretation."[33]

V

Proponents of thickening holism, as I noted at the outset, are by no means limited to the philosophical profession. They are scattered across the humanities and sciences. The influential anthropologist Clifford Geertz is an example of this methodological orientation. In an essay entitled "Thick Description: Toward an Interpretative Theory of Culture," Geertz says:

> The concept of culture I espouse . . . is essentially a semiotic one. . . . [M]an is an animal suspended in webs of significance he himself has spun, [and] I take culture to be those webs, and the analysis of it to be therefore not an experimental science in search of law but an interpretive one in search of meaning. . . . [C]ulture is not a power, something to which social events, behaviors, institutions, or processes can be causally attributed; it is a content, something within which they can be intelligibly—that is, thickly—described.[34]

Recent ("second generation") cognitive science is another domain of inquiry, a highly interdisciplinary domain, in which numerous efforts have been made to advance theories that are thick and holistic. One of the best-known books surveying this research is Andy Clark's *Being There: Putting Brain, Body, and World Together Again*. Clark tells us:

> The nature and bounds of the intelligent agent look increasingly fussy. Gone is the central executive in the brain—the real boss who organizes and integrates the activities of multiple special-purpose subsystems. And gone is the neat boundary between the thinker (the bodiless intellectual engine) and the thinker's world. . . . [I]t may for some purposes be wise to consider the intelligent system as a spatio-temporally extended process not limited by the tenuous envelope of skin and skull. . . . Cognitive science . . . can no longer afford the individualistic, isolationist biases that characterized its early decades. We now need a wider view—one that incorporates a multiplicity of ecological and cultural approaches as well as the traditional core of neuroscience, linguistics, and artificial intelligence.[35]

Mark Johnson has perhaps best canvassed this work and explained its philosophical significance most recently in *The Meaning of the Body: Aesthetics of Human Understanding.* He "attempts to provide a thick description of the bodily origins of meaning in sensorimotor processes and in feelings." He adds: "If mind and body are not two separate and distinct ontological kinds, then thought must emerge via recruitment of various sensorimotor capacities that do not involve representations." Moreover, *"Meaning is not just what is consciously entertained in acts of feeling and thought; instead, meaning reaches deep down into our corporeal encounter with our environment."*[36] He urges that we "stop treating percepts, concepts, propositions, and thoughts as quasi-objects (mental entities or abstract structures) and . . . instead see them as patterns of experiential interaction . . . modes of interaction and action."[37] This embodied cognitive science he often explicitly links with the pragmatist philosophies of William James and John Dewey.

As a final example of thickening let me mention the debates concerning emergence and supervenience that have been raging for many decades. The reductionists have fiercely battled the antireductionists. The pictures offered of the relations between parts and wholes have become ever more subtle and complex. One inescapable product of this seemingly interminable dispute is the conclusion that emergence comes in many degrees and types, and that some types and degrees of emergence under some conditions are compatible with some types and degrees of reduction. Those philosophers of physics who settle on an ontological position somewhere intermediate between unqualified reductionism and unqualified emergentism are adopting a position in philosophy of science comparable to the moderate holism in the philosophy of language of Jackman described above.[38] In both domains of philosophical debate, moderate holism is achieved by *thickening* descriptions of the relations between parts and wholes.

VI

To sum up, since Quine propounded a *thin* holism in "Two Dogmas" in the middle of the last century, there has occurred a historical process in which many investigators working more or less independently with widely different vocabularies in virtually every specialized area of our discipline and in other disciplines in myriad ways have thickened Quine's web. Although no one has directed this zigzagging development and there is lively disagreement among the contributors, there has been remarkable confluence among investigators. As I noted above, we may discern an "invisible hand" at work in this philosophical progress comparable to the invisible hand Adam Smith saw in economic progress. This is not to say that there do not remain large gaps in our understanding. Unsurprisingly, there is no general theory of holism on the horizon since thick holism is, by its very nature, context-sensitive, as we have seen in Jackman's moderate holism. But we are justified in adopting a melioristic attitude toward this trend. With continued effort by investigators in many fields, gains in thickness will be made, and critiques of holism will often enhance thickness as much as fervent support does. However, consonant with the fallibilistic empiricism of pragmatism, we must not suppose that a priori principles will ever be discovered from which can be deduced what specific forms of holism obtain in a specific context. Moreover, we must guard against any assumption that greater thickness is to be identified with more extreme holism. Recall that Jackman achieves greater thickness by *moderating* semantic holism. To aim toward thicker holism is very different from aiming toward *radical* holism. One reason that empiricistically inclined philosophers and scientists are often suspicious of holism is that they fear a revival of the metaphysics of internal relations. They shun any holism that is committed (if only covertly) to the a priori truth that everything is internally related to everything else, a type of holism found in some forms of idealism. They are leery of even a *presumption* of internal relatedness. However, the holism championed by such philosophers as Jackman, White, Rouse, Clark, and Johnson as well as by the anthropologist Geertz is scrupulously based on experimental evidence. Like William James and John Dewey, they appeal to *experience* of both continuities and discontinuities. They attribute a degree of holism in a specific context consonant with the thickest description available. In their methodology we are enjoined to seek the thickest description possible without regard to the degree or type of holism implied. Their grievance is not against those who draw attention to our experience of discontinuities. Their complaint is instead against those who, because they refuse to recognize experience of continuities as well as of discontinuities, are to that extent barred from giving thick descriptions. As we have seen, Quine's holism is unacceptable to White not because no discontinuities can be found in experience but because in an important respect Quine refuses to endorse a thick description of our experience of the world—specifically to appreciate the deep continuities between the normative and the descriptive.

PART FOUR

THE PHILOSOPHY OF RELIGION

Some may find it surprising that a committed naturalist such as Hare was so involved with issues pertinent to religion. Yet many of his most recognized papers contributed to an extended debate with nonnaturalists. He is perhaps best remembered in the philosophy of religion for his views on the problem of evil—how evil can exist in a world many believe was created by an omnibenevolent, omnipotent, and omniscient being. In the first essay provided, Hare argues against many of the most established explanations of the problem of evil, ultimately arguing that the theist's solutions to this problem are frequently inconsistent.

In the second essay, Hare argues for the separation of speculative metaphysics and religious belief. In particular the case he makes here shows Hare's on-going engagement with nonnaturalists on issues in the philosophy of religion. We see this once again in the third essay of the section. Here Hare takes a very uncharacteristic position in that he argues for the apparent compatibility of Justus Buchler's metaphysics and Whitehead's process theology without resorting to humanistic theologies. Readers will find it an interesting and unexpected position for him to adopt. However, on greater reflection, we believe it was one of Hare's most clever essays.

NINE

ON THE DIFFICULTY OF EVADING
THE PROBLEM OF EVIL

with Edward H. Madden

I

There have been many attempts to make religious belief, commitment, and language immune to criticism and to make ordinary and scientific concepts of evidence irrelevant to them. The point of such attempts is to evade the usual critiques of historical religion, the problems posed by higher criticism, conflicts with science, and epistemic discussions about adequate evidence. To some religious people this tactic has seemed to have an application to the problem of evil, although others have felt that while the position in general is right it has no application to the problem of evil. Our contention is that the position not only has no application to the problem of evil but is implausible in general and, hence, that not only is the difficulty with evil a good reason for rejecting religion but that the traditional critiques, for anything this position shows to the contrary, also constitute good reasons for such rejection.

The general evasionist view is established or justified by radically different means even though the final result is identical. Recent attempts to establish the view reflect the influence of Karl Barth and Paul Tillich, on the one hand, and certain interpretations of the later Wittgenstein and J. L. Austin, on the other. We will briefly explain each justification in turn and then show why none of them either has an application to the problem of evil or is tenable in its own right.

(1) According to Barth, the whole of rational theology is not only useless but exhibits on the part of those who indulge in it a sinful nature.[1] It is useless because rational arguments are irrelevant to the true basis of belief and pernicious because it recognizes by implication the legitimacy of the traditional rational critiques of historical Christianity. Rational theology in all aspects is sinful because it puts human reason above revelation. It is the sin of intellectual pride, the old sin of seeking to eat of the tree of the knowledge of good and evil.[2] Barth's advice is to abandon such theology and return to Reformation concepts. Man has a completely corrupt nature and can have no insight into religious truth through any human capacity whatever. Belief and salvation come to some wholly through the grace of God. *Fides sola gratia* is the watchword of neoorthodoxy. Moreover, although revelation is granted to some people, they can never know that they have been the recipients of it. Man, in short, has no point of contact with the divine. The only thing he can do is hope and worship.[3]

While Barth rejects natural theology he is not simply an irrationalist. He does not wholly eschew "reason" but rather locates and interprets it in his own special way. Reason, he thinks, consists in conforming to the object of knowledge, not in ratiocination, and in the case of religion this means conforming to the content of revelation.[4] The Christian Revelation, in turn, he tries to show is the Revelation. It is in this sense that Barth is said by some "to adjust assent to the evidence." Such evidence, he seems to think, is conclusive. If a theologian accepts the Christian Revelation and exhibits believing obedience, he becomes invulnerable to external criticism. "If revelation of this kind is reflected upon by those who claim it and the result is called theology, where is there access for the nontheological critic? The method and structure of theology, thus conceived, can be criticized only in intra-theological debate, which is what Barth intends."[5]

(2) Tillich rejects natural theology on existential grounds. "In every assumedly scientific theology," he writes, "there is a point where individual experiences, traditional valuation, and personal commitment must decide

the issue."[6] However metaphysical or empirical one's concept of God may be, it is really based on an immediate experience of ultimate value and being of which one can become intuitively aware.[7] All rational justifications for believing in God only confirm what was present from the beginning. Conversely, no rational arguments against such a belief are effective because, coming from another frame of reference, they are "foreign," "external," "outside," and hence irrelevant. This is what Tillich calls "the theological circle."

Tillich is eager to show that Christianity, while basically existential and voluntaristic, is not irrational in the sense of being self-contradictory or demanding assent to the absurd.[8] Consider the doctrine of the logos made flesh in Jesus the Christ. This claim that Christ unites universal Being in concrete form is not a genuinely self-contradictory claim. It is not like saying that this table is black and white all over at the same moment. It is rather a *paradoxical* claim that adumbrates a dynamic, Hegelian-like ontology that is at odds with Aristotle's static ontology, not with his law of noncontradiction. While such a paradoxical claim is not self-contradictory, it is, Tillich contends, not a matter of rational apprehension either. Ultimately all Christian paradoxes transcend reason. "This is indicated by the ecstatic state in which all biblical and classical theological *paradoxa* appear."[9] Paradoxes, in short, are simply fumbling cognitive ways of pointing toward spiritual truths that can never be adequately pictured.

(3) The existential theological circle has been transformed by some writers into a linguistic theological circle.[10] Intelligibility takes many and varied forms, the argument goes, but there is no norm for intelligibility "in general." Criteria of logic arise in contexts of "ways of living" or "modes of social life" and only make sense in their respective frameworks. Science, for example, is one such mode of life and religion is another, and each has criteria of intelligibility peculiar to itself. "So within science or religion actions can be logical or illogical; in science, for example, it would be illogical to refuse to be bound by the results of a properly carried out experiment; in religion it would be illogical to suppose that one could pit one's own strength against God's; and so on. But we cannot sensibly say that either the practice of science itself or that of religion is either illogical or logical; both are nonlogical."[11] The specific frameworks themselves provide the criteria for some special kind of sense and logic. The implication

of all this is that any frame of reference, any way of living or mode of social life, provides its own autonomous and unassailable language system. Given the fact that the language-game of religion is played, there simply is no way in which it can be logically inappropriate or improper to engage in it. It simply cannot be criticized from the outside; indeed, it cannot even be *understood* from the outside.

Those who use different variants of the linguistic circle maneuver agree on the importance of distinguishing between "belief in" God and "belief in the existence of" God, and at this point are all agreeing with their neoorthodox and existentialist counterparts.[12] "Belief in" God is a genuinely religious concept while "belief in the existence of" God is a scientific type notion to which rational, nonreligious criteria of evidence are applicable. To ask the question in a religious context is to mix "modes of life" inadmissibly and to invite confusion. The religious man does not talk *about* God but talks *to* him. When someone says "I believe in God, the Father Almighty" he is not asserting that he believes that God exists but is *performing an act* through the use of these words which makes perfectly good sense and is unassailable within its own frame of reference.

Our reply to these evasions, as we indicated, is twofold. We will attempt to show that none of them has an application to the problem of evil and that all are implausible in general and hence no detriment to the many traditional criticisms of religion they were designed to meet.

(i) The problem of evil, it must be noted at once, is neither a part of rational theology nor a criticism that is imposed upon religious belief from some external frame of reference. Thus all the present evasion efforts are simply irrelevant to the problem of evil. To classify the discussion of God and evil as rational theology is to confuse the two notions of rational theology and being rational about theology. The former requires reasons for believing in God, while the latter requires only that beliefs about God, on whatever grounds they are held, cohere and match in some intelligible way. This does not mean that there is no room in religion for paradoxes and mysteries like "the logos made flesh," but it does mean that there is no room for absurdity and incompatibility. Neoorthodox writers certainly agree to this stipulation. Now the point is that there is prima facie gratuitous evil in the world which never gets resolved by the recurring combinations of old solutions, a deficiency which suggests that there is a real incompatibility or nonmatching of beliefs in a theistic framework. This nonmatching of beliefs is not a paradox or mystery in the supposedly admissible sense but is an absurdity or incompatibility of the type neoorthodox writers in other contexts renounce. Moreover, to be puzzled by this difficulty and seek an answer (or even to be persuaded that it has no solution and thus counts as a good reason for rejecting religious belief) is certainly not to exhibit sinful pride. The effort to make one's views a coherent whole is not a matter of sitting in judgment upon God but is rather an effort to understand what it is one believes. Such "reasonableness" can be viewed by a godly man as just as much a divine gift as faith and consequently no more vain than the latter. Indeed, some Christian writers think that the charge of pride and vanity might well be made of neoorthodoxy rather than of those thinkers who try to solve the problem.[13]

Finally, the problem of prima facie gratuitous evil is clearly not a problem forced upon theism from an external frame of reference that has different concepts of evidence and reasonableness. It is a problem wholly indigenous to the religious frame of reference and requires a reexamination of basic concepts within that system. The problem is either how to stretch the three concepts of evil and God's unlimited power and goodness without actually abandoning one or more of them as quasi theists do, or how to match up the three concepts if they are interpreted in a strict and traditional way. In either case, the problem is completely internal and a matter of being reasonable about theology and not a matter of imposing foreign concepts of evidence upon theology.

(ii) Barth's notion that reason consists in conforming to the nature of an object and not being misled by rational artifacts and that this conformity is only legitimately achieved through the Christian Revelation is itself a staggering epistemological claim that would require enormous skill to justify. Barth clearly does not display such skill in his earlier "Kantian" and later "Hegelian-like" philosophical speculations. But the important point for us is that getting involved in philosophical justifications of what counts as being "reasonable" itself detracts in a damaging fashion from the dramatic and appealing claim that philosophy is irrelevant to theological claims and that religious commitment and revelation constitute an unchallengeable frame of reference. It is this claim that has seemed most important to those neoorthodox writers who wish to evade the problem of evil.

(iii) Tillich says that the theological circle is existentially grounded. The argument from existential commitment, however, is a double-edged sword and cuts both ways. A feeling for the depth and pervasiveness of evil is so great in some people that Christianity is not even a live hypothesis for them. They can stand gratuitous evil if it comes from a naturalistic world that knows neither good nor bad or comes from a genuinely evil world, but they could not bear to hear from any providential source whatever that it is not really gratuitous evil after all—that there is some point to it. Tillich sometimes seems to be aware of this existential dimension of the problem of evil, but he does not, after all, understand it.[14] The existential feel for evil, he says, must be taken into account in any adequate conception of divine providence. It rules out optimistic theodicies, progressive theology, and so on. But this response quite misses the point. For some people the existential feel for evil constitutes the grounds for not believing in God at all, or for others like Schopenhauer constitutes the grounds for believing that an evil will dominates reality. In either case the existential feel for evil does not simply set the requirement of pessimism any acceptable theodicy must meet. It is a bit too convenient for Tillich to use existential grounds as the basis of a theological circle and then use counterexistential grounds to provide a particular kind of theodicy!

(iv) The distinction between "belief in" and "belief that" is an important one, to be sure, but both existential and linguistic proponents of "the circle" are misled by it. To say that "I believe in God, the Father Almighty . . . ," as in the Apostles' and Nicene Creed, is to perform an act and not to assert a proposition just as the minister who says, "I baptize you in the name of Jesus Christ," is performing an act and not asserting a proposition. Yet while performative utterances are neither true or false, are not themselves statements, nevertheless they usually entail assertions which are either true or false.[15] Saying the Apostles' Creed is an act of faith, adoration, and commitment without doubt, but it entails the claim that God is almighty and infinitely good. But such claims do not match up with the admitted instances of prima facie gratuitous evil. Then the stretching of concepts begins. If one stretches the concepts too far or abandons one or more of them, then it becomes pointless for such a person to continue the use of performative utterances like the Nicene Creed. And the same can be said, we claim, for every set of performatives that has been put in place of the rejected one. None of them is any more effective in dealing with the problem of evil and hence every alternate set of performatives is equally pointless to pursue. The crucial point is that we are not importing cognitive considerations about "the existence of God" into a framework of "belief in" God. These two notions should be kept distinct. What we have shown is that questions of truth and falsity arise within a theological context and that the inability to match these truth claims causes internal questions about the nature and existence of God. Questions about "the existence of God" are not present at the beginning; they arise, rather, as a result of taking the religious circle quite seriously. Is this not the route traveled by most thoughtful and noncompulsive agnostics, humanists, and naturalists?

(v) The very concept of a theological circle encounters serious difficulty. If the claims implicit in it were true, it would make the use of any particular frame of reference wholly arbitrary. But certainly it is possible to discuss the consistency, adequacy, and genuineness of different frames and hence arrive at good reasons for accepting some and rejecting those incompatible with the ones accepted. It is true that all systematic arguments and justifications of particular judgments must occur within a frame of reference, but it is also true that good reasons (including reference to existential and historical matters as well as "rational" considerations) can be given why one framework should be adopted or rejected. One is inconsistent, inadequate, not genuine, and so on. Or one is apparently consistent, adequate, genuine, and so on. As involved and subtle as this sort of indirect argument is, to deny the possibility of it is to land in skepticism, not Christianity. If there is no way in which it is permissible or appropriate to criticize or evaluate a frame of reference, then there appears to be no way in which it is appropriate or proper to engage in it. One simply engages in it and there is an end of the matter. But the same could be said for *any* frame of reference and hence the notion of the applicability of any frame to our particular world is forfeited. But this conclusion certainly must be unacceptable to the Christian who clearly believes that his performative frame of reference entails claims that are true while all others entail at least some that are false.

The present point may be put another way that may help the "light dawn" or "the penny drop." The concept of a theological circle produces the following alternatives: Either one can insist that the Christian commitment is the right one simply because one feels it to be so, or one can give some reason for accepting it. The first alternative is useless since everyone, including those who have opposite commitments, feels that his "belief in" is the right one. The second alternative is more promising. One can justify his Christian commitment by pointing out both internal and external evidences of divine revelation, by showing how it is morally superior to other religions, by successfully rebutting criticisms of the commitment, and so on. But these reasons for justifying the Christian frame of reference are themselves arguable and hence the notion of a theological circle which is immune to examination has disappeared. The same point can be made again in the context of apologetic theology. Tillich claims that the task of apologetic theology is to "show that trends which are immanent in all religions and culture move toward the Christian answers."[16] But this claim forcibly rejects the notion of all other autonomous frames of reference and hence entails, *even if the claim were a true one,* that Christianity itself does not constitute a frame of reference immune to criticism.

(vi) The previous criticisms apply in large measure to the notion of a linguistic as well as a theological circle. There are, however, in addition difficulties which are unique to the former. In the first place the criteria of intelligibility and rationality implicit in the practice of a society or of a mode of social life are often incoherent and often do not yield one clear and unambiguous answer. "When this is the case people start questioning their own criteria. They try to criticize the standards of intelligibility and rationality which they held hitherto."[17] On the view that a given linguistic circle *defines* such standards, it is difficult to make sense of such criticisms. Yet the criticism is clearly legitimate. Hence doubts arise about the concept of a linguistic circle. In the second place, the dichotomy between some overall criterion of intelligibility "in general" and the complete relativism of criteria determined by discrete linguistic circles is a false one. Criteria themselves have a history. They change, grow, and develop and hence are not simply defined by a given frame of reference. The propositions of Azande witchcraft, e.g., are *in principle* falsifiable but are *in fact* unfalsifiable. There are ways of covering all negative cases. Now how can such a frame of reference be criticized and by what standards? "It seems . . . that one could only hold the belief of the Azande rationally *in the absence of* any practice of science and technology in which criteria of effectiveness, ineffectiveness, and kindred notions had been built up. But to say this is to recognize the appropriateness of scientific criteria of judgment from our standpoint. The Azande do not intend their belief either as a piece of science or as a piece of nonscience. They do not possess these categories. It is only *post eventum*, in the light of later and more sophisticated understanding, that their beliefs and concepts can be classified and evaluated at all."[18]

II

Tillich's thought is relevant to the problem of evil in more ways than we have yet discussed. His own "rational" theodicy is carefully thought out and rewards close attention. For a believer, Tillich says, the existence of prima facie gratuitous evil does not constitute a reason for giving up his belief in God but simply constitutes one of the ultimate mysteries of religion.[19] And yet, he feels, within the religious framework there is not only the possibility of a rational theodicy but also a grave need for it. While prima facie gratuitous evil never constitutes a reason for giving up a belief in God, such evil cannot be ignored. It sets certain rational requirements for Christian theology.[20] It eliminates the teleological optimism which characterized Enlightenment theodicies and the progressivism which characterized nineteenth and early twentieth century theology. And it requires certain modifications of the traditional Christian conceptions of God and divine providence. God can no longer be understood as an all-powerful Being who ultimately turns all evil into good. (In fact, he cannot be understood as *a* Being at all but the Ground of Being.) No future justice and happiness can annihilate or justify the suffering and injustice of the past. And providence can no longer be understood in a deterministic way—as if God had built in a design at creation and occasionally intervenes miraculously when necessary. Providence rather must be conceived as "God's directing creativity" working through the spontaneity of creatures and human freedom.[21] Man is born with the "freedom for good and evil," and his decisions and acts are effectual in bringing about a different future than would have occurred without them.

The crucial question, of course, is how "God's directing creativity" works through the spontaneity of creatures and human freedom. At this point Tillich returns from his rational journey. The way in which it works "is identical with the divine mystery and beyond calculation and description."[22] Hegel made the mistake of trying to describe how it works by applying the dialectics of logic to the concrete events of history. His mistake was trying to understand how providence works overall. It was a grandiose attempt to "set himself on the chair of the divine providence." Fragmentary insights into the workings of providence are possible but that is all; the whole understanding "remains hidden in the mystery of the divine life."[23] Tillich's notion of mystery and his rational theodicy are skillfully enough developed but something seems to be wrong with each at the outset.

(i) The notion of mystery as used by Tillich is dubious in several ways. First, he provides no criterion for delimiting the area of mystery in such a way that not all parties in a fundamental dispute can invoke it. Everyone can protect his own commitment by invoking some notion of mystery and no one thereby gets any closer to resolving whatever question is at issue. And even if he were to provide such a criterion, it is difficult to see how he could apply it consistently, or in a non-question-begging way. Second, and equally fundamental, Tillich's notion of mystery does not really evade the problem of evil. What, after all, does it mean to say that evil constitutes one of the ultimate mysteries of religion? It might mean that evil serves some purpose but it is a mystery what it is. Or it might mean that it is a mystery whether or not evil serves some purpose. In the first case, there must be independent existential, historical, and rational grounds for claiming that God exists and that evil thus serves some purpose though we do not know what it is. However, not only are there well-known difficulties attendant upon the usual existential, historical, and rational "grounds" of belief, but in addition this interpretation simply amounts to a version of the ultimate harmony solution to the problem of evil and thus inherits all the difficulties of this theodicy. On the other hand, if what is meant is that it is a mystery whether or not evil serves some ends, then no evasion, solution, or anything whatever to ease the problem of evil has been offered.

(ii) The rational part of Tillich's theodicy exhibits the same deficiencies found in other quasitheistic theodicies. Tillich is right in believing that the traditional Christian view of God's all-powerfulness and the "mechanical" notion of providence must be abandoned in view of the existence of monstrous moral and physical evil. However, Tillich's alternative encounters equal difficulty. In the first place it is unclear how Tillich's God is religiously available. It seems strange to pray to "the Ground of Being." And it is unclear how any personal attributes are applicable to it. Moreover, it is difficult to see how, on Tillich's view, "the ultimate triumph of God's aims" is assured. The strength of the traditional view is that an all-powerful God can assure such a triumph. On Tillich's view, however, God must work through man's freedom and other restrictions in order to achieve his goals. But it is a little too convenient to deny the unlimited power of God in order to account for evil and yet allow him precisely that amount of power which insures the ultimate triumph of God's aims. And, finally, Tillich never succeeds in making it clear how "God's directing creativity" and man's freedom are ultimately compatible.

(iii) Tillich's tumbling act—going from a notion of mystery, to rational theodicy, and back to mystery—is not without difficulties. He appears to want to play the game of theodicy and yet not. One can have a rational theodicy but never one that can be destroyed by counter-reasons. The notion of mystery is always in the background. Such rules hardly seem fair. It is like playing chess in the following strange way. By virtue of playing you accept the rules that the queen starts on its own color, has the equivalent mobility of a rook and a bishop, and so on. But when you are checkmated you want to avoid disaster by saying that a king, after all, in some mysterious cases, can move two places. You avoid defeat finally by sweeping the players off the board and into the box. You did not lose, to be sure, but then you really did not play the game either.

(iv) Tillich's notions of paradox and symbolism suggest a final avenue of evasion which must be sealed off if our analysis is to be complete. Tillich assures us that Christian paradoxes are not self-contradictory. They point to spiritual truths which cannot be expressed in terms of "the structure of reason" but only in terms of "the depth of reason."[24] Jesus the Christ is the concrete Absolute—this is the most fundamental Christian paradox. Yet if one tries to pinpoint the concrete nature of Christ or the absolute nature of the logos, the paradoxical truth of their union disappears. "The words of Jesus and the apostles point to this New Being; they make it visible through stories, legends, symbols, paradoxical descriptions, and theological interpretations. But none of these expressions of the experience of the final revelation is final and absolute in itself. They are all conditioned, relative, open to change and additions."[25] This viewpoint, it should be clear, permits systematic evasion. Whatever criticism is leveled against Christianity Tillich can allow. "We have constantly to get rid of false conceptions of God." It allows Tillich to be critical of *any* actual form of Christianity and still be committed to Christianity; it allows him to admit deficiencies in every concrete formulation of Christianity and yet say that the Christian way is the true way—a paradox which passes understanding literally. Either Christianity says something or it does not, and it is vulnerable either way. Tillich's strategy at this point seems highly dubious. It amounts to having a blank check which is never written on or writing a promissory note that can never be called in. To write "Love" finally on the blank check neither shows any significant insight into what is unique in Christ's message nor is itself immune to criticism.[26]

TEN

RELIGION AND ANALYTIC NATURALISM

A metaphysical system can be defended without appeal "to *either* logical necessity *or* personal passion." On this point I concur with Professor Arthur Holmes. Moreover, I share his rejection of positivism in favor of speculative metaphysics. But unfortunately Holmes maintains that religious belief is in exactly the same position as metaphysical belief, and hence that defense of the empirical character of metaphysical inquiry is also defense of the empirical character of religious knowledge. In the first place, religious belief and metaphysical belief do not belong to the same logical order, as Holmes seems to think; and in the second place, the transition from an object of empirical metaphysics to an object of religious knowledge that Holmes makes is, to say the least, very dubious. We shall discuss each of these features in Professor Holmes's presentation in turn.

The Nature of Metaphysics

I wish to suggest that metaphysics is explanation of explanation, or second-order explanation. I will offer an illustration of this remark before we consider the various conceptions of the nature of metaphysics in recent philosophy.

If my three-year-old son gives me an explanation of how the spot got on the rug in my absence and the babysitter gives me another apparently incompatible explanation, I do not simply decide that one is false and the other true or that both are false. I try to construct an explanation which will explain both the appearance of the spot on the rug and how they have come in good faith to give me apparently incompatible explanations. I explain their first-order explanations in a second-order explanation. The metaphysician, I suggest, takes as given a collection of types of first-order explanation from the sciences, moral thought, common sense, and so on. He then tries to conceive of how, so to speak, reality could be such as to allow all these types of explanation; that is, he tries to explain how it is that all these types of explanation work. When the types of explanation conflict, he can either try to show how reality gives rise to the conflict (characteristic of Kant in his phenomena-noumena distinction) or he can argue that there is no way of resolving the conflict, and one type of explanation must be in some sense eliminated in order to present a conception of reality such that none of the types of first-order explanation are incompatible with others.[1]

But the metaphysician is not concerned only with the resolution of conflict among types of first-order explanation. He may begin with such a resolution and then go on to try to show how miscellaneous types of first-order explanation not involved in such conflict are related to the other types of explanation: that is, to show how they are explanations of fundamentally the same reality. For example, Whitehead's metaphysics might be considered to have its origin in the resolution, by way of a theory of actual occasions, of the conflict between modern physics and the traditional conception of substance, but he goes on to discuss many other topics in terms of his theory of actual occasions.

The recent discussion of the nature of metaphysics can be divided into two schools of thought—I shall call them "descriptivism" and "linguistic innovationism." The descriptivists, of whom Strawson is the most influential example, hold that strictly legitimate metaphysics is solely concerned with the attempt "to lay bare the most general features of our conceptual structure."[2] The descriptivist's effort to uncover presuppositions is admirable as far as it goes; however, the mere description of presuppositions is not *all* there is to strictly legitimate metaphysics. While the descriptivist conceives of metaphysics as the description of concepts *as they are actually used*, the linguistic innovationist (John Wisdom is the best known example) emphasizes the *revision* of concepts.[3] Wisdom sees the metaphysician as giving his reader not new facts and not primarily even new words but a new way of seeing things, as one might give a person a new map projection. The paradoxical statements of metaphysics are simply, according to him, a way of interpreting; they offer encouragement to rethink the facts in a new way by awakening his intellectual curiosity. We can be grateful to the metaphysicians for the insights which this kind of prodding can lead to.

Unquestionably, linguistic innovation plays an important role in metaphysics, and Wisdom's remarks are salutary as a corrective to the views of the descriptivists, but unfortunately Wisdom fails to give a satisfactory account of what this innovation accomplishes. It is not clear what the nature of these insights gained from metaphysics is. Apparently in Wisdom's mind these insights are not different in kind from insights in mathematics or in art. Certainly in mathematics and art one can be jolted into seeing fundamental new relationships, and in that respect the insights in art and mathematics are no different from those induced by the paradoxes of metaphysics. It is the *terms* of the newly seen relations that are different in metaphysics. In metaphysics one is led to see relations between categorial principles; not merely relations between any two concepts, but between the presuppositions of experience in general, so that one grasps how reality can be such as to require those fundamental explanatory concepts.

Pepper, in his distinctive form of linguistic innovationism, has some idea of what peculiarly metaphysical purpose linguistic innovation can serve. He sees the metaphysician as constructing a world hypothesis by means of a "root metaphor."[4] Metaphysics, he says, is peculiar in that it is not content with a conventionalistic hypothesis to cope with the data; it seeks a hypothesis which will allow us to reinterpret the data so as to interpret all data.[5] Metaphysical theory thus has "cognitive value in its own right" in a way that a scientific hypothesis does not.[6] But Pepper is mistaken in taking the cognitive value to be empirical. To the contrary, the value of a root metaphor becomes apparent when, in a Kantian manner, metaphysical assertions are thought of as rules or "principles of interpretation."[7] A root metaphor helps one to "see" how reality requires these rules. Using a root metaphor, one can incorporate the rules into a second-order explanation. For example, almost all of Whitehead's categorial principles can be found in one form or another in his pre-1925 works, but it was only in his later works that he succeeded in linking them all to an organic root metaphor and thereby constructing a complete metaphysics. This is not to say that this metaphor is somehow the *essence* of Whitehead's metaphysics. It is only to suggest that it is an essential part of his presentation of his view of reality.

When metaphysics is conceived of as second-order explanation, the place of paradoxes can also be more readily understood. Paradoxes are ways of getting others to see how the categorial principles one is proposing are right. Usually one states a rule, and orders or suggests that someone use it. One does not normally make paradoxical statements about rules. But in explanations much time is spent preparing the reader to grasp the point, and often included in this preparation is material designed merely to excite the curiosity of the reader and, as Wisdom suggests, to jolt him out of his old ways of thinking as paradoxical statements can.

Let us now formulate our conception of the nature of metaphysics in terms of the merits of the various views we have considered. A metaphysics must include: (a) the uncovering of the existing rules of interpretation in ordinary language, but also in all other first-order explanation; (b) linguistic innovation, including paradoxes, in order to jolt the reader out of his habitual categorial principles, and (c) linguistic innovation in the use of a root metaphor to link the rules and to allow the reader to understand how reality is such that it requires these rules.

There is nothing in the conception of metaphysics I have presented to make a theistic metaphysics a logical impossibility. It is not impossible that someone be able to show that a theistic root metaphor is better able to explain how all first-order explanations explain the same reality. However, Professor Holmes, who is sympathetic toward the "root metaphor" theory, has done nothing to show the comparative merits of a theistic root metaphor. He has merely assumed that once he has shown that a special use of some root metaphors is legitimate in metaphysics, there is nothing that can be said against any use of any root metaphors that may appear in religion.

A successful metaphysics is not, as I have tried to make plain above, created merely by an individual's determination to use a metaphor consistently. The use of metaphor is only a *part* of the metaphysical enterprise and a part which is utterly dependent for its cognitive success on *first* having an adequate grasp of the types of first-order explanation or categorial principles which are to be linked through linguistic innovation. Nowhere does Professor Holmes do anything to show that a theistic metaphor could do this job adequately. It is as if someone in science were to say that because postulation of theoretical entities in some physical theories is very successful it can be assumed that the postulation of any theoretical entity on any occasion will be equally successful. Surely anyone aware of the vast number of antinomies encountered in the philosophy of religion will agree that the prima facie case at least is against a theistic metaphor being able successfully to link first-order explanations. In view of this strong prima facie case against a theistic metaphor, Holmes failure to attempt to defend the comparative merits of such a metaphor is very surprising indeed.

A Dubious Transition

According to Professor Holmes, a root metaphor is chosen on the basis of what the individual finds he has "ultimate concern" for:

> The selection of a model can also be a largely subjective matter. Where do the personal, subjective factors enter? Whatever guiding image I choose, I do so because of its disclosure value to persons like myself . . . seeking meaning that is both cognitive and existential.[8]

Much later Holmes remarks that

> the most cogent religious position is often that which has most fully articulated metaphysical categories—theistic philosophies like those of Augustine . . . and perhaps Tillich.[9]

I think it is fair to say that Holmes considers Tillich a good example of the combination of cognitive metaphysics and existential commitment that he recommends. However, Tillich's views, I suggest, can be very conveniently used to show the pitfalls of just the sort of elevation of a metaphysics into a religion that Holmes proposes. If we can recognize the dangers involved in Tillich's procedure, perhaps we will be able to foresee the dangers involved in Holmes's suggested procedure.

Tillich's central concept of Being-itself can be interpreted as a piece of eminently naturalistic metaphysics. With this interpretation one supposes that "Being" is a (perhaps bombastic) way of referring to what others have called "the generic traits manifested by existences of any kind"[10] or "the metaphysical categories." "Being" in Tillich can be considered an abbreviated way of referring to the collection of categories *as a whole*. If "Being" in this distributive sense is a way of referring to the generic traits of existence, then it has an intelligible opposite and is not true of every state of affairs. It is easily admitted that the metaphysical categories could be otherwise than they are. To call attention to "Nothing," then, is to call attention to the fact that we know of no reason for the categories being as they are. The term "Nothing" may be bombastic, but it is emotionally effective in drawing the reader's attention to the fact that one has no reason for Being being what it is. To say that Nothing threatens is simply to say that one is stymied by the question of what prevents the categories from being radically different.

However, the situation is complicated by the fact that Tillich uses the term "Being" in another sense in addition to the distributive sense described above:

> Philosophy asks the question of reality as a whole, it asks the question of the structure of being. And it answers in terms of categories. . . .
> But the power of being, its infinitude, ground of "being-itself," expresses itself in and through the structure of being.[11]

The "power of being" is, so to speak, that which sees to it that not nothing happens. To put it misleadingly (but perhaps forcefully) in terms of a bizarre universal, experience presupposes happeningness as well as some set of categories. That which accounts for not nothing happening is neither an entity nor a set of categories, and yet it is something which Tillich (and Heidegger before him) is convinced is absolutely fundamental.

So far, there is nothing nonnaturalistic about Tillich's metaphysics. It is in the notion of "ultimate concern" that we find the dubious transition to religious knowledge.

> It cannot be one being among others; then it would not concern us infinitely. It must be the ground of our being, that which determines our being or not-being, the ultimate and unconditional power of being.[12]

Tillich is convinced that we are obliged to be ultimately concerned with Being-itself. The argument implicitly given is that we are more dependent on Being-itself than on anything else, since without Being-itself there would be nothing else to be dependent on; and since degree of concern always should correspond to degree of dependence, we should be utterly concerned with what we are utterly dependent upon.

The argument is superficially appealing, but if one looks closely at the meanings of "Being-itself" and "concern," one sees that Being-itself is not a proper object of concern. For surely we should be concerned about only those things the taking account of which will help us in achieving our goals. How can taking account of happeningness help us to achieve our goals and hinder the achievement of goals of which we disapprove? "The power of being" is completely *neutral* to individual goals. It is true that without happeningness no goals could be achieved but from that it does not follow that taking account of happeningness in general will help us to achieve any particular goal. Such a concern would neither allow us better to foresee the consequences of our action nor allow us to change outcomes by manipulating the object of concern. It appears to make no more sense to ask someone to have ultimate concern for the power of being than it does to ask him to conjugate his lawn.

It seems to me that it is incumbent on Professor Holmes to show exactly how the object of his cognitive metaphysics can be considered a more meaningful object of religious knowledge than the object of Tillich's metaphysics.

ELEVEN

BUCHLER'S ORDINAL METAPHYSICS AND PROCESS THEOLOGY

with John Ryder

HARE: Students of Whitehead can find much of interest in the metaphysics of Justus Buchler. Buchler, like Whitehead, subjects traditional substance-quality metaphysics to a devastating critique. If we regard, as surely we must, such rejection of substance-quality metaphysics as one of the distinguishing traits of process metaphysics, Buchler is a process metaphysician. But Buchler, again like Whitehead, does much more than find fault with traditional metaphysics—he elaborates an alternative system of categories.[1] Because his alternative categorial scheme is very different, the points Buchler makes in criticism of traditional metaphysics are interestingly different from those made by Whitehead. Indeed, though Buchler draws on the insights of various metaphysicians including Whitehead, his categories are genuinely original.[2] Consequently, Buchler's metaphysics offers to Whiteheadians the illumination of a novel perspective on the shared goal of the rejection of traditional substance. Furthermore, this shared rejection of substance-quality metaphysics leads to a shared rejection of classical Christian theology, and it is Buchler's original perspective on the rejection of such traditional theistic doctrines as creation ex nihilo, which John Ryder explores below. After his account,

I will explore the relevance of this account to the possible development of an ordinal, process theology based on Buchler's categories.

RYDER: In his *Metaphysics of Natural Complexes*, Justus Buchler presents and develops the categorial framework of a general metaphysics. One of the primary functions of a system of this generality is its applicability to a wide range of more specific subject matters. A general ontology is designed to provide a framework for interpretation of such areas as experience, science, art, ethics, and religion. It is the task of this paper to consider some of the consequences of Buchler's ordinal metaphysics for one component of most religious systems, God. Our scope will in fact be limited to two specific issues: the existence of God and God as creator.

The discussion will be framed for the most part by the categories of natural complex, ordinality, prevalence, scope, contour, and integrity. For Buchler, everything is a natural complex, including such things as material objects, fictional characters, ideas, relations, and laws. To say that something is a natural complex is to say that it is not simple, that it consists of subaltern traits. A natural complex is an order of complexes; it locates (i.e., it is a sphere of relatedness for) its subaltern traits. Not only does a complex locate traits, but it is itself a trait located. Every complex is an order that locates traits and is itself located in an order, a context. That every complex is located in some order or orders is Buchler's principle of ordinality. When a complex maintains traits in a particular ordinal location, it is said to prevail, to be prevalent, in that order.

Complexes may prevail in any number of orders, and for each order in which a complex prevails it has an integrity. A clock, for example, has an integrity as a time piece, a piece of furniture, and a wooden object, among others. The totality of a complex's integrities is its gross integrity, its contour. In addition to its integrities, a complex has subaltern traits which do not influence its ordinal locations. The individual splinters of wood in our clock are such constituents. These constituents fall within the scope of a complex. Each of the categories just discussed, i.e., complex, ordinality, prevalence, scope, contour, and integrity, will bear on the forthcoming discussion of God and God's characteristics.

In an ordinal metaphysics, "whatever is, in whatever way, is a natural complex."[3] God, then, is a natural complex. This of course does not imply an affirmative answer to the question "Does God exist?" God is a natural complex in so far as it prevails in some order or another. The order in which it prevails might be the order of literature, or the order of complexes that have had an important influence on the course of human history. To say that God prevails in these orders would not provide the kind of answer called for by the question "Does God exist?" The question must itself be understood in ordinal terms. To ask if God exists is to inquire into the ordinal locations of a discriminated complex. In particular, the question might concern the location of God in the order of complexes to which devotion is due, or the order of complexes that create other complexes. "Does God exist?" is a question that wishes to identify a specific integrity of the complex God.

Given the necessity of understanding the question "Does God exist?" within the terms and categorial framework of an ordinal metaphysics, it may be better to dispense with the question altogether—dispense with it, that is, only in the terms in which it is usually couched. In an ordinal metaphysics, existence outside of some order is an unintelligible notion. To ask if God exists is to ask whether God is in order x or order y. God is already discriminated and to that extent must prevail in some order. To take the question of the existence of God at face value, we would have to answer yes to it. God does exist, at least in the order of myth, or that of symbol. But these are not the sorts of responses that fully satisfy the question. The question "Does God exist?" is not equivalent to the question "Does God prevail?" Outside of prevalence in some order, though, the term "existence" can have very little meaning in an ordinal metaphysics. Thus Buchler says that "the question whether God 'exists' or does not is a symptom of deficiency in the categorial equipment of a metaphysics."[4] It is better—that is, less ambiguous and more clearly meaningful—to ask what orders God is located in rather than if God exists. A complete answer to this question would amount to an articulation of the contour of the complex God.

How can the question of the ordinal locations of God he answered? One way would be to look at several of the traditionally assigned attributes of God and consider whether these attributes can be consistently held along with the workings and conditions of ordinality. One such characteristic would be God as creator ex nihilo. If God is a creator ex nihilo, then certain things must be true. It must be true, for example, that at the point when God had not created the world, there was nothing other than God alone. If an ordinal metaphysics allows for this possibility, then it may allow for the possibility of God's being located in the order of complexes that create, or create ex nihilo. If this characteristic of God is found not to be possible in an ordinal metaphysics, then it is not possible that God is located in the order of complexes that create ex nihilo. If God cannot be located in this order, then God cannot be a creator. The same methodology must be applied to all the traditional traits of God. Once that is done, a picture will emerge of the nature of the God that an ordinal metaphysics can recognize. We will not pretend here to offer an exhaustive analysis of the characteristics of God. Rather we will treat only one of them. This will clarify at least a bit what an ordinal metaphysics does or does not allow for.

To say that God is a natural complex is to say a number of things, or a number of different kinds of things. Consequences follow in different branches of inquiry. One of the kinds of consequences that follow from God's being a natural complex is ontological. If God is a complex, then, by definition, God is not simple or indivisible. As a complex, God, to use an awkward phrase, is composed of constituent complexes. The constituent complexes are what constitute God. This in itself is contrary to one of the more prevalent features of the God of much of monotheism, viz., its simplicity. Further consequences follow from this ontological point, one of which has to do with God as creator. If God is a creator ex nihilo, then there was a point where God had not yet produced his creation, or at least this is the popular conception. Leaving aside the difficult question of how there could be a "before" if time was not "yet" created, there are still difficulties in the notion of a creator God. Presumably, when God had not yet created the universe, there was nothing in existence other than God. But if God is a natural complex, there must be complexes other than God for there even to be God. If God is a complex, then this complex locates other subordinate complexes. That is, it has constituents. These constituents cannot be the same as God, since God, as a complex, is the order within which they are located. In order for God to be, certain subordinate complexes must be as well.

An ordinal metaphysics places further stipulations on the nature of any given complex. Not only must the complex locate subordinate subcomplexes, but it must itself be a subcomplex of another, perhaps more pervasive, complex. All complexes both locate and are located. If God is a complex, then God is located in at least one order. Here again, the image of God (as cause) standing alone, prior to everything else (its effects), is untenable. An order is defined by Buchler as "a sphere of (or for) relatedness. It is what 'provides' extent, conditions, and kinds of relatedness."[5] An order necessarily distinguishes complexes in certain ways and along certain lines; it necessarily delimits complexes and the relations among them. Complexes are what they are by virtue of their ordinal locations. The multiplicity of orders, which includes the idea of orders as delimitors, is what provides the many-faceted nature of complexes. The ordinal location or locations of a complex are what provide, or constitute, its integrity or integrities. The contour, or gross integrity, of a complex is what determines it as that and just that complex. Buchler characterizes identity as "the continuous relation that obtains between the contour of a complex and any of its integrities."[6] In an ordinal metaphysics, the very notion of identity, of a complex being the complex that it is, is a function of the stipulation that every complex must both locate traits and be located in an order of traits. For God to obtain at all, it is necessary that it both locate traits and be itself ordinally located. Neither of these conceptions seem to be compatible with a creator ex nihilo.

Even the principle of ontological parity creates trouble for a creator God. Much if not all of the more Platonic strain in the history of Christian thought turns to a large extent on a principle of ontological priority, but this is not the source of the trouble suggested here. Even though the principle of ontological priority has played such a crucial role in our philosophic and theological development, there is an equally strong tradition wherein the notion of degrees of being does not figure quite as prominently. The point at which the principle of ontological parity interferes with a creator God is in the context of the idea of existence itself. Whatever is, is a complex, and no complex "is" more than any other. Many things, and many different kinds of things, can be said "to be." It has become traditional philosophically to erect as a model of existence a rather crude spatiotemporal paradigm. But this is clearly too restrictive. There are many kinds of complexes that do not seem to fit this paradigm, but yet must be said "to be." Possibilities are one such kind of complex. There has also been a strong tendency in philosophy to consider "being" as in some sense equivalent to actuality. This conception places possibility in some sort of ontological limbo. A more coherent way of looking at all of this is to say that actuality "is" no more than possibility "is." A possibility is no less of a complex, with all of the appropriate ordinal conditions, than is actuality. If either can be said "to be," then so must the other.

If God were a creator, then the possibility of what he creates obtains along with him. It would not do to suggest that God creates this possibility as well, since that would only push the question back one step. The question would then have to do with the possibility of this creation, and this could easily lead to an infinite regress of the possibility of the creation of the possibility of the creation of. . . . The possibility of creation must be understood as a complex, located in certain orders, and as obtaining along with, and in relation of some kind to, God. Again, the idea of a creator ex nihilo is severely hampered by the categorial demands of an ordinal metaphysics.

There is one further point that would be worth making here. It has to do with an issue already raised, viz., the identity of a complex. It was pointed out earlier that Buchler locates the identity of a complex in the continuing relation "between the contour of a complex and any of its integrities." I will try to show why this way of characterizing identity is important for the coherence of an ordinal metaphysics, and in particular how identity in this sense allows for some of the more characteristic features of Buchler's treatment of the question of God. The issue of identity should also show the importance of a principle mentioned earlier, viz., that all complexes must themselves be ordinally located.[7]

One of the more interesting points that Buchler makes in connection with God is that:

> In the metaphysics of natural complexes it could be said that God prevails, not for this reason or that, but because God is a complex discriminated, and every complex prevails, each in its own way, whether as myth, historical event, symbol, or force; whether as actuality or possibility.[8]

On the basis of this, it would be appropriate to say that God prevails in the orders of literature, mythology, historical influences, etc. At the same time, there are orders in which God does not prevail, such as the order of complexes that create other complexes ex nihilo. The body of this paper has been an attempt to show that God could not possibly prevail in this order. The curious thing about this, though, is that the orders in which God cannot prevail are precisely those orders which seem to frame the historically most characteristic and persistent traits of God. If God cannot prevail in the order of complexes that create ex nihilo, as well as others which could be elaborated, then God cannot be a creator, etc.

Yet it seems necessary, especially in light of the principle of ontological parity, to say that God does prevail in some of the other orders already mentioned. However, if God cannot create and do many of the other things customarily attributed to the Divinity, one wonders whether the God that does prevail in the orders of historical influences and literature is the same God that cannot prevail as creator, etc. If the two "Gods" are not one and the same, that is if we are doing something more than viewing the same complex in a number of its ordinal locations, then the point of saying that God *does* prevail in this or that order loses much of its force. Yet it does look as if it is not the same complex under discussion in the two cases. The complex "God" that prevails in these orders *is* the God who has created what is, who may perhaps preserve its prevalence and toward whom persons strive.

It is crucial for an ordinal metaphysics to be able to show that the complex seen in terms of each of these orders, including those in which it prevails and in which it is not located at all, is the same one. This is accomplished by the particular way in which identity is characterized. Another point of considerable relevance here is that complexes are indefinitely ramifiable, which is to say they are amenable to indefinite inquiry and analysis.[9] In so far as they are ordinally located they are relational, and in so far as they are relational, their traits and integrities are inexhaustible.

What this point amounts to is that an elaboration of the traits of a complex must include both the traits of the complex in terms of each of its ordinal locations as well as each of its ordinal locations as among its traits. It would be curious to suggest that at a given point all the ordinal locations of a complex, all of its integrities, have been exhaustively delineated, since this would imply that all possibilities for the complex have ceased to obtain. If the integrities of a complex are indefinitely ramifiable, then so are its traits. The important implication of this, at least for our purposes, is that a discussion of the traits of a complex, if it hopes to achieve any sort of adequate scope, cannot limit itself to a consideration of a complex only in terms of one of its ordinal locations. A proper response to the question "What are the attributes (traits) of God?" must include those traits that obtain for the complex in terms of a number of its ordinal locations. God, then, could not be adequately characterized solely as a creator, preserver, judge, goal etc. The description must include those traits relevant in other ordinal locations as well. God is also a major force in human political and social history, in literature, etc.

If one introduces at this point Buchler's account of the nature of identity, the question of the sameness of a complex across its ordinal locations should be answered. A complex has an integrity for each of its ordinal locations, and identity, to repeat a phrase cited twice already, is the "continuous relation that obtains between the contour of a complex and any of its integrities." The identity of a complex is not a function of this or that integrity. If it were, then we would be forced to say that a complex in one of its ordinal locations is not the same one as the complex considered in another of its locations. Since identity is a function of the relation between the contour, or gross integrity, of a complex and any of its integrities, the possibility of speaking of the "same" complex across ordinal locations is assured. Consequently, the categorial relations of an ordinal metaphysics allow us to say of God that while it cannot be a creator, etc., it, the same God is locatable and identifiable in other ordinal locations.

It is clear, then, that whatever character an ordinal metaphysics may recognize God as having, it does not include God as a creator ex nihilo. As I have indicated earlier, it does not follow from this that it would be appropriate to say that "God does not exist." God prevails in any number of ordinal locations, but not as a creator. Peter H. Hare's remarks that follow consider in further detail the possibilities of examining the traits and functions that can be ascribed to God, which is to say the possibility of an ordinal theology.

HARE: John Ryder has argued that Justus Buchler's metaphysical principles do not allow God to have at least some of the traits he is thought by traditional Christian theists to have. More specifically, using Buchler's categories of natural complex, ordinality, prevalence, scope, contour, integrity, and relation, he argues that God cannot be creator of the world. Ryder's careful account of the conflict between Buchler s metaphysics and the metaphysics of Christian theism is surprising. I find it surprising not because his exposition of Buchler's views is inaccurate. His exposition is faultless. Nor do I find it surprising because I do not think worthwhile the examination of the implications of Buchler's metaphysics. Certainly Buchler's ambitious and original categorial scheme deserves attention, much more attention than it has received. What I find surprising is that Ryder should consider it remarkable that the metaphysical principles of Buchler, or those of any other philosopher, are violated by Christian theology. In the history of metaphysics it has been *common*—it has been the *norm* even—to have metaphysical principles violated by Christian theology. For example, a metaphysician will commonly assert as sound metaphysical doctrine that every event has a cause, and yet will also assert, as a doctrine of Christian theology, that God's acts do not have causes. Or, as sound metaphysical doctrine it is asserted that everything that manifests design must have a designer, and yet as sound theological doctrine it is also asserted that the design manifested in God is without designer. Or, it is asserted as sound metaphysical doctrine that all existence is contingent, and yet as sound theology it is asserted that God's existence is necessary, i.e., noncontingent. This fundamental sort of inconsistency seems to be *endemic* among metaphysicians.

In other words, it would have been remarkable if Buchler's metaphysics had *not* been found to contradict basic tenets of Christian theology. It would have been remarkable not just because Buchler is working in the tradition of American naturalism but also because, as I have just pointed out, such a conflict is common among many sorts of metaphysicians, not just among naturalistic metaphysicians.

Although I applaud the accuracy of Ryder's account of the relations between some of the tenets of Christian theology and Buchler's categorial scheme, I worry that Ryder may unintentionally give the impression that Buchler's metaphysics is narrowly naturalistic and strongly antitheological in character when quite the opposite is the case. It seems to me that, all things considered, Buchler's categorial scheme is a naturalistic metaphysics that is unusually open to theological development. To be sure,

Buchler's metaphysics quite appropriately rules out certain theological tenets of the sort Ryder describes. But Buchler's is not a militantly naturalistic metaphysics of the sort one finds espoused by Sidney Hook, for example. Indeed, I venture the opinion that Buchler's is the most broad and open naturalistic metaphysics yet produced. That breadth and openness is one of his system's most characteristic features, and I would not like to see that admirable breadth and openness obscured by Ryder's emphasis on the conflicts between Christian theology and Buchler's system of categories.

More than any other feature of his system it is Buchler's principle of ontological parity that ensures the openness of his metaphysics. According to that principle, "no complex is more 'real,' more 'natural,' more 'genuine,' or more 'ultimate' than any other."[10] While this principle, of course, rules out any theology in which God is considered the *ultimate* reality, i.e., rules out traditional theism, it does not rule out other sorts of theology. When I speak of "other sorts of theology," I do not have in mind only a Deweyan or a Randallian sort of theology in which "God" is considered a human symbol of the unity of social ideals. It should go without saying that Buchler's metaphysics leaves room for religious humanism. Buchler's metaphysics, I am suggesting, leaves open the possibility of more than a humanistic sort of theology. I can find nothing in his metaphysics that requires that divine reality be reducible to human reality. It is a serious mistake to suppose that the fact that his metaphysical principles preclude traditional theism implies that they allow only humanistic conceptions of God. There is much metaphysical room between the extreme of traditional theism and the extreme of religious humanism. Humanism is by no means the only conceivable religion compatible with the principle of ontological parity. Let us consider the intriguing question of what nonhumanistic theologies Buchler's metaphysics will allow.

Whitehead advised us to seek a concept of God according to which he is the "chief exemplification" of our metaphysical principles, not an exception to those principles "invoked to save their collapse."[11] Whitehead may not have done a very good job of following his own advice, but it is good advice nonetheless. What might be the "chief exemplification" of Buchler's metaphysical principles? Couldn't we develop as such an exemplification a category of "divine proception"? "Proception" is the term Buchler uses to refer to the life-process of a human individual. I can find nothing in his principles which precludes a superhuman form of proception. There seems to be nothing in his characterization of individual experience that precludes a form of proception in which far greater than human powers are exercised. If proception in its human form involves the exercise of powers of assimilation and manipulation of natural complexes, could not a divine form of proception involve much greater powers of assimilation and manipulation? If the cumulative order of complexes which constitute the history of a human being is what Buchler calls the "proceptive domain," is it not metaphysically permissible to conceive of a much more inclusive proceptive domain, a "divine proceptive domain"? If human experience has what Buchler calls "proceptive direction," couldn't we suppose that much more influential forms of proceptive direction can be found—what might be thought of as a process form of Providence?

In short, I can find nothing in Buchler's metaphysics that rules out—or even discourages—the development of an ordinal, process theology. Of course, process theology is associated with the work of Whitehead, and Whitehead has been severely criticized by Buchler for his arbitrary use of a principle of ontological priority.[12] Yet there seems to be nothing in the nature of process theology which requires that some entities be considered "more real" than others. If process theology were freed from Whitehead's "strain of arbitrariness," it would seem to be compatible with Buchler's metaphysical principles.

The theological possibilities inherent in Buchler's metaphysics can, I think, be illustrated in other ways. For example, Buchler has said repeatedly that metaphysicians should cure themselves of the bad habit of treating the spatiotemporal complex as the fundamental entity. Surely this openness to realities that are not spatiotemporal invites the development of the notion of a divine reality that is located in various orders but not in a spatiotemporal order. If part of the motivation behind theistic theology lies in the need to believe that reality is not merely spatiotemporal, then a theology developed from Buchler's metaphysics would satisfy that need without committing the theologian to the metaphysical absurdity of a God that is not a natural complex.

Another feature of Buchler's metaphysics that invites theological development is his insistence on the reality of possibilities, a reality that follows from his principle of ontological parity. If part of the motivation behind traditional theology lies in the demand for a recognition of the genuine reality of possibilities and not merely the reality of here-and-now actualities, that demand could be satisfied without departing from Buchler's metaphysics of natural complexes.

My thesis, then, is that one of the remarkable features of Buchler's metaphysics is that it allows (by virtue of the principle of ontological parity) the development of a nonhumanistic theology, a development not allowed by other systems of metaphysics in the naturalistic tradition and a development that should be welcomed by process theologians.

PART FIVE

PHILOSOPHY PAST AND FUTURE

I n this section we chose to bring two brief articles together that effectively capture philosophy's past, present, and future in Hare's eyes. The
first essay discusses Royce, Mead, Chauncey Wright, and others on symbolic interactionism. While some in social psychology have recognized
the roles played by Dewey and Mead in developing interactionism, others such as Royce have largely been ignored. It is an interesting essay in
which Hare makes a compelling case for recognizing these "neglected"
philosophers.

The second essay, while less dramatic, is no less significant. Here the
reader is given a candid and direct assessment of modern American culture and values. Of particular interest, of course, is the future of American philosophy, where it is headed, what challenges it faces, and what
strategies from our past appear to be the most promising for solving modern problems.

TWELVE

NEGLECTED AMERICAN PHILOSOPHERS IN THE HISTORY OF SYMBOLIC INTERACTIONISM

with John Lincourt

Although historians of social psychology and sociology have given considerable attention to the development of symbolic interactionism,
they have curiously overlooked the fact that at the turn of the century there
was already a well-developed American philosophical tradition of social
interactionism. It is seriously misleading to say, as Talcott Parsons has,
that "it was Cooley who first took seriously the truly indeterminate character of the self as a structure independent of others."[1] It is also unfortunate that the most comprehensive history of symbolic interactionism to
date, written by John W. Petras, contains no discussion of this American
philosophical tradition.[2] To be sure, the roles played by James Mark Baldwin, William James, and John Dewey have been recognized and described
in detail, but the contribution of Josiah Royce, one of George Herbert
Mead's teachers, is seldom mentioned, and Charles Sanders Peirce's interactionism has been adequately treated only by philosophers. The pioneering studies of self-consciousness by Chauncey Wright appear to have
been ignored altogether in this connection.

Mead's approving reference in 1909 to the social theory of meaning presented by Royce in his "Self-Consciousness, Social Consciousness and

Nature" has a significance that has not been fully appreciated.[3] Mead, after all, was exposed to Royce (1887–88) even before he was exposed to Wundt, and Royce's *The Religious Aspect of Philosophy* (1885) contained the germ that in the 1890s developed into his full-blown social interactionism.[4] Probably Mead himself is in large part responsible for the neglect of Royce. When discussing explicitly the history of the movement in his well-known essay on Charles Horton Cooley, Mead discusses Baldwin, Tarde, and James but never mentions Royce.[5] Although he was glad elsewhere to give Royce somewhat dubious credit for opening his mind to "the realm of romantic idealism,"[6] Mead appears to be so eager to emphasize functional mechanisms and to disown what he regards as Royce's somehow un-American metaphysics that he pointedly avoids considering him a significant figure in the history of social interactionism.

Perhaps also responsible for the neglect of Royce is the widespread ignorance of his stature in the philosophical community at the turn of the century. Royce was the leading American exponent of idealism at a time when idealism was the dominant philosophical school, and consequently his influence on the American philosophical community may have equaled, for a brief period, that of his older colleague, William James. However, fashions in philosophy, as in other disciplines, are such that in a very few years a philosopher's reputation can change drastically. It was not long before realists and pragmatists, who vehemently objected to Royce's idealism, had seen to it that Royce's work was no longer taken seriously except perhaps as metaphysics of the most speculative sort. It was then an easy step to the assumption that Royce's work never *had* been taken seriously except as speculative metaphysics. Once this assumption was made, it was natural to overlook Royce's work in social psychology or to suppose that his social psychology had been of an amateur sort without impact at the time it was published. Fortunately, in recent years a convenient edition of Royce's chief writings has appeared,[7] and a number of thorough studies of his work have been published by historians of American philosophy. Perhaps the intellectual biography just published by Bruce Kuklick will at long last lead historians of social psychology to a proper appreciation of Royce.[8]

This is not to belittle, of course, the influence on Mead of Wundt, Cooley, and others already mentioned. However, even if it were true (as we doubt) that Royce had negligible influence on Mead, that would be no reason to overlook Royce's interesting contribution. It is important for the history of ideas to recognize that Royce, a philosophical giant of his time, was partly responsible for the main themes of social interactionism being very much in the American intellectual "air" at the turn of the century. Royce represented a living philosophical tradition of social interactionism, a tradition whose origin was independent of such figures as Cooley. Behind Royce in this tradition lay the work of Wright and Peirce. The existence of this tradition is not called in question by such facts as that Dewey said that his ideas stem "in part from Peirce and Royce, but only after and through Mead,"[9] any more than it is called in question by the fact, if it is a fact, that Royce had negligible influence on Mead. Although we think it likely that Royce had more influence (direct and indirect) on Mead than Mead was conscious of or willing to acknowledge, what is more important to recognize is that this social interactionist tradition existed and has been neglected, whatever its causal influence on the figures whose names are usually associated with the movement. Let us now very briefly sketch the contributions of these neglected philosophers.

Chauncey Wright (1830–75) contributed a number of key ingredients to the tradition without himself being, strictly, a symbolic interactionist: (a) Darwinian orientation, (b) self-consciousness as an emergent, (c) signs as essential to the emergence of self, and (d) the social nature of man as enhancing self-consciousness.

Although Wright's views were adumbrated in a short essay probably written in 1852 before Darwin published *Origin of Species*,[10] he provided a full statement of the above ingredients in "Evolution of Self-Consciousness," a monograph written at Darwin's request and published in 1873.[11] Since Darwin was concerned to explain the evolutionary transition from animal instinct to the rational faculties of man and shared Wright's view that language played an essential role in the transition, he asked his enthusiastic American disciple to use his analytical powers to determine when a thing may "be properly said to be effected by the will of man."[12]

The evolutionary gap which Wright is attempting to bridge is between two levels of mental activity. On the lower level—which men and animals have in common—knowledge is produced by "outward attention."

> When a thought, or an outward expression, acts in an animal's mind
> or in a man's, in the capacity of a sign, it carries forward the move-
> ments of a train, and directs attention away from itself to what it sig-
> nifies or suggests.[13]

On this level there is a reaction to outward effects or signs without any
recognition of the relation between the sign and the thing signified. However, on the upper level of mental activity, which is peculiar to the minds
of men, further knowledge is produced by "reflective attention" to signs
as signs. Internal images and outward perceptions are operative as signs
in inference, and the recognition of the difference between them, Wright
argues, is the crucial step in achieving self-consciousness. The step becomes possible when there is an extension of memory to recall or revive
impressions and an increase in the power of attention, so they can be directed to an examination of the external and internal signs as such.

There is another factor, Wright believes, which enriches man's knowledge of himself as subject, a factor of special interest to historians of interactionism: the social nature of man.

> Motives more powerful than mere inquisitiveness about the feebler
> steps or mere thoughts of a revived train, and more efficient in con-
> centrating attention upon them, and upon their functions as signs, or
> suggesting images, would spring from the social nature of the animal,
> from the uses of mental communication between the members of a
> community, and from the *desire* to communicate, which these uses
> would create. And just as an outward sign associated with a mental
> image aids by its intensity in fixing attention upon the latter, so the
> *uses* of such outward signs and the motives connected with their em-
> ployment would add *extensive* force, or interest, to the energy of at-
> tention in the cognition of this inward sign; and hence would aid in
> the reference of it and its sort to the subject *ego*.[14]

However, having identified the social dimension in Wright's account of
the emergence of self, we should not conclude that he advocated a thoroughgoing social explanation of the self. He is concerned primarily with
how the race developed self-consciousness biologically, not with how
an individual child develops a concept of self in the present social context. Wright takes the view that, at the present stage in evolution, self-
consciousness is a largely instinctive given, though it is a given that was

achieved specifically by the use of signs. In his view the present social nature of man serves only to enhance the self-consciousness already given biologically.

For many years Charles Sanders Peirce (1839–1914), like William James, was a younger companion of Wright.[15] The companionship is vividly described by Peirce:

> It was in the earliest seventies that a knot of us young men in Old Cambridge, calling ourselves, half-ironically, half-defiantly, "The Metaphysical Club," . . . used to meet, sometimes in my study, sometimes in that of William James. . . . Chauncey Wright, something of a philosophical celebrity in those days, was never absent from our meetings. I was about to call him our corypheus; but he will better be described as our boxing-master whom we—I particularly—used to face to be severely pummeled.[16]

Peirce was influenced by Wright in a number of ways, not the least of which was in his preoccupation with the theory of signs.[17]

Examining our consciousness of self, Peirce asks whether, as Descartes held, we directly intuit the self. He answers that knowledge of the self is an inference—knowledge of the self is learned. Since the self is a learned entity, not an intuited entity, and since everything that is learned is a thought, and every thought is a sign, Peirce concludes that the self is a sign: "man is a sign . . . my language is the sum total of myself."[18] His argument from his theory of signs to his theory of self is complex, much too complex for us to explain in the present paper where we wish merely to draw attention to an independent American tradition of social interactionism. Fortunately, we can refer the reader to an illuminating discussion of Peirce's difficult argument recently published by Duane H. Whittier in a Festschrift for Max Fisch.[19]

In addition to presenting many of the themes of social interactionism in terms of his theory of signs, Peirce provided a metaphysics, or theory of categories, appropriate to such themes. His categorial scheme, in which the self is understood in terms of "Firstness," "Secondness," and "Thirdness," is an important attempt to extend many tenets of social interactionism beyond human activities to reality as such. Social psychologists inclined to view such metaphysical extensions with dismay should be reminded that Mead similarly extended the concept of sociality in his later work.[20]

Although Peirce's metaphysics of social interactionism is developed from the point of view of the logic of relations, and Mead's metaphysics is developed from the point of view of naturalistic social psychology, this difference in approach should not be allowed to obscure basic conceptual similarity.

Before he came under the spell of Peirce's logic and theory of signs, Josiah Royce (1855–1916), influenced by Darwinian evolutionism as well as by German metaphysics, was already a determined advocate of social interactionism.

> My idea of myself, as empirical Ego is on the whole a social product, due, strangely enough, to my ideas of other people. . . . I believe, and in believing conceive myself as demanding the approval of good judges, I esteem myself, and in so doing conceive myself as esteemed by others.[21]

> I . . . exist, for myself, as the beheld of all beholders. . . . If I sink in despair and self-abasement, my non-Ego is the world of the conceived real or ideal people whose imagined contempt interests, but overwhelms me, and I exist for myself as the despised Ego, worthy of their ill will.[22]

> [A] man becomes self-conscious only in the most intimate connection with the growth of his social consciousness. . . . I am dependent on my fellows . . . for what I take myself to be.[23]

In numerous papers, using current theories of imitation as a point of departure, Royce developed an elaborate account of the social origins of the self in terms of imitation and what he called "reflection." This account was intended to be social psychology free of the metaphysical presuppositions of German idealism. A few years later, under the influence of Peirce's semiotic, Royce found that by using the concept of "interpretation" he could rework his social interactionism in such a way that he no longer needed the mechanism of imitation and could integrate his social psychology into a comprehensive and much more naturalistic theory of reality. This reworking culminated in Part II of *The Problem of Christianity*, published in 1913.[24]

THIRTEEN

THE FUTURE OF AMERICAN PHILOSOPHY

P resented at Southwest Texas State College, November 20, 1997
(i) What I bring to any discussion of the future of American
philosophy—my experience may be unusual in many respects:

(1) For about twenty-five years I have been with Dick Robin editing a
     journal that specializes in the American philosophical tradition—
     Transactions of the Charles S. Peirce Society. In that quarterly we have
     tried to nurture the American tradition. We have published histori-
     cal studies but studies which attempt to *advance* the American tra-
     dition by critical analysis of historical texts. In other words, we aim
     to be both historical and constructive in the American tradition.
(2) I have long been a member of a department at Buffalo that since Mar-
     vin Farber joined the department about seventy years ago has tried
     to be one of the most *international* philosophy departments in the
     world. As many of you know, for decades Farber's journal, *Journal
     of Philosophy and Phenomenological Research*, was really the only
     philosophical journal published in English that was seriously inter-
     national. For more than thirty years, many of those as department

chair, I have labored to build on Farber's internationalism. In regular faculty, visiting faculty, and graduate students I think we now have as international a department as any.

(3)   In recent years I have visited philosophy departments in many parts of the world—various Asian countries, Russia, Central Europe, Eastern Europe, as well as Western European countries. This has given me considerable knowledge of the attitudes of philosophers abroad about American philosophy.

(4)   Also important in what I bring to the topic of this talk is my role on the APA Board of Officers as chair of the Committee on Career Opportunities. In the last year or two, I have given a lot of thought to the present and future of philosophy as a *profession* in this country and elsewhere in the world. I have also given a lot of thought to the question of how advanced training in philosophy may be useful in careers *outside academia*. Another concern that I've discussed with many people is how the *general public* perceives philosophy, philosophical education, and the profession of academic philosophy.

(ii) Having provided those autobiographical remarks I want to assert that *internationalization* is going to be the dominant reality in philosophy in the coming decades, and it is crucial that we recognize this fully and that American philosophy in general and individual philosophers in the country respond to the challenge of internationalism in the most constructive, responsible, and just way. This is not going to be easy.

We have heard much about global markets in goods such as cars, clothes, electronic devices, etc. But I think there is little appreciation of how rapid is the acceleration of the global distribution of intellectual products. In this area the Web is only beginning to have the staggering effects it will have over the coming decades. My journal is a microcosm of this. Articles on such arcane topics as Peirce's theory of infinitesimals and mysticism were pirated and put on the Web almost immediately after we published them. If the entire journal does not already appear somewhere on the Web, I expect it to happen very soon.

Also significant is that the winter issue of the *Transactions* has more contributors from outside the United States than inside. And this, remember, is a journal that specializes in the history of *American* philosophy.

My colleague Barry Smith edits the *Monist* and the contributors to that journal are overwhelmingly from outside the United States.

There are many reasons for this ongoing internationalization besides the Internet. One obvious reason is that English has become virtually a *universal* language among those who have received higher education in the last twenty years.

(iii) You may suppose that such internationalization of intellectual products, including philosophical scholarship, is a blessing that we should all welcome. You may anticipate that much internationalization brings a healthy free trade in ideas. As liberals in the tradition of John Stuart Mill, you may hold that the widest possible competition among ideas can only lead to intellectual and consequently social and political progress. I am not so sanguine. In the present world situation there are, I want to suggest, real dangers in such internationalization in intellectual products.

Thanks to the end of the Cold War, the United States is the sole superpower. This country dominates the world militarily and in many respects economically as well. Having "defeated" the Soviet bloc, Americans assume that this "victory" was made possible by the superiority of Western, particularly American, *ideas*, political ideas, social ideas, economic ideas, and by *convenient extension* of all our ideas from ideas in science, to ideas in philosophy and art.

I am not suggesting that commonly Americans with overaggressiveness demand that their ideas be adopted throughout the world. Only on the radical right fringes do Americans make demands of that sort. I am suggesting that commonly Americans cheerfully assume that the superiority of American ideas follows as a logical consequence of this country's economic, military, and political triumphs. Americans with often sincere generosity of spirit offer their ideas to solve the world's problems. We seem to say to the rest of the world that we offer our ideas free of charge on the belief that the use of our ideas is bound to make it possible eventually for those in other societies to enjoy the freedom and prosperity that Americans enjoy. I submit that the assumption that American ideas if adopted abroad will maximize freedom and prosperity needs to be subjected to close and continuous scrutiny.

Let me give you an example. In our department this semester, one of our visiting faculty is Svetozar Stayonovic from the University of Belgrade in the former Yugoslavia. I've been attending his weekly seminar on the breakup of Yugoslavia, the fall of the Soviet Union, and related topics. Stayonovic agrees that in American foreign policy it is assumed that rights of self-determination require that ethnic groups be allowed to break off from the rest of Yugoslavia. In other words, American political leaders cheerfully, generously, assumed that American ideas of freedom give justification to the breakup. This assumption also prevails among representatives of the media. Over the years Stayonovic has been interviewed by journalists countless times. Almost invariably when he has tried to give extensive historical background to explain his analysis of the present situation and his proposed remedies, journalists, including highly educated journalists from the elite media in America, say, "I'm not interested in history!" It is what Stayonovic and others call Western *triumphalism* and a kind of naive paternalism. Americans suppose that there is not anything especially intellectually complex about applying American ideas to the realities of other countries. After all, are we not doing this with the best intentions? Surely, if our intentions are good, we needn't take the trouble to understand complex local histories that lie behind current conflicts.

(iv) Also of fundamental importance in the accelerating internationalization of philosophy is *the fact* that there has recently developed *in the West* a remarkable convergence in philosophical viewpoint. Last August I participated in a two-hundred-speaker symposium on *pragmatism* in Austria in the Twentieth Wittgenstein symposium. Speakers from more than twenty-five countries spoke on pragmatist themes of every description. Paper after paper made absolutely clear the similarities between the ideas of the later Wittgenstein and the ideas of classical American pragmatists. But pragmatism was not limited to those with links to Wittgenstein or to American pragmatism. It seems that pragmatist themes are "breaking out all over" the world. I confess to experiencing a thrill at the worldwide popularity of philosophical pragmatism. After all, I'm someone who has spent his entire career laboring to preserve and develop the pragmatist tradition. Up until recently pragmatism was a small minority position even in America. And even if we look to the past in the United States, I think that during the career of John Dewey there was only a decade or two in which it could be said that pragmatism was the most influential philosophy in the United States. To be sure, there was an enormous amount of *discussion* of pragmatism in the first half of this century, but a very modest number of American philosophers actually identified themselves as pragmatists or advanced one or another pragmatist theme.

Pragmatism today has far more adherents than it ever had during the American classic period. I mean by pragmatism such news as that philosophical method should be continuous with scientific method but not identical with it, that understanding is possible only when a problem is contextualized, that mind must be understood in broadly Darwinian terms, that knowledge does not entail certainty or incorrigibility, that any sharp distinction between logical truths and factual truths is to be rejected, that our body of beliefs form an independent web of belief, that the correspondence theory of truth is to be rejected, that the human self must be understood in terms of social processes that are constitutive of it.

The broad consensus in support of these now is not limited to America. Jürgen Habermas, who many regard as the most influential living European philosopher, quite openly agrees in broad terms with American pragmatism, classical and contemporary.

Much is made, of course, of disagreements within this broad consensus. Academic philosophers thrive on disagreements. An academic philosopher advances his or her career by finding fault in the work of other philosophers. So you won't often find academic philosophers in this country or elsewhere celebrating or even admitting the existence of philosophical consensus.

Some of these disagreements are more important than others. I happen to think that the disagreement between the antirealist pragmatism espoused by Richard Rorty and the various forms of pragmatist realism is one of great importance. In some moods I feel so strongly about this disagreement that, like the transplanted British philosopher Susan Haack, I like to call antirealist pragmatism "vulgar" pragmatism. But this antirealist pragmatism is fast disappearing. If one looks closely at Rorty's writings in recent years, one finds him slipping and sliding between realism and antirealism. A couple of weeks ago Rorty told me that though he used to think that pragmatic realism was an oxymoron, after reading such works as Robert Brandom's big book *Making It Explicit*, he now wonders whether it is an oxymoron after all. I recently gave him a copy of Westphal's collection of Frederick Will's articles in the hope that Will would serve to strengthen the case made by Brandom. We'll see what happens.

The question of just how the details of a theory of truth is to be worked out within a framework of pragmatist realism is one I find utterly absorbing. There is still much work to be done on this. In particular, pragmatic realists do not yet have an adequate account of the semantic relations between the content of beliefs and the world known. Fascinating as it is, this is still very much a quarrel among close friends— pragmatist friends.

I'd like to mention another respect in which there is now a remarkable degree of consensus among American philosophers. Less and less it is supposed that there is an unbridgeable gulf between *analytic* philosophy and nonanalytic philosophy. Admittedly, there are significant differences in the degree to which techniques of formal logic are used, and some philosophy is written in what might be called *essay style* without carefully structured, detailed argument. But it is almost universally accepted that, for example, philosophy of science is appropriately written in a style that is tightly and technically argued.

(v) So what I have been saying is that there is now a remarkable philosophical consensus in American and European philosophy and this consensus threatens, thanks to the internationalization of philosophy and America's enormous geo-political power, to exert intellectual dominance over the entire globe. I submit that this is something that we should worry about. It is dangerous to assume that having everyone in the world *buying* the same ideas is as benign as having everyone in the world buying the same TV sets or cars. To be sure, the natural sciences and mathematics have been greatly internationalized for a long time, and these are *intellectual products* internationalized, not just TV sets or cars. But I want to suggest that the internationalization of philosophical ideas has much more profound implications. But it is not so much internationalization of ideas that I'm worried about. To be quite blunt, I anticipate that in the coming decades something is going to come into existence that might be described as an *American philosophical empire*. I deliberately put that provocatively. But I don't think I exaggerate. I believe that we should take very seriously the reality of *intellectual* imperialism that is growing with each year. Of course, I am speaking of philosophical ideas quite broadly—I'm not concerned only with what *academic* philosophers produce, though I think they are an important part of this intellectual imperialism.

Though I believe that America's relative *economic* and *military* strength is going to shrink and shrink over the coming decades as Asian, South American, and African nations develop economically and militarily, I'm convinced that America's philosophical influence, especially so-called political ideas, are going to increasingly dominate the world. In other words, the future of American philosophy is becoming to a considerable degree a global philosophy. Yet I see no philosophers giving attention to the implications of that global dominance.

(vi) An important part of the current situation that I have yet to mention is *immigration*, immigration into the United States. As many of you are aware, the United States is making it increasingly difficult. A friend who is a lawyer specializing in immigration has recently abandoned her practice in immigration law because there is now so little she can do to get people in.

Elected officials and those who elect them increasingly forget or ignore the role that immigration has played in the history of this country. Or they say that large-scale immigration was justified in the past but *not today.*

Immigration policy is a big and complex topic that I cannot here discuss adequately, but I'd like to make some point about immigration as it played a role in the development of American philosophy. As some of your know, George Santayana, considered one of the most important philosophers of the classic period in American thought, never became an American citizen; he remained a citizen of Spain throughout his distinguished Harvard career.

As is well known, many important philosophers immigrated to the United States in the 1930s during the rise of Hitler—Alfred Tarski, Kurt Gödel, Gustav Bergmann, Herbert Feigl. This wave of philosophical immigration was not limited to Jews—Rudolf Carnap immigrated in the same period. These philosophers had a profound impact on American philosophy.

The immigration of the Jewish philosopher Hannah Arendt had a significance quite different. Though she had little impact on technical American philosophy, her impact on American intellectuals generally has been enormous. Indeed, I think there is more extensive secondary literature on her life and work than there is on Quine.

More recently, there has been much philosophical immigration from Britain. Susan Haack is an interesting example. A graduate of Oxford and Cambridge who taught for a number of years at University of Warwick in England, she moved to the United States about 1980 and is now, in my judgment, one of the most skilled proponents of *pragmatist* epistemology. She thinks of herself as working within the *Peircean* tradition, the tradition of the founder of American pragmatism. I must also mention that the most erudite *historian* of American philosophy is Ignas Skrupskelis of the University of South Carolina—Skrupskelis is an immigrant from the Baltic states. I could go on and on. Let me just mention one more example. John Lachs of Vanderbilt, who many think of as one of the most important proponents of the American philosophical tradition, is a native of Hungary.

I submit that the development of the American philosophical tradition is inconceivable without the crucial role of immigrant philosophers and immigrant ideas, ideas from abroad. In my view, one of the most distinctive strengths of the American intellectual tradition is its ability to weave into the fabric of the tradition immigrant ideas. I know of no other country that is more creative in the absorption of ideas from abroad. Perhaps this is America's greatest philosophical strength.

But I see no philosophers concerned about US immigration policy. The American Philosophical Association has not made a *peep* about this. Perhaps there have been no protests because American universities believe that it will always be possible to bring to this country the highly trained people they especially want. I'm not so optimistic. I fear that it is going to become harder and harder to bring philosophers and other intellectuals to this country. If the flow of immigrant philosophies is stopped, this will have a major impact on the future of American philosophy, a philosophical tradition that, as I have illustrated, has been continuously enriched by immigration.

In other words, I am suggesting that this is another serious problem in the internationalization of philosophy. However, in this case, it is the problem of internationalization being reduced or eliminated inside the United States, whereas before I was discussing the problem of American ideas being exported in such a way as to dominate the world.

If we take the two problems together, I think you can see that philosophers need to give serious attention to the implications of *both* internalization of ideas and the *lack* of internationalization. *I believe that the future of American philosophy depends very importantly on how American philosophers meet and do not meet the challenges, problems, and benefits of internationalization.*

(vii) Also importantly influencing the future of American philosophy is the way the profession understands the role of philosophical training in society. Until recently, the profession gave little attention to how philosophical training on both the undergraduate and graduate levels related to society. A start has been made in a booklet just put out by Stephanie Lewis, chair of a subcommittee of my committee—she is chair of the committee on *nonacademic* careers. Her committee has found that it is difficult to generalize about nonacademic careers in which philosophical training is especially useful—they are extremely varied. The best one can do is give examples to illustrate the variety. One example I might give from my own department—one of our graduate students works in the robotics research team at Carnegie Mellon. Clearly, training in philosophy of mind is helpful as a member of an interdisciplinary team in robotics.

Another example I might give relates to your area. In Austin I believe there is a software firm that is developing software to do the work of a white-collar manager. A noted British philosopher is involved. As I have heard him explain, this is a program in applied metaphysics, applied ontology. An interdisciplinary team including philosophers is working out the most appropriate set of ontological categories to incorporate into the software.

He mentioned that there is a rival software firm that has a very different approach to the same problem of applied ontology. I believe that is the firm that not long ago advertised on the Internet that it was looking for fifteen ontologists to hire.

I am also pleased to report that Richard Schacht of the University of Illinois has just completed an essay to appear in the May APA proceedings, an essay which explains how he thinks we should rethink the role of philosophical education and its role in society. He calls his proposal the *Open Field Model*. In his model, employment in academia would be only *one* of the many ways that philosophical training is used. I asked

Schacht to write that piece because I am convinced that his model calls for serious discussion. We should not assume that we can continue business as usual. I am persuaded that the future of American philosophy must involve the development of many more connections between philosophical training and the nonacademic world.

However, I want to stress that I do not think that that means that the most rigorous, technical philosophy can be abandoned in favor of *popular* works, accessible to the public. I see no reason why both cannot be practiced as legitimate philosophical enterprises, and I see no reason why one should be confused with the other. I also see no reason why often an individual philosopher cannot practice both types of philosophy on different occasions for different purposes. It seems to me absurd to believe that, if the profession strongly encourages applied philosophy, there is a risk that philosophy will not be taken seriously as a profession.

(viii) Another concern I have is with the lack of attention given to how the general public perceives philosophical training and the profession of philosophy. The APA has made almost no efforts to correct this. However, I'm pleased to report that I am on an APA panel set up by Eric Hoffman (executive director of the APA), a panel at the December meetings in Philadelphia to discuss what sort of magazine might best make philosophical thinking interesting and accessible to the general educated public. Another member of the panel will be the fellow who edits *Philosophy Now*, a British philosophy magazine.

This is a beginning in the effort to make *philosophy more public*.

These are, as I say, interesting beginnings, but much, much more needs to be done, much more thought is needed about the problem of how best to relate philosophical training and philosophical research to the society in which they are done. I am convinced that the future course of American philosophical training and research should be related to society. This is not something that will take care of itself. Certainly there are social and economic forces over which the profession has little or no control. Even developments in higher education can be difficult to control. Some of you have read about the University of Phoenix, a vast institution offering courses in branches around the country using only part-time, temporary, nontenured faculty. This is a *profitable* business enterprise of a type that many believe will come to dominate all but the most elite parts of American higher education. The implication of such institutions for the relations between philosophical training and research and society are enormous. How should we approach those implications? To my knowledge, philosophers have given little or no attention to this challenge. But, as many earlier remarks indicated, this is only one of many ways in which philosophers have failed to give serious attention to how philosophical training and philosophical research can best be related to society.

(ix) Now I want to draw this little talk to a close. Let me summarize. I have suggested that the future of American philosophy crucially involves internationalization both in the relations between this country and the rest of the world and within the philosophical country in America. I have also suggested that the future of American philosophy depends importantly on how philosophical training and research relates to society. I have noted that philosophers have given precious little attention to these factors so importantly affecting the future of American philosophy. I have implied that this failure is irresponsible. Although I recognize that the control that can be exerted over these developments is limited, it seems to me irresponsible for philosophers not to give serious thought to these realities and consequently not to be able to exercise a significant influence over these changes, over these developments.

PART SIX

POETRY

H are's affinity for poetry is well known to those with any familiarity with his work. It is therefore fitting to include some of his thoughts on poetry and philosophy. Readers will find that Hare had much to offer on this topic. For instance, he asks, what are poets for? It is a familiar question, but Hare's answer is far from conventional. His belief that a function for poetry cannot be context-neutral is at odds with nearly every major thinker on the topic. Yet, his case is convincing, and it sets up some of the points he would build on in later essays.

The second article focuses on the lives of (poet) Wallace Stevens and (philosopher) Paul Weiss. Hare finds that in the course of their troubled correspondence many points of confusion led to an unfortunate distance between poet and philosopher. More importantly, Hare finds that their misunderstandings are a microcosm for the discord between poetry and philosophy more generally. This helps to set up Hare's eventual point that philosophy has much to gain from the conceptual creativity of the poet.

Hare would use the Stevens–Weiss correspondence to develop what he called "deep conceptual play." It is the modification of certain core concepts which come to bear on our actions, on how we interpret our environment, and on many of our most fundamental values. Hare felt that this kind of play was especially prevalent in thinkers who succeed in bringing together wide-ranging branches of thought. He saw it in Stevens and Stein, but also in William James. The third essay, then, reconceives of philosophy as a way of structuring our experiences through the concepts we use. Hare argues that this motivation is at the heart of James's philosophy.

FOURTEEN

WHAT ARE POETS FOR?
CONTEXTUALISM AND PRAGMATISM

N ever has more angst been felt about how to answer the question
"What are poets for?" than is felt today. In the most recent issue of
the official magazine of the American Academy of Arts and Sciences appears a letter by a member of the academy that mocks as unintelligible
the poetry published in the magazine by fellow members of that august
body. And in an essay just published in the newsletter of the St. Mark's
Poetry Project in New York, Dale Smith bemoans what he perceives as
today's lack of attention to what he calls "the communicative force of
poetry." Poetry, he says, "has grown increasingly self-referential, rarely
able to extend arguments beyond a small tribe of practitioners and
students."

Needless to say, such doubts about what contemporary poetry is good
for are not expressed only by representatives of high culture such as those
I have just mentioned. No less powerful an arbiter of middlebrow culture
than Garrison Keillor in his bestselling poetry anthologies *Good Poems*
and *Good Poems for Hard Times* has few kind words to say about contemporary poets and specialists in poetics. In his characteristically colorful and mildly risqué way, he says most contemporary poems are "like

condoms on the beach, evidence that somebody was here once and had an experience but not of great interest to the passerby."[1]

There is nothing new, of course, about attacks on poetry. Plato's assault on poetry is perhaps the most memorable ever written. However, it is not my intention today to survey attacks on poetry over the last 2500 years. Instead I wish to make a case for a *contextualist* and *pragmatist* approach to the problem of what function poetry has. It is my contention that any context-neutral account of the nature and function of poetry is doomed either to be defeated by counter examples or to becoming banal. And this banality cannot be avoided by a Wittgensteinian move in which the competing forms and functions of poetry are said to share family resemblances.

If I may be allowed a homely analogy, a context-neutral attempt to state the function of poetry is as pointless as a context-neutral effort to state the function of human hands. Only when one has specified a context—say, a sculptor in his or her studio with some specified aesthetic ideals, commission, tools, etc.—can one say interesting things about how human hands function in shaping a piece of wood into a work of art. The ability to use language in which metaphor and rhythmic sound are markedly integral to meaning is such a fundamental human capacity that nothing interesting can be said about the function of such language without limiting one's attention to a specific context.

In my contextualism I have no quarrel with Heidegger's account of poetry in terms of his philosophy of Being—*provided that* Heideggerians refrain from applying what they say about unconcealedness and poetry *outside* the overall framework of Heidegger's metaphysics and epistemology. I am confident that certain kinds of poetry can perform an epistemological function for those who are committed to Heideggerian philosophy, but I am doubtful about attempts to justify this understanding of poetry in a context independent of Heidegger's work.

With an analogous proviso, I have no objection to the theory of poetry propounded by my teacher Justus Buchler in his book *The Main of Light: On the Concept of Poetry*. Buchler presents a splendid account of how poetic discourse can be fitted into his overarching theory of judgment and ordinal metaphysics, but I share Roland Garrett's view that Buchler's theory does little to "illuminate the internal dynamics of a poem, how the features sound, rhythm, language, imagery and meaning develop in the poem. . . . Does a universal concept of poetry actually help to identify the mechanisms by which *this* poem has its effect on *me*?" Though I would be the last to say that Buchler's philosophical system is banal, I fear that his theory of the nature and function of poetry borders on the banal, albeit banality couched in novel vocabulary such as "the sense of prevalence."

And to mention the theory of poetry of another teacher of mine, if I may, I think that Cleanth Brooks's belief that a poem functions as a formal, symbolic structure is useful as a corrective to the excessive zeal of his contemporaries who insisted that we understand poetry biographically and historically, but I am skeptical of any attempt to apply that "close reading" approach to poetry universally, outside the context of debates between literary critics of Brooks's era.

"New criticism" of the early twentieth century was by no means the first account of the function of poetry that can be said to have served as an appropriate corrective to dominant trends in its cultural context. Plato notoriously offers an account of what he perceives as the *pernicious* function of poetry, that is, the view that poetry does dreadful harm to its audience by fueling the nonrational parts of the soul. Cultural contexts in which poetry has such a *dis*function are entirely conceivable.

I also have no problem with the Greek view of poetry common before Plato, the belief that poets sometimes function as moral authorities. Nor would I question Whitman's poetry, in its mid-nineteenth century context, functioning as praise of the nation's spiritual promise.

Though it is unfashionable to say so, I even have no problem—with the same proviso—with the notion that the primary function of poetry is didactic. Hesiod, one of the earliest known Greek poets, exalts honest labor and denounces corrupt judges. It seems to me quite plausible that in Hesiod's cultural context it was appropriate for poetry to have a plainly didactic function.

However, I am enough of an intellectual snob to wince in the face of some of Garrison Keillor's comments on these matters. "The goodness of a poem," he says, "is severely tested by reading it on the radio."[2] But I concede that if the contextual constraints are a daily five-minute show called *The Writer's Almanac*, many fine poems will not function well.

Keillor's dictum that "the meaning of poetry is to give courage" prompts in me a reaction more serious than a wince. The idea that the sole function of a poem is "to get you to buck up" in the face of "hard times" strikes me as a reductive view not plausible in any context—even in the context of a truck driver in an army convoy in Iraq listening on an iPod to a reading of Walt Whitman's *Leaves of Grass* while dreading the next roadside bomb.

I confess to being personally attracted to one of the aphorisms to be found in Wallace Stevens's *Adagia*. Stevens writes: "After one has abandoned a belief in god, poetry is that essence which takes its place as life's redemption."[3] Echoes of Emerson, Dickinson and Santayana are obvious. But I recognize that my own sensibilities have always been firmly in the American tradition so powerfully represented by Emerson, Dickinson, Santayana, and Stevens. There are many continuities between Stevens's context and my own, so this notion of the function of poetry naturally resonates with me. It is also important to note that elsewhere in his writings Stevens expresses scores of other views on the nature and function of poetry, some of these appear to be in conflict with the redemption view and others are seemingly complements to that view. If one takes Stevens's writings as a whole, one appreciates how nonreductive and pluralistic his views on the function of poetry are. Such pluralism also resonates strongly with me.

As I draw these comments to a close, I would like to return to the current controversies with which I began. Intellectuals, including some prominent poets, charge that most poetry published today is intelligible only to coteries of academics and their students; they claim, in effect, that much of the poetry of our time is more or less pointless. It is again well to remember that attacks of this sort on poetry are nothing new. In the early twentieth century Harriet Monroe, editor of the magazine *Poetry*, famously accused Hart Crane of using obscure and "illogical" metaphors in "On Melville's Tomb," and Crane tried to explain how metaphors can be effective without being logical.

One of the most interesting such critiques of contemporary poetry and poetics I know of is that by Jeffrey Walker. Walker's targets are Charles Altieri and Charles Bernstein. Altieri takes the view, Walker says, that "the essential role of lyric is *not* to argue for particular beliefs, that 'rhetoric' and 'ideology' are forms of 'duplicitous' false consciousness and that lyric poems present 'acts of mind,' in other words, embody a state of subjectivity."[4] Bernstein, Walker alleges,

> retain[s] a more or less traditional romantico-modernist suspicion of what Bernstein calls "argument," "rhetoric," and "rationalistic expository unity" as forms of socially constructed false consciousness. Bernstein thus tends to project a basic understanding of "poetic" or lyric discourse as in essence "a private act in a public place" that serves to represent or embody "thinking" liberated from the shackles of discursive reason *rather than* to present an argument for the reader's judgment.[5]

In a detailed argument that I do not have the time to go into here, Walker claims that lyric poetry—or at least lyric poetry that we should take seriously—*does* present genuine argument, albeit *enthymematic* arguments. I take it that Walker believes that poetry that *only* embodies a state of subjectivity is poetry that has no significant function other than perhaps a psychotherapeutic one. Some of Sylvia Plath's "confessional" poetry may come to mind in this connection, but there are vast differences between the states of subjectivity Altieri and Bernstein are talking about and the states embodied in Plath's poetry. Bernstein's postmodern "language poetry" and "experimental poetry" and Plath's poetry inhabit different universes. The Altieri-Bernstein subjective states are so intellectually complex that the poetry that embodies them can function, many critics believe, only as material on which graduate students can exercise their decoding skills. And Walker seems to hold that once an example of language or experimental poetry has been laboriously decoded, if it does not present a genuine argument, it does not have a poetic function worthy of the name.

In the spirit of my contextualist pluralism and pragmatism, I want to leave it as an open question whether the poetry Bernstein and Altieri champion has the genuinely poetic function of presenting an enthymematic argument. In any event, being hermeneutically challenging alone should not disqualify literature from having a genuine poetic function. On the other hand, I reject also the view that in our postmodern world all *serious* poetry *must* be difficult to decode.

The Academy of American Poets fancies itself as the official gatekeeper of the pantheon of poetry in the United States. If the academy answered the question "What are poets for?" in the way I have just recommended, if it became less a bastion of conservatism in its views about the nature and function of poetry, it would not only elect Bernstein as a chancellor, it would also elect Bob Dylan. Today America's cultural context is sufficiently heterogeneous to accommodate both as major poets. However, I expect neither of these elections to take place any time soon.

I would like to conclude with some suggestions of how modernist and postmodernist poetry might function within the context of pragmatist epistemology. William James told a poet that "the power of *playing* with thought and language" is "the divinist of gifts."[6] He was convinced that wordplay (e.g., in the writing of Benjamin Paul Blood) could sometimes make accessible realities otherwise inaccessible. In playful use of words we move freely between conceptual structures. If one believes, as James did, that concepts, especially intellectualist concepts, block our perception of reality, then the more flexible one's use of concepts, the better one's perception of reality (e.g., modal realities). As Harvard students and thereafter, modernist poets Gertrude Stein and Wallace Stevens famously absorbed James's thought. Significantly, no poet is more noted for her wordplay than Stein. Stevens's poetry, I suggest, plays with epistemological theories as alterative metaphorical structures. Charles Bernstein's postmodernist "language" poetry and poetics has recently developed this poetic epistemology in radical ways.

FIFTEEN

MISUNDERSTANDINGS BETWEEN
POET AND PHILOSOPHER: WALLACE STEVENS
AND PAUL WEISS

I am confident that most readers of this journal believe, as I do, that Wallace Stevens was the greatest philosophical poet in America in the twentieth century. But I wonder how many readers know the story of how, a few years before his death, when Stevens was being showered with honors, Paul Weiss, editor of *The Review of Metaphysics*, rejected a lecture submitted by Stevens on the philosophy of poetry, a paper that Weiss had helped Stevens write and one that Weiss had earlier praised. Stevens refused to consider submitting the paper to a nonphilosophical magazine. Sadly, the lecture, "A Collect of Philosophy," was Steven's last attempt to contribute to the philosophy of poetry.

Here I wish to discuss this breakdown in communication between poet and philosopher. Their misunderstanding I find interesting not because it is an extreme example of the growing fragmentation of cultural life in the last century and in our time. When one measures what happened between Stevens and Weiss against what has become commonplace even within separate disciplines, the relationship between Stevens and Weiss appears intimate by comparison. Stevens's intense interest in philosophy was matched by Weiss's interest in poetry. What concerns me is how

Stevens and Weiss failed to understand one another despite each author's deep respect for the other's discipline.

The Stevens–Weiss relationship is of additional interest because many other poet–philosopher relationships can be found which are similar. I feel sure that every reader of these pages can think of such examples.

By the time of Weiss's earliest personal interactions with Stevens in the 1940s, he had already been familiar with the poet's work for many years. He had first read Stevens's poetry at the suggestion of his wife, Victoria Brodkin, in the late 1920s, when she was a graduate student in the English Department at Harvard and he was a graduate student in Harvard's philosophy department. Although this is not the occasion to attempt to summarize Weiss's exceptionally long and active career—when he died in 2002 at the age of 101 he was still publishing prolifically—I want to stress how unorthodox Weiss was as an American academic philosopher in the middle decades of the twentieth century.[1] Although literary scholars who comment on the Stevens–Weiss interchange seem to assume that Weiss was a typical academic philosopher of that period—a period in which the various forms of analytic philosophy dominated the profession in the United States, especially in the top tier departments; in fact, *no* senior member of an elite philosophy department was as much of a maverick as Paul Weiss was. Even his Yale colleague Brand Blanshard, a staunch absolute idealist, was more acceptable. Blanshard was at least aligned with a philosophical movement that had been in the ascendancy in the recent past, where Weiss had no clear alignment with any school of philosophy past or present. His Harvard dissertation under Whitehead was on logical systems, and some of his early publications were on technical topics in the philosophy of logic. At the beginning of his career he had coedited Charles Peirce's papers and found himself as much absorbed by Peirce's pioneering work in mathematical logic as by Peirce's highly speculative and imaginative metaphysics, cosmology, and theology. Weiss also studied with and was influenced by the French historian of medieval philosophy, Etienne Gilson. After he moved from Bryn Mawr to Yale, he founded *The Review of Metaphysics* in 1947 and the Metaphysical Society of America in 1950. At the time metaphysics was completely out of fashion among ambitious philosophers in the United States. Perhaps the best illustration I can give of Weiss's stubborn independence is his difficulty in 1956 in getting *Modes of Being* published, despite his full rank at Yale and four earlier books. In desperation he put out the two-volume manuscript on metaphysics in mimeographed form. Only in 1958 did he find a publisher for a drastically revised version. Weiss also published books on the philosophy of sport and philosophy of the cinema when no other well-placed American philosopher produced books on such subjects. He also published numerous volumes of idiosyncratic notebooks called *Philosophy in Process*. It may be of some significance that, during roughly the period in which Weiss corresponded with Stevens, he directed Richard Rorty's dissertation on potentiality. Perhaps also relevant is the fact that during his period at Yale I was both an undergraduate major in philosophy and a member of the board of *The Yale Literary Magazine*.

In 1944, while still teaching at Bryn Mawr, Weiss first wrote Stevens after reading "The Figure of the Youth as Virile Poet," an essay Stevens had just published in the *Sewanee Review*. There was much in this piece to provoke Weiss. Here are a few quotations.

> The poet, in order to fulfill himself, must accomplish a poetry that satisfies both the reason and the imagination.

> [I]f the end of the philosopher is despair, the end of the poet is fulfillment since the poet finds sanction for life in poetry that satisfied the imagination. Thus poetry, which we have been thinking of as at least the equal of philosophy, may be its superior.

> [F]or the poet, the imagination is paramount . . . if he dwells in his imagination, as the philosopher dwells in his reason. . . .

> For all the reasons stated by William James, and for many more . . . we do not want to be metaphysicians.[2]

Weiss objected to Stevens basing his understanding of philosophy on his reading of James and Bergson, and asked, "Why not grapple with a philosopher full-sized?"[3] Although Stevens, who habitually played down his wide reading, had studied full-sized thinkers more carefully than he cared to admit, in this piece he largely ignored them. In Stevens's report on his correspondence with *Paul* Weiss to the literary scholar *Theodore* Weiss, who had recently started to publish *The Quarterly Review of Literature*, he said that he asked the philosopher Weiss what specific "full-sized" philosophers he had in mind and was told "Plato, Aristotle, Kant and Hegel, and then, as a relief from these divinities of the Styx, suggested Whitehead, Bradley and Pierce [*sic*]. I think [Stevens continued] that most modern philosophers are purely academic, and certainly there is very little in Whitehead contrary to that impression. I have always been curious about Pierce [*sic*], but have been obliged to save by [*sic*] eyesight for THE QUARTERLY REVIEW, etc."[4]

Although Weiss was familiar with the tradition, especially among the Romantics, of poets making strong claims for the philosophical importance of poetry, he was unaware of the special context in which Stevens had composed this paper, and Stevens did nothing to enlighten Weiss or any other readers on the background. Stevens had written the essay in the context of a "project for poetry" that he had developed with Henry Church, a friend who edited the important French language literary magazine *Mesures*. Church had discussed with Stevens the possibility of endowing a chair of poetry at Princeton. No such chair existed anywhere in America. "The Figure of Youth" piece was an attempt to marshal arguments in favor of the establishment of such a chair whose occupant would have the job of teaching poetry in an academic setting. Writing with that purpose, it was natural for Stevens to try to show that poetry was a discipline "superior" to a discipline, philosophy, that such institutions as Princeton considered obviously worthy of teaching by holders of endowed chairs. Princeton, like many universities in America, had a long history of philosophy being taught by the *president* of the University.

Notice the irony here. While dismissing as "purely academic" the recent philosophers Weiss urged him to consider, Stevens strained to find *academic* arguments to prove to *academic* leaders at Princeton and elsewhere that poetry was superior to philosophy.

Possibly distracted by having his discipline "put down" in favor of poetry, Weiss in large part missed the chief points Stevens was making. Stevens was insisting that philosophy lacks the imagination found in poetry. Focusing on full-size philosophers would not necessarily have provided Stevens with evidence of lots of imagination in philosophy. Indeed, the less full-size philosophers he discusses, Bergson and James, are generally considered *more* imaginative than the philosophers Weiss recommends. Weiss would have responded more effectively if he had directed Stevens to specific writings of Peirce and Whitehead that are highly imaginative.

Also, instead of taking umbrage at Stevens quoting James against meta-physics, a type of philosophy dear to Weiss's heart, Weiss should have simply pointed out that the type of philosophy condemned by James was rationalistic metaphysics unconnected to the world of everyday sensory and emotional experience. Peirce, James, and Whitehead (and Weiss himself), he should have added, all propound metaphysical systems rooted in everyday experience.

Weiss's appeal to full-sized philosophers was also to no avail in responding to Stevens's comments about philosophy and despair. In his letter he should have done what he did many years later when discussing "The Figure of Youth" with Stevens's oral biographer, Peter Brazeau. He might have pointed to specific philosophers whose works are clearly optimistic.

The regrettable miscommunication of this exchange was not enough to discourage either Weiss or Stevens from further interaction. Four years later, after he read "Effects of Analogy" as a Bergen Lecturer, Stevens wrote Theodore Weiss that "Weiss, the philosopher, came to the lecture at Yale and spoke to me afterward. I liked immensely what I saw of him. He has the same eager interest in everything that you have."[5] When Brazeau quoted this letter to Paul Weiss in the interview mentioned above, Weiss replied:

> That's interesting that Stevens had this reaction to me, and yet he didn't move on it. I don't remember the lecture at all. I just remember being so disappointed because I couldn't make contact with him. . . . [I was amazed] that a man who was so successful in business and so big in physical presence was so shy. He spoke hardly above a whisper. Had I not been in the first row, I would not have heard anything. After, I went over and introduced myself. Then a number of people came over and spoke to him. Afterward, I sat with him for ten, fifteen minutes. I found him very shy, almost timid. I found it difficult to make contact with him. Then I discovered he was in awe of somebody who might be a philosopher and was sort of frightened that he might have to talk to me [about] some of the things he had said. He was so damned shy that he didn't say to me, "Now let's sit down and talk about this. . . ." He apparently didn't realize the great respect I had for him, how highly I thought of him, and how willing I would have been to sit down and go over matters that bothered him.[6]

Although Brazeau and others who knew Stevens often noted that he tended to keep "his distance from those he met at his public appearances with whom he felt affinities,"[7] Weiss's personal manner probably contributed to their problems in communication. I can testify from personal experience that Weiss had a loud volubility in asking questions that could intimidate fellow *philosophers* even when Weiss intended his questions to be sympathetic.

In early 1951, Stevens accepted an invitation to give the Moody Lecture at the University of Chicago in November of that year. Having chosen as his subject the question of whether there are philosophical ideas that are inherently poetic, during the summer he wrote to various philosophers—Weiss among them—for suggestions. He thanked Weiss for taking the trouble to write several letters in an effort to help, letters in which Weiss gave in summary form a slew of doctrines from the history of philosophy and commented on the relations between poetry and philosophy. In the lecture Stevens quoted extensively from these letters.

Puzzlingly, in this correspondence preliminary to Stevens writing his lecture, Weiss seems to have seriously misunderstood Stevens. He wrote Weiss:

> The truth is that I referred to the idea about perception merely as an example of a philosophical concept. I don't want to concentrate on that single concept. Don't let me bother you, but, all the same, if you can think of a few of the big ideas of modern philosophy, it would be a great help. I am not thinking of style nor, when all is said and done, the subject, but of ideas not intended to be poetic but which actually are. For instance, the mere phrase nature of man because of a certain grandeur about it becomes poetic although it was never intended to be anything of the sort. The idea of man's place in the universe is a poetic idea and there are a multitude of things of this sort. The idea of God is a poetic idea, but I believe that the idea of God is not a philosophical idea, that is, is not of philosophical origin. Bergson's *Elan Vital* has a measure of poetry about it. I speak of these as instances.
>
> Now, I have never read Peirce notwithstanding all that has been said about him. Are any of his main thoughts (not his discussion of other people's thoughts) what might be called poetic concepts?[8]

A few months later, not long after Stevens delivered the lecture, Weiss wrote to ask him to send the paper for possible publication in *The Review of Metaphysics.* To which Stevens responded: "You are most welcome to it if it is of any interest to you. On the other hand, from the point of view of a technical publication, you may not find it suitable, and in that case I shall be glad to have you return it. In any event, I am most grateful to you for your help. I may also say I greatly appreciate being able to have contact with you."[9]

Whatever may have been the problems with the piece that Weiss later discussed with Brazeau, when Stevens first sent it to him, Weiss responded encouragingly. Let me quote the letter in full:

> This is one of your splendid pieces. As you surmised it is not technical enough for a technical periodical. It belongs in some journal as the *Yale Review, Partisan, Kenyon, Thought.* If none of these will have it—a prospect hard to imagine—send it to me. I would rather bend the boundaries defining the content of our magazine than have this go unpublished.
>
> Do keep me posted on these basic explorations. What you say is always suggestive and often profound. Philosophers and poets are made to learn from one another.
>
> With every good wish, I am
Cordially,
Paul Weiss[10]

As we have seen, in the letter accompanying his paper, Stevens had frankly told Weiss that his submission was not technical philosophy. Also, by calling the piece "A Collect of Philosophy," he had plainly signaled that the essay was in some ways like a prayer.

Some weeks later, having heard from his Yale colleague Norman Holmes Pearson that Stevens's feelings had been hurt by his letter, Weiss wrote him again: "I do hope you did not take amiss my purely editorial decision that your paper, excellent and perceptive though it was, did not fit inside the frame of a purely technical periodical devoted to enlightening professional philosophers on purely professionally respectable topics. I try to break the conventional bounds, but your paper would require me to destroy them entirely. I hope you will publish the paper soon elsewhere and let me know, for I would like to refer people to it."[11]

Shortly thereafter, having talked to Pearson again, he wrote: "I hope you will consent to have your paper printed by the *Yale Library Gazette.*

Mr. Pearson told me that they want it. What you have to say is important and should be made available."[12] But Stevens had written Pearson that he now didn't think well enough of his lecture to publish it anywhere.

Unfortunately, many years later when Weiss discussed this correspondence and subsequent essay with Brazeau, he persisted in his misunderstanding. Weiss said that he thought what Stevens should have been trying to do was to explain "what poetry and philosophy have in common" and "*what it is* that philosophy and poetry both see."[13] Although Stevens surely would not have denied that those are questions that could be usefully discussed, they were not the same ones he was addressing in the Moody Lecture, where, in discussing "the idea of the infinity of the world," Stevens makes plain what he considers the crucial mark of the inherently poetic nature of a philosophical idea. A philosophical idea is inherently poetic because "it gives the imagination sudden life."[14] A philosophical idea's powerful stimulus to the imagination is what is of special interest to Stevens.

Much of the lecture is taken up with Stevens's efforts to explain what he is *not* talking about. He is *not*, he says, speaking of a poetic style of *writing* and *thinking* as can be found in Plato, Nietzsche, Bergson, and James—a style of philosophy in which metaphors are prominently used and/or where there is "incessant euphony." Nor is he speaking of "philosophical poetry," as can be found in Lucretius, and in some of Milton and Pope—where the poet has chosen as subject a philosophical theme.

There are parts of the essay in which Stevens wanders from his announced topic of inherently poetic ideas in philosophy. He attempts to make generalizations about what poetry and philosophy share and where they differ. "The habit of forming concepts unites them [poetry and philosophy]," he says. "The use to which they put their ideas separates them."[15] In forming concepts they both seek integration, but they differ in the type of integration sought. "The philosopher searches for an integration for its own sake . . . the poet searches for an integration . . . for its insight, its evocative power or its appearance in the eye of the imagination."[16] Another such generalization Stevens offers is this: "The probing of the philosopher is deliberate . . . the probing of the poet is fortuitous."[17] It is unclear how these generalizations help us answer the question whether there are philosophical ideas that are inherently poetic. Weiss gave his attention to these generalizations and ignored Stevens's announced topic.

What seems to have most distracted Weiss from full attention to what Stevens was trying to do was the poet's frequent use of an elementary textbook in philosophy in searching for possible examples of philosophical ideas that are inherently poetic. As Weiss later told Brazeau, "it was the sort of reference that made me think I couldn't possibly publish it in a highly technical magazine."[18] He was probably also embarrassed by the fact that in his lecture Stevens had quoted from his (Weiss's) letters at some length. He may have felt that those quotations would give readers of the *Review* the impression that Weiss was not a disinterested editor.

Though he didn't remember exactly what he had written Stevens some twenty-five years before, in 1976 Weiss remorsefully told Brazeau that his letters were "undoubtedly brash and stupid, evidencing a younger philosopher. (Philosophers are young, I now think, at 75, when they are below 60.) In any case, I read the essay again, and found it penetrating but not altogether clear. Yet I felt that it was my fault, my insensitivity that made me not get it all. It leaves me with the conviction that I must read it again and again."[19]

In this misunderstanding, who was at fault, if anyone? If you are inclined to assign blame, I suggest that you assign blame equally. Weiss was at fault in failing to appreciate the chief question addressed in the paper. Also, in a laudable effort to be supportive, he made the mistake of telling Stevens that he would publish the paper if it was rejected by other magazines. In light of the serious problems he found in the paper, it was unwise to give him such assurances. He must have known that it would not be feasible to ask someone of Stevens's stature to make significant revisions such as eliminating all use of an elementary textbook.

Stevens, in turn, may have been at fault in being hypersensitive to criticism by academics. Furthermore, his lecture did often wander confusingly from the announced topic. Finally, he was naïve to believe that a philosophical periodical of any kind would publish an essay in which an elementary textbook was used heavily.

What lessons can be drawn from my narrative of misunderstandings between Stevens and Weiss? Does it provide reason to be pessimistic about the benefits to be derived from philosophers studying poetry and poets studying philosophy? No. Emphatically no. There is ample historical evidence that such readings between poetry and philosophy are mutually beneficial. It is well known that Gertrude Stein was influenced by Whitehead, though the extent of that influence has not been appreciated. In particular, the influence of Whitehead's work in mathematical logic has not been recognized. William Carlos Williams's reading of John Dewey has recently been discussed. And no one can doubt the influence of Wittgenstein's work on poets today. However, personal cooperation between individual poets and philosophers is a different matter. It was one thing for Stevens to read the works of philosophers such as Bergson, James, and Whitehead, and quite another thing for Stevens to interact cooperatively with a living philosopher such as Weiss. In merely reading published works, a poet can cherry-pick whatever aspects of a work seem stimulating and ignore any ideas that lack such appeal. A poet, for example, can make use of Whitehead's notions of field and process and ignore what he says about abstract objects, what he calls "eternal objects." Likewise, a philosopher can cherry-pick in the work of a poet according to his or her philosophical purposes.

The benefits of personal interaction between poet and philosopher are more problematic. In such interactions both poet and philosopher are, understandably, unhappy when their interactions ignore major parts of their work. And seldom do a poet and philosopher agree on the natures of their disciplines. This disagreement is often a serious barrier to cooperation. We had best be modest in our expectations of the benefits of personal exchange. However, the relationship between Stevens and Weiss— with all its disappointments—teaches us that such encounters can be stimulating and productive.

I would like to close with an estimate Weiss gave of Stevens's work after his death, along with lines from a poem that Weiss considered insightful, and remarks Weiss made in response to questions by Rorty.

> [Stevens] is a phenomenologist—that is, somebody who is alert to what he confronts and gives it its full value, doesn't reduce it by virtue of some preconceived concept, but tries to accept the things in their immediacy and their full richness. . . . [H]e is involved in the immediate, confronted data . . . which then he sees with . . . a philosophic or even metaphysical depth but interprets in phenomenological terms. . . . I think of him as one who thinks that the world that we see every day is encrusted with all kinds of conventional meanings and the whole function of the imagination is to penetrate beyond those and catch

what the phenomenon really is as it is there in its nakedness and full phenomenological clarity. And that is why he is constantly thrusting in, breaking up the images, challenging the ways, and even, I think, opposing the philosophers because he thinks they're encrusting it in another [way]. Therefore, I think it is right to say that he is a man of metaphysical insight who then uses the result as an object for phenomenological examination.[20]

Here are the lines Weiss thought illuminating. They are the opening lines of "Description without Place."

It is possible that to seem—it is to be,
As the sun is something seeming and it is.

The sun is an example. What it seems
It is and in such seeming all things are.

Thus things are like a seeming of the sun
Or like a seeming of the moon or night
Or sleep.[21]

Weiss found that these lines expressed something "very close" to what he was thinking. But he immediately adds—note the cherry-picking—that there are other parts of the poem "which seem to indicate something quite different from what I intend, as if there were nothing to the reality but the appearance. And this I would say is an error. But that it is the reality that is really there when it appears seemed to me a very good and vital insight and put by him in a most arresting way."[22]

In another part of the interview, a section that Brazeau did not publish, Weiss made revealing remarks about how he—and perhaps most philosophers—derive benefit from poetry:

Stevens is a difficult writer for me. . . . But if I give myself to it and also come with my own ideas then I find him really enriching them rather than giving me a new insight. Now that may be a defect of my own thinking, and maybe the fact that I am by nature occupied with concepts and perhaps I even do this when I read the poetry, though I do not think so. Perhaps I cannot learn from someone unless I capture it within the compass of a concept. And this means perhaps that I will never learn from a poet, except in the area that I already somewhat understand. And what he provides me with is depth rather than another kind of thought.[23]

In a reply to an inquiry by Rorty concerning his views on Derrida, Weiss said that the distance between philosophy and poetry is not so great as the above remarks might suggest:

> Derrida is right, I think, to look at philosophical writing as a type of literature, involving the use of images, metaphors, and other agencies by means of which basic visions and insights are portrayed and communicated. The distinctions that are pertinent to recording, reporting, dialectic, argument, and systematization are then rightly neglected or minimized; but that does not mean that they are not present, unchanged in role and import. Poets can report, judge, and claim, at the same time that they attend to the weight and affiliations of their words. Philosophic discourse, though not a type of poetry, resonates in multiple ways at the same time that it represents, refers, humanizes, socializes, and austerely formulates the nature of what is true everywhere and always.[24]

SIXTEEN

DEEP CONCEPTUAL PLAY IN WILLIAM JAMES

Let me begin by saying how much pleasure it gives me to be part of a conference honoring John Smith. I have fond memories of being one of Professor Smith's students while I was an undergraduate here at Yale in the mid-1950s. Dick Bernstein was a graduate student here for roughly the same period I was an undergraduate. I am sure that he would agree that Yale's philosophy faculty was especially glorious in that era. But at the time I was an innocent, naïve undergraduate, who simply took for granted the extraordinary resources of the Yale philosophy department. It was the only philosophy department I knew much about. I was in no position to compare the Yale philosophers to those at Harvard, Princeton, Brown, and Stanford.

However, now, with a half century of hindsight, I recognize that Yale in the mid-1950s probably had a more genuinely pluralistic and diverse group of philosophers than any philosophy department in the United States before or since. No single "ism" or philosophical approach dominated the department. I could be a student of philosophers as different in outlook as Brand Blanshard and Arthur Pap. Working with such different philosophers, I took it as a matter of course that fundamental philosophical disagreement did not preclude productive coexistence in the same department. In particular, Yale's philosophy faculty demonstrated to me concretely that representatives of analytic philosophy could work constructively with sharp critics of analytic philosophy, and that scholars in the history of philosophy could work constructively with philosophers whose efforts were focused on contemporary philosophical problems. That Yale model of a pluralistic philosophical community, of which John Smith was such an important member, has stuck with me for more than fifty years. Through my entire career I have tried to create the conditions for that sort of pluralism in everything I have done. In many years of chairing the department at Buffalo, I attempted to develop such pluralism in faculty and students. Although my personal philosophical allegiance has been to classical American pragmatism and naturalism, I have never attempted to create a department where my personal philosophical outlook is the *dominant* outlook. Similarly, in more than thirty years of coediting the *Transactions of the C. S. Peirce Society*, I have struggled to have the rich diversity of American thought represented in the journal. This has always been and will always be an uphill battle. For me, an ideal issue of the journal is one in which we publish articles on topics as diverse as Peirce's logical graphs and Emerson's metaphysics. Although it is pedagogically convenient when teaching the history of American philosophy to overstate what American philosophers have in common, by offering, for example, a pragmatist narrative, this convenient fiction obscures something enormously important in philosophy in America. It obscures the fact that the American philosophical tradition has many strands, strands of many colors. Moreover, new strands are constantly joining and enriching this tradition. Overstating the continuity and homogeneity also has the destructive effect of encouraging philosophers in this country to be overly defensive. It encourages American philosophers to be hostile to what I like to call "immigrant ideas." Just as I believe, as many do, that much of the strength of our general culture can be attributed to this country's ability to absorb constructively wave after wave, generation after generation, of persons immigrating from other parts of the world, I believe that much of the strength of philosophy in America can be attributed to our ability to absorb constructively wave after wave of immigrant *philosophies*. During the twentieth century, the chief among them were, of course, logical empiricism and linguistic philosophy. While conceding that there is much in those philosophies that I personally reject, I am convinced that those philosophies have enriched the American philosophical tradition. That is not to say that such approaches should not be critiqued from any number of alternative perspectives, as analytic philosophy has been. It is rather to say that energetic and even fierce dialogue between immigrant philosophies and well-established currents of thought is healthy and intellectually productive in the long run, however frustrating, irritating, and exhausting it may be in the short term.

So I want to salute John Smith for the leading role he has played in that dialogue over many decades at Yale and in the broader community. No one has contributed more to the ever-evolving spirit of American philosophy than he has. Now I would like to turn to the announced topic for my talk today, "Deep Conceptual Play in William James."

I must begin by making some remarks about the cultural matrix in which Charles Peirce and William James developed their ideas in the 1860s, 1870s, and 1880s. In the mid and late nineteenth century, there were not the sharp divisions between science, literature, mathematics, art, philosophy, and religion that we have come to take for granted since early in the twentieth century. James in *The Principles of Psychology* thinks nothing about quoting from Virgil's *Aeneid* in Latin. In that work he also quotes at length Jane Austen's description of Miss Bates in the novel *Emma*. A lengthy quotation from Alexander Pope can be found elsewhere in *The Principles*. He appeals to Robert Browning's poetry when expounding the nature of space-relations, cites the novelist Samuel Butler in explaining how necessary truths are related to experience, and draws on Mozart, Shakespeare, Dante, Dumas, Goethe, Coleridge, and William Dean Howells on a wide range of topics. James puts together on the same page some abstruse results of experimental psychology and a reference to a novel or poem. Such crossing of boundaries is also common in Peirce's work, especially in his manuscripts. Not infrequently, on a sheet of paper filled with mathematical calculations will also be found a line or two of poetry carefully written out.

In what follows I would like to suggest that today we would sometimes do well to return to such a rapprochement between what are conventionally considered radically different subject matters. To be sure, today the terms of fusion will be somewhat different from what they were in the late nineteenth century, but there are instructive similarities. I believe that recent work in cognitive linguistics and brain science sheds light on an activity that fascinated both Peirce and James, what I shall call "deep conceptual play." In cognitive linguistics I have in mind what George Lakoff and Mark Johnson call "conceptual metaphors," and in brain science I have in mind the striking finding that most of our thinking is *unconscious*. Although the unconscious has been explored by a host of writers from the early nineteenth century through Freud and Lacan to the present, what is remarkable about recent discoveries is the overwhelming conclusion that *formal* thinking, *logical* thinking, *mathematical* thinking is largely unconscious. Hitherto it has been assumed that whatever thinking was going on unconsciously, it could hardly be considered to have the cognitive status of logic and mathematics or of "rational thought." In other words, some unconscious thinking is now considered by brain scientists (and psychologists and philosophers familiar with their experimental conclusions) to have a cognitive status radically different from what it was previously thought to have. But I am getting ahead of myself.

Let me begin to explain what I am proposing by telling you [as is fully developed in the preceding chapter] about the interaction between the philosopher Paul Weiss, a longtime Yale colleague and friend of John Smith, and the poet Wallace Stevens, often considered the most *philosophical* of American poets of the twentieth century. In commenting on what he finds valuable in Stevens's poetry, Weiss says:

> [Stevens] is a phenomenologist—that is, somebody who is alert to what he confronts and gives it its full value, doesn't reduce it by virtue of some preconceived concept, but tries to accept the things in their immediacy and their full richness. . . . [H]e is involved in the immediate, confronted data . . . which then he sees with . . . a philosophic or even metaphysical depth but interprets in phenomenological terms. . . . I think of him as one who thinks that the world that we see every day is encrusted with all kinds of conventional meanings and the whole function of the imagination is to penetrate beyond those and catch what the phenomenon really is as it is there in its nakedness and full phenomenological clarity. And that is why he is constantly thrusting in, breaking up the images, challenging the ways, and even, I think, opposing the philosophers because he thinks they're encrusting it in

another [way]. Therefore, I think it is right to say that he is a man of metaphysical insight who then uses the result as an object for phenomenological examination.

Here are the lines Weiss thought illuminating. They are the opening lines of "Description without Place."

It is possible that to seem—it is to be,
As the sun is something seeming and it is.

The sun is an example. What it seems
It is and in such seeming all things are.

Thus things are like a seeming of the sun
Or like a seeming of the moon or night

Or sleep.

Weiss found that these lines expressed something "very close" to what he was thinking. But he immediately adds—note the cherry-picking— that there are other parts of the poem "which seem to indicate something quite different from what I intend, as if there were nothing to the reality but the appearance. And this I would say is an error. But that it is the reality that is really there when it appears seemed to me a very good and vital insight and put by him in a most arresting way." [See Chapter 15 in the present volume—ed.]

As I read Weiss's comments, he is saying that the poet Stevens has "metaphysical insight" because he recognizes that both our ordinary experience and the language of philosophy are "encrusted with" "conventional meanings" and "preconceived" concepts but he is also able by "breaking up the images" to make the reader aware of "things in their immediacy." Weiss is suggesting that philosophers' talk *in the abstract* about our experience, including our philosophical experience, is conceptually encrusted and poets appreciate that abstract philosophical point, but a poet like Stevens is able concretely to bring the reader into immediate contact with things in a way that a philosopher cannot or at least in a way that a philosopher qua philosopher cannot. As I hope will become clear in what follows, Weiss is, I think, on the right track in making that contrast between philosophy and poetry. But Weiss goes astray when he suggests that there is "an error" in Stevens's poem because part of the poem suggests that there is "nothing to the reality but the appearance" while another part of the poem correctly (in Weiss's eyes) suggests that things really are as they are experienced in their "full phenomenological clarity." [See Chapter 15 in the present volume—ed.]

Weiss mistakenly assumes that a poet qua poet should—at least within a single poem—espouse an epistemology that is both sound and self-consistent. He applauds part of the poem for its realistic epistemology and faults another part of the poem for its unsound, phenomenalist epistemology. That is not to suggest that in this poem or in any of his other poems it was Stevens's intention to present an epistemological viewpoint. I am rather suggesting that Stevens regarded each of the competing epistemologies as *metaphorical structures*. It is difficult perhaps for those of us whose daily bread is earned by grappling earnestly with epistemological arguments to "get our minds around" the notion of an epistemological theory as a metaphor, but I submit that this is not a difficult notion for a poet with strong philosophical, especially epistemological interests, as Wallace Stevens was.

If epistemological theories are, for Stevens, metaphorical structures, there is no reason to suppose that only one epistemological theory can appear in a single poem, and no reason to suppose that the poet is committed to the *truth* of one of the epistemologies. After all, no one doubts that it is appropriate to have more than one *metaphor* in a single poem. Furthermore, no one worries about whether a poem's various metaphors are logically self-consistent.

Some of Weiss's further remarks are also helpful in clarifying the relations between *some* philosophers and *some* poets:

> Stevens is a difficult writer for me. . . . But if I give myself to it and also come with my own ideas then I find him really enriching them rather than giving me a new insight. Now that may be a defect of my own thinking, and maybe the fact that I am by nature occupied with concepts and perhaps I even do this when I read the poetry, though I do not think so. Perhaps I cannot learn from someone unless I capture it within the compass of a concept. And this means perhaps that I will never learn from a poet, except in the area that I already somewhat understand. And what he provides me with is depth rather than another kind of thought. [See Chapter 15 in the present volume—ed.]

Weiss is saying that, though a poet cannot give him a new concept, a poet can provide "phenomenological clarity" that roots more deeply in experience a concept Weiss already employs. The assumption seems to be that it is in the nature of a philosopher to be concerned primarily with concepts and it is not in the nature of a poet to provide conceptual knowledge. The contrast is between the *conceptual* knowledge appropriate to philosophy and the *phenomenological* knowledge appropriate to poetry. Although I am suspicious of this dichotomy, there is a valuable insight to be found in this contrast. What Weiss misses, however, is that what a poet does with concepts, using them as metaphors, can loosen the grip that a concept has on the reader, including the philosophical reader.

William James is another philosopher strongly interested in poetry and literature in general. Although there are parallels between the thinking of Weiss and James on this topic, the differences are important. Much has been written about James's use of metaphor, and his prose is sometimes considered prose poetry. This is not the occasion to attempt a comprehensive survey of everything James had to say about literature (after all, he was the brother of Henry). But it is important to note that James had no "literary theory." Indeed, he was dismissive of the very idea. But he cared deeply about the *psychological and epistemological* significance of the arts. Charlene Haddock Seigfried has written most perceptively about this aspect of James's thought. Poetry, as she points out, was one of the arts in which what James calls "sympathetic concrete observation" is central. "Scientific rational thinking always involves extracting a partial aspect of the whole phenomenon thought about, while poetic empirical thinking always compares phenomena globally. . . . Both the scientist and the artist abstract partial aspects of the total phenomenon, but the degree of simplification and their intentions in doing so differ significantly,"[1] she says. "Experiences are originally global and artists do less violence to the 'much-at-oneness' . . . so their work, like the originating experiences themselves, can be returned to again and again to discover new connections. Since experiential reality has an infinity of aspects, the differing ones discovered and communicated by scientists and artists are not rivals so much as complementary angles of vision. The ability to recognize unusual couplings, to discern relationships where no one has yet seen them, is the basis for scientific and poetic genius."[2] When artists "judge rightly, classify cases, characterize them by the most striking analogic epithets, but go no further,"[3] this should not be considered evidence that artists have not reached the highest levels of human thought. Rather, these preferences should be considered to reveal "a mind fertile in the suggested image." The comparison here with Weiss is instructive. Although both philosophers value the "phenomenological clarity" found in the arts, the contrast between philosophy and art and between the conceptual and nonconceptual is quite different in the two thinkers. James is much more suspicious of the conceptual preoccupations of philosophers than Weiss is. Although he recognizes that such preoccupations are common among philosophers, James in *his own* philosophical enterprise is attempting to reveal "the richness of experience through analogy and refusal to transcend it by ratiocination."[4] I submit that *James intends his method to be a blend of the method of poets and method traditionally employed by philosophers.*

Megan Mustain has extended Seigfried's account of James's metaphorical method. James recognizes, Mustain says, that an indefinitely large number of terms can be used to describe the world's character, no one of which is "inextricably connected to the referent."[5] When James exchanges, for example, the term "field" for the term "datum," he is not looking for a term that has a one-to-one correspondence to reality. For James, "our terms are better thought of as evocative—of responses, actions, and consequences—than as strictly denotative."[6] In other words, every one of his philosophical terms is avowedly a metaphor, and "a metaphor is always insufficient . . . never capturing a whole experience at one stroke . . . a metaphor is explicitly a product of human interest; we choose our analogies to suit our purposes. . . . Yet analogies, unlike most propositions, reveal the limitations that come with selective interest."[7]

But how then does James distinguish between better and worse philosophical metaphors? "[For James, t]he test of a philosophical metaphor," Mustain writes, "is twofold. First does, the metaphor harmoniously satisfy our interests? And second, to the extent that it does fully satisfy the vast range of human interests, does the metaphor disclose its conditions and limitations, announcing itself *as a metaphor*?"[8]

James's metaphorical method "asks us," Mustain concludes, "to loosen our notion of objective reference in the manner of a poet. It asks us to see the philosophical systems to the past and present as originating in and responding to human needs—needs which may or may not be compelling in the current context."[9] James sees "the task of philosophy as the creation and reconstruction of metaphorical images of the world which better suit the needs and interests of human beings in their personal and collective lives."[10] It is significant, I suggest, that some of James's lecture notes read, as Mustain points out, like the free verse found in Walt Whitman's *Leaves of Grass*.

There is an additional aspect of poetry that James finds of philosophical importance, an aspect that goes unnoticed by Seigfried and Mustain— the element of *play*, word play. Anyone even superficially familiar with James's biography knows that playfulness and a closely related gift for hyperbole were typical of him. Indeed, the playfulness that comes out so clearly in his correspondence is one of the reasons that so many find his personality attractive. Without for a moment denying the biographical significance of James's general playfulness, I want to draw attention to a specific form that his playfulness sometimes took.

Consider this passage in a letter James wrote to the poet Emma Lazarus:

> I am myself a prosaic wretch, and find myself reading little poetry, especially little that is not lyric, but I must say that when I *do*, I enjoy it very much. To you gifted ones who can float and soar and circle through the sky of expression so freely, our slow hobbling on *terra firma* must sometimes be a matter of impatience. // I think the power of *playing* with thought and language that such as you possess is the divinist of gifts.[11]

I am not suggesting that there was anything *casual* about James's approach to the use of language. No philosopher was ever more self-conscious about his writing style than James. He took pains to engage in word play appropriate to the context, the audience, and his purposes. He expressed admiration for word play in philosophical writing as well as in poetry. He wrote of his colleague and friend Josiah Royce that he had the traits of "play with earnestness" in his philosophical writing. Undeniably, he found word play effective as a means of holding the attention of readers or a live audience and of making himself popular as a speaker and writer. His numerous drawings in correspondence are also often a form of play. But I suggest that something much more philosophically *substantive* was also involved, what we may call "deep play." I call it "deep" because it involves concepts of an extremely high level of generality and abstractness and because our work with them is largely unconscious.

Perhaps James's correspondence with Benjamin Paul Blood reveals this commitment to deep play more than any of James's other writing. James wrote Blood:

> You seem to be a man after Walt Whitman's own heart—and I've got much good from that man's verse—if such it can be called—I see you as a man of discontinuity and insights, and not a philosophic pack-horse or pack-mule. . . . Your thought is obscure [he told Blood]— lightning flashes, darting gleams—but that's the way truth is. And although I "put pluralism in the place of philosophy," I do it only as far as philosophy means the articulable and the scientific. Life and mysticism exceed the articulable, and if there is a *One*, (and surely men will never be weaned from it) it must remain only mystically expressed. . . . For single far flung & far flashing words and sentences, you're the biggest genius I know, but when it comes to constructing a whole argument or article it seems to be another kettle of fish.[12]

Although James called Blood a "pluralistic mystic" and commentators have correctly pointed to his comments on Blood as an example of James's most speculative mysticism and pluralism, scholars have failed to note what James *most* values in his cast of mind. What James finds *most* valuable is the *conceptual flexibility and versatility* exhibited in his work. Blood has an extraordinary gift for juggling philosophical concepts. In deep word play of vivid metaphors he was able to move quickly back and forth between radically different "way[s] of treating the world."

Such conceptual flexibility and versatility is of epistemological value to James because it loosens our bonds to any one conceptual structure, and such loosening allows us to extend the reach of experience, allows us to penetrate more deeply into the real. Recall my earlier comment that Wallace Stevens employs competing epistemological theories as metaphorical structures in an effort to extend our experiential encounter with the world beyond what language with encrusted conventional meanings allows. Blood's writing is a more florid effort of the same kind.

By any measure the poet most directly influenced by James was his student Gertrude Stein. Much has been published about the influence of James's psychology on Stein, an influence she often acknowledged. However, it has not been recognized—even by Stein herself as far as I know—that the importance James attached to word play in the use of philosophical concepts had an influence on her. That is not to deny that other influences were present in this aspect of her writing—cubism in painting was one additional influence. However, I wish to suggest that her early exposure to James's thought as a student may have been one reason that she was later attracted to cubism. Stein's work *Tender Buttons* is filled with odd, apparently self-inconsistent juxtapositions of philosophical concept-metaphors. Here is an example:

> *A Substance in a cushion*
> The change of color is likely and a difference a very little difference is prepared. Sugar is not a vegetable.
> Callous is something that hardening leaves behind what will be soft if there is genuine interest in there being present as many girls as men. Does this change. It shows that dirt is clean when there is volume.[13]

Here is another example. Under the heading "Food," Stein writes the following:

> *Roastbeef*
> In the inside there is sleeping, in the outside there is reddening, in the morning there is meaning, in the evening there is feeling. In feeling anything is resting, in feeling anything is mounting, in feeling there is resignation, in feeling there is recognition, in feeling there is recurrence and entirely mistaken there is pinching. All the standards have steamers and all the curtains have bed linen and all the yellow have discrimination and all the circles has circling. This makes sand.[14]

Note the riot of conceptual clashes in what I have just read. It should be clear that the above discussion of metaphor and word play implies a blurring of the distinction between poetic knowledge and philosophical knowledge. Although blurring of distinctions is, in general, typical of pragmatist thought, there is a reason why James wanted to blur this particular distinction. For James, one of the chief tasks of a philosopher is to exploit every cognitive resource that can be found, and he has an exceptionally catholic attitude toward cognitive resources. Most notoriously he devoted himself to exploring psychical research as a possible cognitive resource. His treatment of feelings as cognitive, though highly controversial during his lifetime, is now widely accepted. James was not urging that philosophical knowledge be *replaced* by poetic knowledge. He was not suggesting that Benjamin Paul Blood serve as a model for what philosophers should be doing. Instead, he was recommending that philosophers find a way to incorporate Blood's poetic knowledge in their philosophical knowledge. This, he believed, would be possible only if philosophers met the poets half way. For that reason, the account that Seigfried and Mustain have given of James's metaphorical method is of particular importance. Only if we come to understand how philosophical concepts are to be evaluated as metaphors can we appreciate how the metaphors of poets can be an important cognitive resource. If we continue to insist, as philosophers have traditionally done, that there is an unbridgeable epistemological gulf between the metaphorical and the propositional, we will confine philosophical knowledge to thin abstraction, shut off from concreteness. What is needed is the *thick* use of the philosophical.

Among recent thinkers in the English-speaking world, probably Richard Rorty makes the strongest claim for the philosophical value of poetry. Perhaps not coincidentally, Rorty was a student here at Yale at the same time that Dick Bernstein and I were, the mid-1950s. And, interestingly, both Bernstein and Rorty were students of Paul Weiss.

Rorty uses the term "poet" in what he recognizes is a wider sense than is usual. A poet, for him, is "one who makes new" by developing a new vocabulary. Galileo and Hegel count as poets as clearly as Yeats. He sees "human history as the history of successive metaphors" and sees "the poet, in the generic sense of the maker of new words, the shaper of new languages, as the vanguard of the species."[15] He borrows from Harold Bloom the term "strong poet" to help distinguish what he has in mind from what is conventionally thought to be poet. I have much sympathy with Rorty's views on the role of metaphor in conceptualizing our experience of the world. I also share *some* of his enthusiasm for blurring distinctions between literature, philosophy, and science. I applaud as well his endorsement of the playfulness he finds in Nietzsche and Derrida. However, I have serious reservations about Rorty's stress on linkage between conceptual play and irony, when irony is construed as a species of skepticism. Although no one can deny that James, Stein, and Stevens sometimes are ironical, the deep conceptual play I find in James, Stein, and Stevens is a very different animal. This form of play is employed as a way of loosening our bonds to any particular structure of philosophical concepts, thus giving us access to realities otherwise inaccessible. Deep conceptual play increases our cognitive powers; it does not *suspend* them, as Rorty's irony seems to do. James perhaps best describes this access in the context of religious experience: "*He becomes conscious that this higher part is coterminous and continuous with a more of the same quality, which is operative in the universe outside him, and which he can keep in working touch with.*"[16] James readily concedes that such prayerful states involve overbeliefs, because in James's ethics of belief overbeliefs do not always lack epistemic justification. We often speak of those contexts as poetic or religious or mystical or paranormal but we should not allow such question-begging labels to discredit indiscriminately this fallibilistic cognitive strategy.

As I mentioned at the outset, the cognitive linguists Lakoff and Johnson have developed a theory of "conceptual metaphors." Their theory helps to explain what sort of concepts are involved in the deep conceptual play that is the subject of my talk. One of their examples is the metaphorical concept "argument is war." Such a conceptual metaphor, they maintain, structures not only how we perceive and how we think, but also what we do. "It is important to see," they write, "that we don't just *talk* about arguments in terms of war. We can actually win or lose arguments. We see the person we are arguing with as an opponent. We attack his position and we defend our own. We gain and lose ground. We plan and use strategies. . . . Many of the things we *do* in arguing are partially structured by the concept of war. . . . [This conceptual metaphor] structures the actions we perform in arguing."[17]

In another example, "Time is money, time is a limited resource, and time is a valuable commodity form a single system based on subcategorization. . . . These subcategorization relationships characterize what we will call 'entailment relationships' between the metaphors. Time is money entails that time is a limited resource, which entails that time is a valuable commodity." "This isn't a necessary way for human beings to conceptualize time; it is tied to our culture. There are cultures where time is none of these things."[18]

In a systematic way in any culture each of its conceptual metaphors structure experience, thought, and action in that particular culture. This is the sort of *deep* metaphor or concept that I believe that James, Stein, and Stevens wish to play with.

Before I conclude this talk, I must comment briefly on the form that deep conceptual play took in the work of Charles Peirce, who was of course a lifelong friend of James and his collaborator in founding pragmatism. Although I know of no comment by James on Peirce's work in this area or of any comment by Peirce on James's thinking on this subject, the similarities between their views are remarkable. The well-known biographical fact must first be noted that Peirce traced the beginning of his philosophical career to his reading of the German poet Friedrich Schiller's *Aesthetic Letters* in 1855 shortly after he had entered Harvard as an undergraduate. It was Schiller's notion of *Spieltrieb* that especially fascinated Peirce. This notion of play as a free kind of doing he later came to call "musement." He also later linked Schiller's idea to the idea of chance in the doctrine he called "tychism." Many decades later he recalled concluding that "esthetics and logic seem, at first blush, to belong to different universes . . . [but] that seeming is illusory, and that, on the contrary, logic needs the help of esthetics."[19] This notion of free play of ideas also became central to his account of scientific creativity. He held that scientific thought grows through discovery by a process of what he called "abduction," and abduction he understood to be creative hypothesis formation. Repeatedly in his writings over many years Peirce argued that creative hypothesis formation could not be explained in terms of induction or deduction. Creative hypotheses are highly unlikely to be arrived at by any amount of induction and deduction. We must, he said, have an "instinct" for guessing. Only such an instinct could explain our success in imagining novel hypotheses that turn out to be empirically confirmable.

As Douglas Anderson has shown, Peirce saw a kinship between *artistic* abduction, *artistic* creativity, and *scientific* abduction and creativity. Anderson's student Daniel Campos has recently extended Anderson's account by explaining how for Peirce the creation of *mathematical* hypotheses is *poietic*, but not merely *poietic*. "Scientific considerations also inhere in the process of hypothesis-making, without excluding the *poietic* element. . . . [H]ypothesis-making in mathematics," Campos argues, "stands between artistic and scientific *poietic* creativity with respect to imaginative freedom from logical and actual constraints upon reasoning."[20] However, Peirce's most widely known discussion of such play or musement is in his late essay titled "A Neglected Argument for the Reality of God." There he says: "But let religious meditation be allowed to grow up spontaneously out of Pure Play without any breach of continuity; and Musement will retain the perfect candor proper to Musement."[21] He claims that anyone who practices Musement will be brought to belief in the reality of God, as an *instinctive* response to the idea of God.

Note that Peirce's discussion of musement, an instinct for guessing, and poetic creativity pointedly does *not* separate the artistic from the philosophical, the philosophical from the scientific, or the philosophical from the religious, or the philosophical from the mathematical. The mental activity that so fascinated him from his earliest philosophical reflections until his death spans all these forms of inquiry; it lies at the *intersection* of the artistic, the philosophical, the religious, the mathematical, and the scientific. Empirical psychology was still in its infancy during the lifetimes of Peirce and James, so they lacked the means to do more than speculate about what this mental activity is. As I have suggested earlier, thanks to recent developments in cognitive linguistics and brain science, we now know a great deal more about conceptual thinking, particularly about *unconscious* conceptual thinking, than was known by Peirce, James, and their contemporaries. Indeed, those scientific fields are still developing at an astonishing rate. My hope is that this rapidly developing science will be used to revisit the deep conceptual play that the founders of pragmatism grappled with so suggestively. If James and Peirce were alive today, they would be eager to bring to bear on their philosophical views the latest findings of empirical science.

PART SEVEN

SOCIAL CRITIQUE

In the final section readers will discover some of Hare's political and ethical views. These essays are occasional in nature. We begin with an account of civil disobedience and then move to Hare's critique of what he calls the American mind. Here he discusses some of the problems systemic to modern American values as they relate to topics such as religion and race. Readers are then introduced to Hare's views on the death penalty and finally to his analysis of the American intellectual class.

These essays reveal an individual deeply committed to social change and yet troubled by the direction of the political process. They also show a pragmatic temper insofar as Hare raises issues that are bound to the historical context of his life. His essay on civil disobedience, for example, is set against the backdrop of the civil rights movement and resistance to the Vietnam War in the 1960s. It is fair to wonder how Hare would have reacted to the presidency of Barack Obama. Perhaps some of his fears would have eased. There is no doubt, however, that he would have felt an affinity for Obama's pragmatic ideology.

SEVENTEEN

REFLECTIONS ON CIVIL DISOBEDIENCE

with Edward H. Madden

I

The concept of civil disobedience is extremely rich and diverse, not at all precise and specific—the way it is with most words outside of a formal system. Yet much can be done to analyze and clarify the concept, though not formally define it, if two opposite tendencies are pointed out and avoided. On the one hand, some authors generalize "civil disobedience" until it loses any special designation and becomes vacuously synonymous with "disobedience to any authority." On the other hand, different authors, for varying purposes, restrict the concept to one of various types of action, all of which ordinarily would be called cases of civil disobedience. The vacuous generalizations result from inattention to actual usage and the lack of ability to prune suggested generalizations and so sharpen up a concept that has a genuine use. The restrictive definitions result from confusing definitional and conceptual concerns over the meaning of "civil disobedience" with the problem of justifying civil disobedience. Authors of restrictive definitions reserve the phrase either for acts of dissent they think justified or for those thought unjustified, depending on what emotive overtones the phrase has for them. Needless to say, the results are mutually incompatible definitions all of a persuasive sort in which different groups try to put the phrase to work for *them*.

We do not claim that our own work is value free; far from it. We only try to get the conceptual analysis and the justification sorted out so that discussions of each can have a significant effect on an issue badly in need of both.

II

(1) The concept of civil disobedience presupposes, first of all, some formal structure of law, enforced by established governmental authorities, from which an individual cannot dissociate himself except by change of citizenship. Disobedience in the contexts of family, clan, church, lodge, or business does not count as civil disobedience.

Sit-ins protesting university policies might seem to be acts of civil disobedience since they constitute public resistance to a system of rules and policies just as surely as protests against the rules and policies of civil government. Moreover, the attitudes and techniques applied in student resistance of university authority are often the same as those applied in resisting governmental authority; and universities, like governments, have elaborate systems of sanctions and penalties. However, if all such cases of resistance counted as civil disobedience, then the countless examples of resistance to ecclesiastical and other nongovernmental authority would also qualify as civil disobedience and the term would lose any special meaning altogether, becoming synonymous simply with "resistance to any authority." Student resistance to university authority does not become civil disobedience unless or until civil laws, as distinct from academic rules, are broken and the protest is aimed primarily at university complicity in government policy, for example, the Vietnam War and Selective Service.

(2) Although civil disobedience presupposes some system of enforced civil law, it is not necessary that an individual ultimately accept the governmental framework in which he acts disobediently; he may be accepting it only conditionally at a given time as a necessary but

temporary fact of life or a step in the direction toward the framework he ultimately accepts.

To insist on the ultimate acceptance of the framework in which the act occurs, as some writers do, has the awkward consequence of denying that Thoreau, Tolstoy, and Gandhi engaged in acts of civil disobedience, since Thoreau and Tolstoy were anarchists and Gandhi was protesting colonial rule.[1] However, it is also true that if acceptance of the framework is not required, then it is difficult to see how it is possible to distinguish between civil disobedience and the early stages of revolution, whether peaceful or violent. Here the wisest course seems to be that of admitting mixed cases. Insofar as an individual in his disobedience temporarily accepts the governmental framework in which he is acting, and the other criteria of civil disobedience are met, the act is one of civil disobedience; and insofar as the individual in explanation of the act expresses the wish ultimately to change the entire system of government, the act is one of incipient revolution even though the revolution may be planned as entirely peaceful.

(3)   Civil disobedience, then, consists in publicly announced defiance of specific laws, policies, or commands (or absence thereof) of that formal structure which an individual or group believes to be unjust and/or unconstitutional.

The defiance must be publicly announced, since the point of it is to bring the unjust and/or unconstitutional laws, policies, or commands to the attention of the public and government for the purpose of stirring their consciences and/or pressuring them into helping repeal the laws, change the policies, or mitigate the commands; or to get the attention of the courts so that their constitutionality can be judged. A person who secretly helped a slave escape to freedom was doing something morally admirable; a doctor who secretly performs illegal abortions may be doing something morally justified; such individuals may even in some cases be doing things which lead to the repeal or nonenforcement of the unjust laws faster than civil disobedience would (if enough people secretly disobey, and the government decides that the laws are unenforceable), but they are not performing acts of civil disobedience. The notion of civil disobedience entails not only the breaking of a law on moral grounds but pointing up the disobedience itself for its symbolic and pressure-exerting value.

A number of writers would disagree with our "unjust and/or unconstitutional" dichotomy, some of them insisting that only acts of disobedience performed in the belief that the law disobeyed is unconstitutional are acts of civil disobedience, and others holding, with equal confidence, that only disobedience of laws held to be unjust yet constitutional can be considered acts of civil disobedience. However, there are serious difficulties with both these restrictions. If civil disobedience is confined to disobedience of laws believed to be unconstitutional, it is not clear what we could call an act of disobedience performed in the belief that a law is unjust despite the fact that the Supreme Court has recently ruled it constitutional. And if we attempt to restrict civil disobedience to disobedience of laws held to be constitutional but unjust, we are forced to conclude that the vast literature in which the civil rights movement is spoken of in terms of civil disobedience is based on an entirely erroneous use of the phrase.[2]

(4) Civil disobedience may also consist in publicly announced defiance of just laws if such disobedience is not itself repugnant to conscience and if it appears to be the only effective way to focus attention on the nonenforcement of other just laws or on the unjust absence of certain legislation, policy, or commands. The only restriction is that the just law chosen be such that disobedience of it will in a dramatically effective way focus attention on the injustice and that the practice not be so widespread as to lead to riot, insurrection, or rebellion.

Tax and trespass laws, for example, have been broken sometimes to protest the *nonenforcement*, both in the North and South, of civil rights legislation and Supreme Court decisions, while similar laws, again, are violated to protest the *absence* of open-housing legislation. Some authors, fearing that such disobedience would lead to unrestrained lawlessness, have refused to call such activity "civil disobedience," but clearly they are thereby confusing the categories of definition and justification. Such activity counts as civil disobedience since it does not necessarily imply any rejection of its framework and hence is not an example of revolution, either incipient or full-fledged. Even if such activity always tended to promote unrestrained lawlessness (itself a highly dubious claim), this fact would show that such activity was an undesirable form of civil disobedience not that it was no form at all.

(5) Civil disobedience may take the form of doing what is prohibited, or failing to do what is required.

An example of the former would be burning a draft card, while an example of the latter would be refusing to report for induction.

(6) Civil disobedience must be a premeditated act[3] understood to be illegal by the perpetrator, and understood to carry prescribed penalties. Willingness to accept such penalties is a crucial part of that sort of civil disobedience which hopes to stir the public conscience, while eagerness to escape punishment is perfectly compatible with that sort of civil disobedience which aims to pressure government officials and the public.[4]

An example of the latter is public school teachers who disobey laws against strikes by public employees. They are involved in genuine acts of civil disobedience since they meet all the above criteria even though they take satisfaction in the government's inability to find effective punishment. These antistrike laws are virtually unenforceable because to put all the teachers in jail still leaves the community with no teachers. Part of the point of this sort of civil disobedience is to change the law by making it impossible to enforce the law, or by making the price of such enforcement extremely high.

(7) In civil disobedience the defiance, finally, may be either nonviolent or violent and still count as civil disobedience.

To restrict the concept of civil disobedience to nonviolent acts, as some authors do, ignores the difficulty of finding a precise dividing line between "nonviolence" and "violence" (is *rigidly* blocking the doorway of an induction center violent and so not a case of civil disobedience?) as well as the facts of usage. Defiant acts of a violent sort, if they are in response to institutional violence, or if they are premeditated but nevertheless controlled and minimal (that is, used for dramatic effect) and are focused, at least for the present, on specific laws, policies, or commands (and hence are well short of unrestricted defiance of the whole government), and meet the above criteria, are in fact called acts of civil disobedience just as much as those which meet the same criteria but are "nonviolent." The pacifist or the advocate of nonviolence on prudential grounds should argue that violent civil disobedience is never justified, either as a matter of principle or a matter of prudence, not that any defiance which has any element of violence, however small, ceases to be an instance of civil disobedience.[5]

III

To summarize our clarification of the concept of civil disobedience: The concept of civil disobedience presupposes a system of laws enforced by governmental authorities from which an individual cannot dissociate himself except by change of citizenship. The individual may ultimately accept this governmental framework or he may accept it only conditionally as a temporary fact of life or a step in the direction of the framework he ultimately accepts. Civil disobedience consists in publicly announced defiance of specific laws, policies, or commands (or absence thereof) which an individual or group believes to be unjust and/or unconstitutional. The defiance may take the form of disobeying a just law if the protesting individual is not in a position to disobey the unjust law or laws, or if it is an absence of laws, policies, or commands that is being protested. In either case, the breaking of a specific just law must not itself be morally repugnant to a protester. The defiance involved in civil disobedience may take the form of doing what is prohibited or in failing to do what is required. The defiance must be a premeditated act, understood to be illegal by the perpetrator, and understood to carry prescribed penalties. Willingness to accept such penalties is a part of that sort of civil disobedience which hopes to stir the conscience of the public and the government, while eagerness to escape punishment is compatible with that sort of civil disobedience which aims to pressure the public and the government. The defiance may be either nonviolent or violent. If violent, the violence must be planned, minimized, and controlled for maximum effectiveness in focusing the public and governmental conscience on specific injustices and/or in pressuring the government and public to change specific laws, policies, or commands (or absence thereof).

IV

Assuming that the notion of civil disobedience is reasonably clear, the question immediately arises why anyone should be civilly disobedient. Is it ever legitimate? If so, under what conditions? The two most important justifications of civil disobedience traditionally have been the Higher Law doctrine and some version of Natural or Human Rights.[6]

(i) The Higher Law doctrine asserts that God's law takes precedence over civil law whenever it can be shown that the two come into conflict. Man is ordinarily duty bound to obey the civil law and magistrates since the benefits of orderly government are large indeed; on the other hand, man cannot, out of higher duty, obey the civil law or magistrates if they command him to break the word of God. In our more humanistically inclined modern world, the Higher Law doctrine frequently is formulated as a moral doctrine without any religious foundation whatsoever. The law of justice or moral law, according to this version, takes precedence over positive law whenever it can be shown that the two come into fundamental conflict. Man should in general be dedicated to upholding positive law, but he cannot, out of respect of higher duty, obey positive law if it commands him to be immoral.

There is a possible misunderstanding of this viewpoint which must be avoided at the outset. That what counts as "moral law" is decided by an individual does not entail the subjectivity or lack of grounding of moral law. All judgments about justice and moral law must be defensible or no reasonable man would pay the slightest attention to them, let alone act upon them. The intelligent agent of civil disobedience offers more than his moral feelings in defense of his action; he presents arguments. He argues, for example, that if the community is to live up to the fundamental ideals on which the legitimacy of a government rests—and in the case of *this* country, if it is to live up to its *own stated political commitment*—then some law, practice, or command must be changed, or some law which is valid but unenforced subsequently *enforced*, or some law needed to erase injustice *enacted*. Moreover, the resisting citizen is not asking for special privilege based on his private feeling; he is asking that basic human rights be given to the members of a minority as they have been "given" to members of the majority. Moral law, in short, though it be accepted, announced, and acted upon by individuals, is itself a universal, social, and community commitment. It asserts that the right to liberty not universally shared ceases to be a right but is a seizure of power. It believes that only the *denial* of the moral law is private, individual, and subjective, a direct result, in fact, from demonstrably selfish desires and transparent rationalizations.[7]

There is really only one significant way of arguing against Higher Law doctrine, namely, that following it entails a spreading effect of lawlessness and ultimate chaos. If everyone is to judge for himself what laws are moral and hence to be respected, then there is really no law at all and we are all deprived of the benefits of civilized society. However sobering this argument is—and should be—it is not ultimately a convincing one. Proponents of the Higher Law recognize the importance of stability and so are willing to obey many questionable laws; they claim only that some laws and policies are so stridently immoral that they must be publicly disobeyed as well as disavowed unless one is to renounce his own humanity. Moreover, the man of principle who will not obey a vicious law is the kind of person who can be counted upon as the strongest upholder of law in general since he will not break laws for selfish reasons or obey the law only when under surveillance. Nothing is more disgusting than the refrain heard nowadays from so-called pillars of society that civil disobedience will lead to lawlessness when they not only openly break laws for their own advantage, or refuse to enforce just laws, but *admit* this, nay, even point it up by joking about it!?—wouldn't anybody do it!?—and by insisting that you cannot legislate a change in attitudes. Finally, a person who would obey *any* law just because it is a law is utterly immoral, for the vilest crimes are often committed on the excuse of following orders of a legally constituted superior. It is also well to keep the Nuremberg judgment in mind here and to realize that there no longer may be adequate *legal* sanction for always following orders.

There are also many who fear that if civil disobedience is considered justified, the society will be constantly disrupted over trivial injustices. But responsible proponents of civil disobedience have always believed that there must be a reasonable proportion between the magnitude of the injustice and the magnitude of the means used to resist. No one has suggested that an individual who holds, for example, that a law against jaywalking is an infringement of his rights is justified in gathering a crowd of thousands to block traffic for a week as a protest. Similarly, an intelligent government's means are proportional to its ends and it refrains from shooting down looters.

Finally, there is widespread fear that an individual can organize disobedient crowds merely to take out his personal grievances on the government without concern for community welfare. However, as anyone who has ever tried to organize a demonstration will report, it is amazingly difficult to persuade citizens to take part in a public protest even when those citizens admit the existence of a shocking injustice; it is well nigh impossible to persuade others to take the risks of public ridicule and imprisonment entailed by protest when they do not share the view that the injustice is shocking. No campaign of civil disobedience can even be begun unless it has strong popular support and is much more than the expression of the peculiar moral feelings of a few individuals.

(ii) The notions of "natural rights" and "human rights" are by no means identical since the former usually involves an absolutistic and rationalistic outlook in moral philosophy and is usually based on a theological foundation such as "God-given rights," while the latter does not usually entail such conceptions but leaves open the possibility, at least, of relativistic, voluntaristic, and humanistic foundations for man's basic rights. The concept of human rights is the one usually used these days, not simply because ours is a more voluntaristic and humanistic era but because this concept includes many social and economic freedoms which seem important to our age, along with the more traditional concept of freedom as "freedom from" various restraints. For example, the Universal Declaration of Human Rights, adopted by the United Nations in 1948, recognizes, among others, the rights to life, liberty, personal security, and equal protection of the law; freedom from slavery and degrading punishment; freedom of thought, conscience, speech, religion, and peaceful assembly; and the right to an education, choice of one's own employment, favorable working conditions, and protection against unemployment.

The concepts of natural and human rights, with all their differences, still have a core of common meaning, namely, that there are certain rights which belong to a person independent of his or her position in a civil society. Since society does not bestow these rights, it cannot justifiably take them away. This is the point in saying that such rights are *inalienable*. The function of society, far from interfering with these rights, is to sustain and protect them and to adjudicate conflicts that arise in the common pursuit of these rights. If a civil government subverts these rights in a wholesale fashion, it is not fulfilling its proper role and hence the people are justified in overthrowing that spurious government (with the least violence possible) and erecting a legitimate one in its place. It follows as a corollary of this general principle that if a government which on the whole respects its proper role nevertheless infringes or denies some specific rights, either for a majority or minority of people, then they have the right to civilly disobey the offending laws, policies, or commands in a way which is consistent with the continued existence of that governmental framework. What measures are consistent with such continued existence will depend wholly upon time, place, conditions, and the specific nature of the government involved, and no general principle, except that of the rational consideration of the facts and the likely consequences of various types of action, can be depended upon for guidance.

Again, there is really only one significant way of arguing against the doctrine of human rights, namely, that it is fine in principle but visionary in fact, since implementing it always entails a loss in social stability and a spreading effect of lawlessness. All that was said in the context of Higher Law doctrine is again applicable here, with these added considerations. It is odd that so many people, while they believe that an act of civil disobedience will spread the contagious and fatal disease of illegality, ignore the genuinely serious spreading effects on community respect for law caused by official attempts to enforce manifestly unjust laws at the same time that just desegregation laws are minimally enforced or totally ignored. The spectacle of its government's flagrant evasion and disobedience of its own laws while it condemns civil disobedience is one of the sources of disaffection that many youths have for their country. When they commit acts of civil disobedience and are told that they must suffer the penalties with dignity, they may justly ask why there are no corresponding penalties for administrative nonenforcement of just laws, a type of disobedience no one in authority seems to worry about.

There are, to be sure, genuine dangers in civil disobedience, well understood by its intelligent agents, but the dangers are to be *weighed* by a believer in human rights and not used as a rationalization for doing nothing when he has the security and someone else's human rights are infringed upon. The point is simply this: If a person is so concerned about civil stability that he cannot conceive any conditions that would justify disobedience, then he really has abandoned any tenable concept of human rights.

The notion of human rights, it should be noted finally, strongly supports the contention that a majority vote cannot decide what is right or wrong and helps put the concept of democracy in its proper perspective. The doctrine of popular sovereignty espoused by Stephen Douglas in pre–Civil War days was supposedly the democratic answer to the problem of slavery in the territories. Let the settlers in each territory vote on whether or not to have slaves! This concept of democracy, of course, subverts the whole notion of human rights and is the rule of the majority to which Thoreau so strongly objected. The democratic principles envisioned by most of the architects of the Bill of Rights of the United States Constitution and of the Declaration of Human Rights of the United Nations is that the rule of the majority is the best way known to man of adjudicating the conflicts which inevitably arise in the common pursuit of their human rights by millions of people; it would have been shocking indeed to these people to have envisioned the democratic principle as deciding who is going to be allowed to have human rights.

V

Assuming that at least in some cases civil disobedience is justified, the question of what form it should take immediately arises. Should it always be nonviolent in nature or is the use of violence ever justified? And if violence is ever justified, what limits must be set upon it?

The question of whether violence is ever justified cannot be fairly considered unless persuasive definitions of the term "violence" are avoided. Often "violence" is given a definition such that it becomes self-contradictory to speak of "justified violence," and whatever force is deemed justified is called national defense, self-defense, law enforcement, or punishment. Care must be taken to avoid all such question-begging discussions of violence. In our discussion we understand "violence" to be synonymous with "the use of force on human beings (or their property or institutions) against their wills."

The defense of nonviolence has taken two radically different forms, one a matter of principle, the other prudential in nature. Those who justify nonviolence as a matter of principle usually appeal to the religious and moral belief that love is necessarily good and hence that violence by its very nature is evil; that only love of others brings happiness and the realization of a moral self, while anger and violence debase the character of the agent as well as wounding and killing others.

To Gandhi the concept of passive resistance came to seem inadequate to capture the full scope of nonviolence practiced as a matter of principle. One must not only resist passively the injustice of government but do so without feelings of animosity or hatred. Complete commitment to the love of fellow men is necessary not only as intrinsically right but as providing that "truth force" which is crucial to the success of civil disobedience. The adjective "civil" in the phrase "civil disobedience" meant for Gandhi peaceful, courteous, "civilized" resistance, and it is for this reason that some scholars have insisted that nonviolence is part of the very meaning of "civil disobedience." Admiration for Gandhi's views and campaigns, however, is not a good reason for making these definitive of a network of views only more or less closely related. Such admiration is also not a good reason for overlooking the historically relevant use of the adjective "civil" in speaking of the civil government or the civil magistrate simply to distinguish them from ecclesiastical, military, and other authorities. Thoreau in the earlier title of his famous essay, "Resistance to Civil Government," surely did not wish to imply that the American government was distinctive in its courteousness.

Many arguments have been offered against the view that nonviolence is always right in principle and that acts of civil disobedience therefore must always be wholly peaceful. It should be borne in mind, of course, that arguments which claim to show that violence is not in principle wrong are not arguments to show that violence is always right or that any degree of violence is right and no other. When violence is justified and to what extent, are further questions that need to be answered by further arguments. Indeed, it is possible to believe that violence is not in principle wrong and still believe, on prudential grounds, that violence is never justified.

While the arguments against nonviolence-in-principle are numerous and complex, the general strategies involved are few and clear. Some people reject the pacifistic interpretation of Christianity and certain other world religions, while others reject entirely a religious viewpoint from which any moral position, pacifistic or otherwise, can be deduced. Still others reject the deontological view of moral philosophy which gives rise to the absolute commitment to nonviolence. Others point out that a utilitarian justification of nonviolence is useless, since it would never yield the absolute quality necessary to the pacifist commitment.

It must also be pointed out that unfortunately some of the most eminent proponents of nonviolence-in-principle mix together, unwittingly, incompatible deontological and utilitarian justifications. Such proponents of nonviolence first insist that under no conditions should violence be used to right a wrong. Yet when they are confronted with a hypothetical situation in which the use of violence produces a world which, on balance, has less violence in it than would be the case if nonviolence were used, they switch to a utilitarian justification and argue that, as a matter of empirical fact, the hypothetical situation is purely hypothetical, and the use of violence never produces a world of less violence than that produced with nonviolence. If this empirical claim is challenged, a move, overt or covert, is made back to the deontological justification. However, it must be admitted that a proponent of nonviolence is in an awkward position indeed if the very absoluteness of his commitment to nonviolence leads him to permit unnecessary violence. The most consistent course for the proponents of the deontological justification of nonviolence appears to be to argue that we have a prima facie duty to act nonviolently which can be overridden by our duty to minimize violence and injustice in the world. Once the deontological justification is put in this form, however, it is not clear how it differs in practice from the teleological.

Moreover, there are various crucial roles that anger and other emotions condemned by nonviolence doctrine play in the psychological health of individuals and communities. In the American community at least it seems to be a psychological and sociological impossibility to gather large numbers of citizens who are both highly motivated to resist and without animosity; it is also likely that many Americans hate far more intensely the strange spiritual arrogance of a Gandhi-like figure than they hate the militancy of a leader who straightforwardly demands his minority's share of the American dream and whose motives can be easily understood.

The absolutist view of nonviolence, finally, is based on a mistaken view of man's present nature and future possibilities. The majority of persons simply are not moral in nature and are incapable of responding to the call of conscience sounded by the advocates of nonviolent civil disobedience. Psychiatrists assure us that some people are *incapable* of the moral point of view because the affective tone of their emotional life is so dulled that they are incapable of fellow-feeling. Experience assures us also that many more people simply reject the moral point of view as a piece of outright foolishness; they are selfish as a matter of self-evident principle. Others are selfish unwittingly, never having given any matter of principle a moment's thought. Still others are deceived by their own moralistic rationalizations of their selfish attitudes. Certainly nonviolent civil disobedience is just so much chaff in the wind to all these people—and always will be. If anything will work it will be the use of pressure tactics. To be sure, pressure tactics are also irrelevant to those of seriously dulled emotions, but such tactics do have desirable effects on those who are selfish-on-principle or thoughtlessly selfish if they are reasonably enlightened. Such tactics may not convert these people, of course, but they will increasingly help justice be done as these people become convinced that their own welfare depends on it; and, hopefully, what they are at first pressured to do out of enlightened selfishness they will gradually out of habit come to regard as moral.

The prudential argument against any sort of violent civil disobedience, however minimal, is that nonviolent disobedience is effective in producing good results, while the use of violence courts disastrous results—the white backlash usually being given as an example of the latter. By now, it seems clear, the facts do not wholly or even largely support this position. Nonviolent demonstration produced largely sham progress because the civil rights legislation enacted as a result of it remains for the most part unenforced. And as far as bad results are concerned, *any* sort of dissent, even that covered by the First Amendment, is accompanied by a white backlash.

Those who insist that not even the smallest amount of violence can be justified on prudential grounds are the ones who are really inviting disaster. By damning violence of every degree, by denying the right of fighting back, by damning even the threat of violence, and by refusing to make comparative judgments, the advocates of absolute nonviolence are encouraging oppressed minorities, who have found nonviolent protest to be ineffective, to adopt immediately the most violent techniques instead of gradually and imaginatively escalating their threat of violence until the necessary social changes come about.[8]

To those who recoil at the thought of the use of violence of any kind or degree it should be pointed out that we live every day with an enormous amount of institutionalized and officially sanctioned violence. Official violence is no less real for being veiled in talk about "law and order" and "keeping the world safe for democracy." Even less often recognized is the incalculable psychological violence done to oppressed minorities by the government and the majority. Although normally the justification of the use of violence in self-defense is not questioned, many apparently think that oppressed minorities are not justified in so defending themselves; in this connection it is well to recall how the labor movement began its struggle against the industrial giants.

There is, finally, a nonabsolutistic prudential argument that has much to recommend it. This argument holds that if government forces and/or public prejudices are so strong and oppressive that they would retaliate with death or ruin against any violence, then they should be opposed only nonviolently or by "passive resistance." If the situation changes, however; if the strength of the oppressive government and public prejudice declines, then it may be resisted by as much violence as seems rational at any given moment. There can be little doubt that this was the attitude of the valiant civilians in Norway and Denmark during the Nazi occupation and that it is a wholly defensible viewpoint for one who both wishes to live and fight again and who cherishes the concepts of human rights and democratic procedures.

VI

Recently Abe Fortas has offered a new justification of nonviolent dissent which does not view violence as necessarily wrong in all societies but as *unnecessary* in a free society like that in the United States of America. There is no *need* for disruption and destructive violence, he says, when there are constitutional and rational means of dissent in this society unparalleled in previous history. Universal suffrage allows the majority of people to express their dissent by voting out of office those officials whose policies and commands are objectionable. Moreover, individuals and groups are guaranteed the right to bring pressure to bear on their government by writing, speaking, organizing, picketing, and demonstrating, provided only that laws governing public safety, etc., are obeyed. They may also challenge unjust laws through the courts, claiming that the laws are unconstitutional as well as unjust. And when they sue the state or its officials, they are equals with the state in court and have the protection of elaborate procedural rights. This is possible because the courts are totally independent of the executive and legislative branches of government. This path of legal dissent was the one taken by African Americans in their famous dissent over school segregation in *Brown v. Board of Education*, in which the Court ruled that state-maintained segregation of public schools was unconstitutional.

The nature of civil disobedience endorsed by Fortas is wholly procedural and never violent or wholesale. An unjust law which is judged to be unconstitutional is disobeyed so that a court test can be made. If the decision of the Court bears out the judgment of the dissenter he is justified and exonerated, but if the decision goes against him, he must accept the penalty of disobeying that law with dignity, the mark of his respect for the overall system in which he is operating. Furthermore, it is crucial that in disobeying a law which he judges to be unconstitutional the dissenter not violate laws which are clearly valid as a way of publicizing a protest and exerting pressure on the public.

A good example of this sort of admissible civil disobedience, Fortas thinks, is the work of Martin Luther King Jr., who pledged that African Americans would openly and peacefully disobey "unjust laws"—defined as laws that only a minority are compelled to obey—and that they would accept whatever penalties might result. "This is civil disobedience in a great tradition. It is peaceful, nonviolent disobedience of laws which are themselves unjust and which the protester challenges as invalid and unconstitutional."[9] It is part of the valid framework of dissent and disobedience provided by the Constitution and constitutes a workable alternative to violence. Fortas concludes that "the experience of these past few years shows, more vividly than any other episode in our history, how effective these alternatives are." It has been "through their use—and not through the sporadic incidents of violence—that we have effected the current social revolution."[10]

This view of dissent and disobedience has many merits and is worthy of the deepest respect. One only wishes that it were the whole story, but, alas, it does not seem to be so. There is grave doubt that any social revolution has really taken place, even though a splendid legal one certainly has. Recently it is often not unjust law that is being protested but instead the unjust *absence* of policies of enforcement. Almost 85 percent of school-age African Americans still go to segregated schools in the South in spite of the 1954 Supreme Court ruling. At least that percent must attend de facto segregated and/or inferior schools in the North. Poverty funds have been frequently used for political purposes or, in any case, for something someone else thought would be good for the black population. Title VI of the 1964 Civil Rights Act, which allows federal withdrawal of funds in cases of discrimination, has been ignored in many cases of unequal treatment, such as segregated hospital facilities, and used only sparingly in regard to schools. Under the 1965 Voting Rights Act only a pitifully small number of federal registrars have been sent to the South. And, most crucially of all, because of our computer revolution and the declining need for unskilled and semiskilled workers, the employment situation of African Americans, in spite of feeble efforts to aid them, is worse than it was ten years ago. Instead of a social revolution, one writer sees "little more than federally approved tokenism" and "a continuation of paper promises and ancient inequities."[11] And Martin Luther King in his later work sadly concluded that "there is a tragic gulf between civil rights laws passed and civil rights laws implemented." There is "a double standard in the enforcement of law and a double standard in the respect for particular laws."[12] King still offered universal love and nonviolence as the only answer to the new difficulties but many black persons found the old answer utterly irrelevant given these new revelations. Stokely Carmichael's odyssey from "sit-ins" to militancy is instructive on this point. For better or worse, black militants of all varieties marched in, and civil disobedience using various types and degrees of pressure is now very much part of the scene.

Fortas does not appear to recognize that a major part of the problem lies in the fact that the oppressed are a minority, a minority which even when organized often cannot control enough votes to put out of office those who do not respect their human rights. The problem is aggravated by the fact that the democratic process as it actually exists with its party machines and conventions, our democratic ideals notwithstanding, is something less than perfect. Regrettably, it is also a political fact of life that there is little chance of persuading a majority to respect the rights of a minority without persuading them that it is in their interest to respect those rights. Too many Americans (like people everywhere) allow themselves the luxury of respect for human rights only when such respect does not cost them anything or, preferably, is to their advantage. The chief purpose of the most recent civil disobedience is not so much to change the hearts of the majority, though such a change should be encouraged and sought by every means, but rather to convince the majority that in the long run they would save themselves much difficulty and expense by respecting the rights of the minority.

EIGHTEEN

THE AMERICAN MIND

I t should go without saying that "The American Mind" is not a unified, coherent substance. It is instead a tangled web of beliefs and attitudes, filled with ever-changing tensions and knots seemingly impossible to untie. However, I shall attempt to throw light on some of its salient features. My remarks will be grouped around four topics: class, race, religion, and empire.

Class

Central in American mythology is the notion that we are a classless society or at least a society whose class divisions are much less marked than those in other countries. When confronted with brute facts such as huge income differentials, Americans fall back on the notion that classes in America are exceptionally *porous*; our land is "a land of opportunity" in which any hardworking and talented individual can move from the bottom of the social ladder to the top over the course of a mere twenty years or so. Pollsters tell us that roughly 20 percent of Americans believe that they are already in the top 1 percent in income, and roughly 40 percent believe that they will *soon* be in the top 1 percent. Such is the peculiar form that belief in the porousness of class takes in America. Anyone who challenges this extravagant claim of class porousness is accused of promoting "class warfare," and in the American political lexicon to be a "promoter of class warfare" is to be a "Communist sympathizer," a "pinko." Widely published statistics have shown that the gap between the poorest Americans and the richest has been growing rapidly. Whereas in 1970 the top corporate leaders had incomes forty times the pay of the average worker, now these business executives are paid a thousand times what the average worker is paid. When the accusation of being a communist sympathizer is not sufficient to discourage complaints about the ever-more-shocking inequalities in wealth, Americans appeal to the Social Darwinism that has had a firm grip on the American Mind since the late nineteenth century. The more grossly large the pay of an executive, the more that very grossness demonstrates that that person has exceptional survival skills in the brutal jungle of the business world. An executive with an annual "compensation package" of $50 million is a near perfect biological specimen in a Darwinian universe.

It is difficult to overstate the corrosive effect that this mythology about class has been having on democracy in America. American democracy has always been imperfect and myths about class have been prevalent for centuries, but in the last twenty years this mythology has become so bizarre and so powerful that a sociologist friend of mine insists that America is now better described as a society of "oligarchic liberalism" than as a democracy.

Race

Nothing bedevils the American Mind as much as race. While no American doubts the moral depravity of slavery and few consciously approve the overt discrimination against blacks that has persisted since slavery was outlawed some 150 years ago, racial issues more than ever distort and scramble American thinking about how their society can be improved. Race has become a "weapon of mass destruction" that, when dropped into an American discussion of how, for example, problems of poverty are best addressed, produces massive collateral damage—conceptual confusion, intellectual dishonesty, self-deception, and sheer stupidity. The catch phrase "political correctness" hardly begins to capture the logical fallacies and pathetic hypocrisies that dominate much American discussion of social issues. To ensure that one's argument is not dismissed out of hand one must take elaborate precautions to preclude the possibility that even the most hostile and ingenious interpreter will see your point as "racist." The desperate desire to avoid being seen as supporting racial discrimination or "reverse discrimination" often leads to advocacy of policies that in fact *increase* discrimination. A recent example is the attack on the use of race as one of many factors in deciding who is admitted to a university. Advocates of "race-neutral" admissions policy urge that the top 10 percent of every high school class be automatically admitted to college. Given racial distributions in high schools across the country, this policy would mean that race, in effect, would matter *more* rather than less in university admissions. It is difficult to overstate the degree to which race has "poisoned the well" of public policy discussion. We have reached the sorry state where often whichever side of a debate is more clever and ruthless in "playing the race card" wins the argument. Some of you will remember reading about the appointment to the US Supreme Court a few years ago of Clarence Thomas. When nominated by the president, Thomas was an extremely conservative black lawyer of mediocre intellect with a shabby record as a civil rights administrator. Yet, after lengthy televised hearings, the Senate confirmed him. During his service on the court, Thomas has perhaps done as much as any American to poison further the well of social and legal discussion. In other countries civil rights is a relatively self-contained social problem. In America civil rights issues are entangled in *every* part, *every* layer, of our social fabric. Tragically, in recent decades every well-intentioned effort to disentangle the rights of minorities from other problems has led to still greater entanglement. Although we are justly proud of the achievements of such African Americans as Colin Powell, Condoleezza Rice, Michael Jordan, Tiger Woods, and Serena Williams, the price paid in the quality of public discourse has been horrific. And, I regret to say, multiplying the Colin Powells in America will do little to solve this serious defect in the American Mind.

Racism with regard to African Americans is linked in the American Mind with anti-Semitism. I am not aware of an adequate explanation for this link in historical sociology, but the link seems obvious. Americans, especially American intellectuals and media pundits, quickly learn that their occupational survival demands that they take pains to avoid the slightest appearance of anti-Semitism. The fear of being seen as anti-Semitic has become a social pathology, a pathology that has had catastrophic effects on our Middle East policy. This is, I know, difficult for Europeans to understand, though they have grappled long and hard with anti-Semitism in their own countries. I suggest that one can begin to understand this American pathology only if one first understands that, in obscure but deep ways, it is linked to the place of race in the American social fabric, as I described that place a few minutes ago. Strange as it may seem, what America is doing now in the Middle East is partly caused by what race issues have done over many generations to scramble the American Mind.

Religion

The latest polls show that almost 50 percent of Americans consider themselves evangelical or born-again Christians. Most significantly, President George W. Bush counts himself in that group. Bush, a graduate of two of the most distinguished universities in the United States (Yale and Harvard), does not believe in biological evolution, or, more precisely, he is agnostic on the subject of evolution. Religious fundamentalism in America is, of course, nothing new. However, in the last twenty years this worldview has achieved a dominance of American life, public and private, that is novel. With the election of Bush as president, America reached a "tipping point" in its religious life. But the dominance of religious fundamentalism means something very different in America than it does in other parts of the world. In America from its beginnings to today religious fundamentalism has been characterized by radical pluralism. Nothing do Americans love more than to design a novel form of worship and a modified concept of the deity. Religion in America takes a staggering number of different forms, and the number continues to grow. The American Mind remains vigorously committed to the idea that there are an unlimited number of ways to the One Truth of God. Partly as a consequence of this epistemological pluralism, Americans are not attracted to a theocratic state, as is the case in other countries where religious fundamentalism dominates. Americans are not attracted to a single religious *institution*, as, for example, Russians traditionally have been. Complicating further the role of religion in the American Mind is the Constitutional doctrine of the separation of church and state that Thomas Jefferson did so much to establish in the eighteenth century. This doctrine is still treated as sacred even by US courts dominated by recently appointed right-wing jurists. This means that religious fundamentalism expresses itself, powerfully expresses itself, in American public life in distinctive ways. It expresses itself in the *moral* domain—in vicious debates about abortion, about cloning, about capital punishment, about drugs, even about gun control. There is, I submit, a raging religious impulse behind the fact that a much larger percentage of citizens are in prison in the United States than in other countries.

Since the 9/11 attack on the World Trade Center, America's religious fundamentalism has been vividly expressed in President Bush's use of Biblical language in speaking of the war on terrorism and now the war in Iraq. His call for "moral clarity" is a thinly disguised call for the worldview of his religious fundamentalism. Only an American religious fundamentalist could be so outrageously self-righteous in contrasting America's "goodness" with the "evil" of the rest of the world.

Horrified by this self-righteousness and religious fundamentalism, American intellectuals are now desperately trying to use secular reasoning to change America's thinking. I fear that this won't work. Only competing forms of religious fundamentalism will sway public opinion, as well as the opinions of the president and members of Congress. Distasteful as it may be to them, American intellectuals need to get on their side a few religious fundamentalists who will publicly condemn Bush's policies as morally bankrupt. Even *one* such religious fundamentalist would do more to reduce the administration's frightful self-righteousness than a thousand intellectuals from Harvard, Yale, and Princeton universities. We can change American policy only by drawing on the rich American tradition of radical pluralism in religion.

Empire

For centuries Americans, especially American intellectuals, had a cultural inferiority complex in relation to Europe. Since World War I we have confidently boasted about the preeminence of the US economy, but we were in awe of European literature, art, music, philosophy, and science. That awe has gradually diminished since World War II. Many factors have contributed to this diminishment. One important factor has been the huge public and private investment in American higher education since the last world war. What some call "the knowledge industry" in the United States has come to dwarf the rest of the world. For example, the number of magazines of academic philosophy published in the United States is now larger than the number of such magazines published in the rest of the world combined. In the sciences one needs only to look at the proportion of Nobel Prizes that have gone to researchers working in the United States to appreciate how dominant the United States is in that important area of cultural achievement. In music, jazz and rock have notoriously influenced people even in the most remote regions of the world. And who can measure the global influence of American films and television?

But the tipping point came with the collapse of the Soviet Union and American ascendancy to the status of being "the world's only superpower." Except in some corners of academe, the remains of the American inferiority complex vanished overnight. More exactly, it vanished except in the form of what we call "a chip on the shoulder." Those many generations of feeling inferior left Americans resentful toward European cultural pretensions and eager to humiliate their former "betters." This first became obvious in relation to Russia. American leaders took every opportunity to tell the world that the collapse of the Soviet Union came about not only because of the misguidedness of Marxism but also because Russian culture was utterly bankrupt. By some feat of mad logic American leaders supposed that this exercise in national humiliation would encourage Russia to cooperate with America in world affairs. By a still greater feat of mad logic, American leaders are now trying to promote international cooperation by humiliating "old European" countries such as France and Germany. Those in the White House openly declare their intention to establish a new sort of world empire by spreading "democracy" (in scare quotes) around the world. In their religious zeal they believe that if they preemptively use their vast military and economic power to establish a democracy in a country such as Iraq, that national democracy will, by a miraculous domino effect, cause nondemocratic regimes throughout that region and even the world to collapse and be replaced by democratic societies. This is a breathtaking vision of world history comparable in its fantasy to the fantasy of Soviet Marxism.

A Hopeful Note

I recognize that I have presented an exceedingly grim picture of the American Mind. Let me end these remarks on a somewhat hopeful note. America still has extraordinary strengths. Not only does it have the most powerful economy and military the world has ever known, it also has the rich tradition of radical religious pluralism that I have described. As well it has the most formidable knowledge industry ever seen. Even more important, it has a robust and stubborn tradition of freedom of information and speech despite Attorney General Ashcroft's attempts to undermine that tradition. And not to be underestimated is the crucial role that women now play in the American economy and public life. I harbor some hope that we Americans will find ways to draw on those remaining strengths in the American Mind so as to save America from itself and to save the rest of the world from America's newfangled imperialism. However, I am cynical enough to believe that this will happen only if Europe invests in enough military strength to counterbalance America's military power. Distasteful as it is for me to sound like Henry Kissinger, I have regretfully come to the conclusion that at this stage of the development of world civilization there is still no viable substitute for old-fashioned "balance of power." Balance of economic power is necessary but not sufficient. Balance of military power is needed as well.

NINETEEN

THE DEATH PENALTY DEBATE: A HUMANIST'S UNDERSTANDING OF AMERICA'S SOCIAL PROBLEMS

Although I am optimistic about the social benefits of scientific humanism, the story I tell below illustrates how little influence science has on public policy in America. This story also illustrates how entangled in a web American social problems are. Russia, too, I wish to suggest, has such a web, though not, to be sure, the same web as we have in the United States. I invite the reader to think about Russia's web after reading the narrative that follows.

The death penalty is inextricably tied up with a huge number of firmly established aspects of American society. This entanglement means that it is doubtful that in the foreseeable future any protest movement will succeed in removing it from all the states. This is indeed a repugnant state of affairs, but I fear that the number of executions in the United States is more likely to increase than to decrease in the near term. I hope that the remarks I am about to make will make it clear why that is the sad truth.

First, let me give some history. In the seventeenth and eighteenth centuries, many, many types of crimes were capital crimes, crimes for which the penalty was death. But, contrary to today's popular belief, there were not a lot of executions in the early history of the United States. We like to congratulate ourselves on how much more civilized we are now in matters of capital punishment than we were three or four centuries ago, but perhaps the reverse is the case. In those early centuries of our history pardons in great quantity were given in capital cases. True, when there was an execution, it was usually a public hanging attended by a large proportion of a town's population. But many people reached a considerable age before there was a hanging in their community that they could attend.

From the beginning, great discomfort was felt by the general public about the pain inflicted in the process of putting someone to death. Strenuous efforts were made to make the manner of hanging as painless as possible. For example, horror was generally felt when the spinal cord was not severed and the condemned died by slow asphyxiation. Such horror in no way implied an objection to the death penalty. I cannot stress too strongly the importance of this strange psychological fact—as much a fact today as it was in the seventeenth and eighteenth centuries. At one and the same time, a person can feel intense revulsion from the pain experienced in the process of execution and fervent belief in the justification and necessity of the execution. This psychological paradox has meant that passionate advocates for abolishment of the death penalty have usually seen their superbly organized efforts lead only to change in the *means* of execution—from hanging to electrocution, from electrocution to the gas chamber, and from the gas chamber to lethal injection. And once a less painful means of execution has been adopted, advocates of the death penalty are more comfortable with an *increase* in the number of persons executed. "The road to Hell is paved with good intentions." In their valiant efforts the abolitionists have only made things worse! Also, in this sense, it can be said that the technological advances represented by the electric chair, the gas chamber, and the lethal injection aggravated an already terrible problem since they all decreased the repugnance felt.

Legal advances brought about by well-intentioned lawyers have sometimes been as self-defeating as technological advances. The insanity defense is an example. Though there had always been some form of the insanity defense—a defense in which, if it is successful, the accused is judged innocent by reason of not knowing right from wrong—gifted and aggressive lawyers with the help of expert testimony from psychiatrists made the insanity defense into a powerful weapon for the defense. But soon states, fearing that juries facing mandatory death penalty for first-degree murder would not convict someone who was clearly guilty, abandoned the death penalty in favor of life in prison. But this change represented anything but a belief that the death penalty was morally unjustified. And in recent decades the insanity defense has become almost totally discredited in the public mind. The public is convinced (with considerable justification) that highly paid psychiatrists can be found willing to support almost *any* claim about an accused person's mental health. For example, some years ago in a widely publicized case of a woman who obviously was seriously mentally ill in postpartum depression when she drowned her children in the bathtub, the insanity defense was not given serious consideration.

Still, in the late eighteenth and nineteenth centuries there were *some* forces that tended to discourage the death penalty. For one, prisons came into widespread use and provided a viable punishment alternative. And religion's role in public life declined. Perhaps most important, the rise of social sciences led to belief in determinism and more and more serious doubts about criminality being *voluntary*. Most famously, in 1924 Clarence Darrow argued that causal determinism undermined all justification for the death penalty. The boys Loeb and Leopold, he insisted, could not have done otherwise than murder, given everything that had happened previously in their lives and in the social and biological environment in which they lived. It was not long, however, before the determinism argument, like so many other valiant abolitionist efforts, began to backfire. Prosecuting attorneys found it easy to persuade the public and the legislatures that acceptance of belief that human acts are determined undermined *every* claim of guilt, *every* justification of punishment, not only capital punishment. The public and its elected representatives found such massive exoneration of wrongdoing unacceptable. In vain did legal scholars and attorneys try to explain that human acts could be caused in very different ways, and some of those ways excused behavior and some did not. Advocates of the death penalty argued that *any* appeal to determinism to excuse criminal behavior would put society on a slippery slope at the bottom of which *every* sort of criminal would be exonerated by appeal to social and biological determinism.

Perhaps the most devastating self-defeat by legal abolitionists was *Furman v. Georgia*, the 1972 decision by the US Supreme Court. In the late

1960s, at the highpoint of the civil rights movement, there was a huge backlog of condemned people on death row—620 of them—and there were an impressive number of challenges to the constitutionality of the death penalty by brilliant, well-financed lawyers. There was even an abolitionist on the Supreme Court, Associate Justice Arthur Goldberg, one of whose clerks was the now-celebrated defense attorney Alan Dershowitz. This impressive group of lawyers fashioned a powerful argument that the various death penalty laws on the books in the various states were unconstitutional. The nine justices of the court produced more pages of reports (233 pages) in this case than in any case in the entire history of the court. Each justice had his own distinctive way of thinking about this constitutionality issue. A majority of the court decided that the law was unconstitutional on various grounds, including the grounds that the law was applied randomly and was not in accord with the so-called "standards of decency" in the American public and thus that the penalty was "cruel and unusual punishment." What happened, in short, was that a majority of the court ruled that the past *administration* of the death penalty was unconstitutional. Only a small minority of the court took the view that the death penalty itself was unconstitutional *regardless* of how it is administered. So, immediately death penalty advocates set to work to change state laws so that their death penalty statutes met the standards required by the Supreme Court. This often led to laws more draconian than any of the books before 1972. In an effort to avoid the randomness the court had objected to, these laws *required* the death penalty under certain conditions. By 1976 no fewer than thirty-five states had new death penalty laws, and there were more death sentences than ever. And public opinion *in favor* of the death penalty was much stronger than it had been in 1972. Before *Furman v. Georgia*, supporters outnumbered opponents 50 to 42 percent. By 1976, supporters outnumbered opponents by 65 to 28 percent. Lawyers who had battled to get the Supreme Court to abolish the death penalty had created a monster!

In this period, in the mid-1970s, the society-wide backlash against the radical late 1960s and early 1970s (the civil rights era and the Vietnam War protest) was in full swing. Such figures as Robert Bork, a brilliant conservative Yale law professor who had been appointed solicitor general of the United States, became media celebrities. Bork seized on death penalty abolitionism as a symptom of the nation's moral decay. Though no longer solicitor general, Bork continues to fulminate to this day. In the 1990s he published an enormously successful book which argued in the strongest terms that almost every shred of morality had departed from American society. By the 1980s, it was clear that it was political suicide to support abolition of the death penalty. In 1988, for example, Michael Dukakis lost any chance of becoming president by expressing his opposition to the death penalty. Mario Cuomo, governor of New York State, was the only political office holder of major significance who managed to remain in office while opposing the death penalty. And Cuomo is widely regarded as one of the most shrewd and brilliant politicians of the second half of the twentieth century. For the first time in US history, the death penalty became bound up with a comprehensive moralistic ideology. The death penalty became inseparable from a moralistic-religious crusade to save the country from the devil and his many secular associates. There were no more constitutional challenges to the death penalty because it had become obvious that any challenge to the death penalty was understood by most of the public to be a challenge to all traditional American values.

While teaching ethics to undergraduates in the 1970s and 1980s, I was often shocked by how hardened opinion on this subject had become. I naively supposed that, if it could be empirically demonstrated in numerous sophisticated scientific studies that the death penalty did not deter people from committing murder, people would abandon their support for capital punishment. I was wrong. Many of my students, like the American public in general, read about the elaborate statistical studies of the alleged deterrent effect of the death penalty and dismissed the results as irrelevant. The brightest of these stubborn people argued that these studies did not constitute a case against the death penalty because it was likely that if the death penalty were given more quickly and more frequently, it *would* have a deterrent effect. The most fundamental obstacle in the way of people taking seriously the empirical studies showing that the death penalty had no deterrent effect was similar to the problem with the appeal to determinism and the problem with the insanity defense that I have already discussed. People looked at elaborate graphs and equations produced by statisticians on both side of the controversy and concluded that statisticians can prove anything they want. The statisticians argued fiercely about which variables were relevant, and few members of the public, few people in the media for that matter, had the faintest idea of what a dependent or independent variable is. The statisticians might as well as have been speaking in the language of some remote tribe in the Amazon jungle. It is a sad fact, I believe, that it is now pointless to refer to scientific evidence in an effort to show that the death penalty has no deterrent effect. The overwhelming majority of the American public—and such intellectuals as Robert Bork—simply consider it *common sense* that the death penalty deters.

The increase in violent crime in the 1970s and 1980s also played an important role in how the death penalty has been perceived. Statistics clearly show that support for the death penalty is strongest in those parts of the United States where the incidence of violent crime is the highest. Much has been written about the various causes of this increase in violent crime. For example, sometimes it is obvious from any perusal of the statistical analysis that a major cause is simple demographics—there is a higher percent of males between the ages of eighteen and twenty-five in the population of a particular geographical location at a particular time. Such statistics are so much chaff in the wind to the American public and their political representatives whose *common sense* tells them the higher incidence of violent crime is the result of inadequate punishment.

There has also come to be a powerful psychological and political bond between the death penalty issue and the gun control issue. In vain do statisticians show that the availability of firearms leads to an increase in homicide. *My* common sense tells me that, although Americans today have no more or less hostile feelings toward others than they did one or two or three hundred years ago, *when* they have such feelings today and act on them, they do much more damage because the weapons available to them are much more lethal. Indeed, by an absurdly twisted logic the American public and government concludes that we need *more* availability of firearms so that citizens can protect themselves against the violent criminals we would not have if the death penalty were much more frequently and quickly used. In short, there is a ghastly synergy between the gun control and the death penalty issues. It seems impossible to pry the two issues apart.

There is also a horrible synergy between issues concerning the US prison system and the death penalty issue. As everyone knows, a much higher percent of the American population is in prison than in any European country. It is also widely conceded that the prisons in the United States do very little to reform inmates. Indeed, even the most statistically obtuse recognize that prisons do a superb job of training inmates to become more effective criminals when they are released. Advocates of the death penalty suggest that the best way to reduce the problems with our prisons is to execute the incorrigible criminals. They also say that we could save much tax money if we executed those criminals instead of keeping them in jail for long periods. They are unpersuaded by the fact that the lengthy legal process needed to put someone to death is much more expensive than keeping him or her in prison for life. As far as they are concerned, we would be better off without due process of law in these circumstances.

The death penalty issue is inseparable from still another issue—drug laws. In the last decade numerous studies have demonstrated that our draconian drug laws have been utterly ineffective in reducing the number of people using drugs. However, the drug laws which mandate imprisonment without giving discretion to judges and juries are largely responsible for creating the huge increase in prison population, an increase which, as I have said, is taken as a reason to increase the use of the death penalty. Even the moderately conservative British newsmagazine *The Economist* has long supported the legalization of most drugs that are currently illegal. Again the statisticians in vain show that these draconian drug laws greatly increase the incidence of violent crime. The absurdities of these drug laws are too numerous for me even to list, much less describe. But I want to mention an absurdity I read not long ago. Anyone who is released after a prison term for a felony is ineligible for student loans from the government. Given the laws according to which doing almost anything with illegal drugs is a felony, most of these people released from prison who cannot get educational help are former drug offenders, victims of our wildly counterproductive drug laws. This means that the government in its self-defeating moralistic crusade against drugs is going out of its way to avoid helping former drug offenders to rehabilitate themselves by getting the education necessary to get a good job and become productive members of our society. In short, the political support for the death penalty is firmly linked to the support for the drug laws. The public and its political representatives passionately believe that the death penalty requires the draconian drug laws and the draconian drug laws require the death penalty. We must, they insist, have both—as well as the availability of firearms—if our society is not to be overrun by "evildoers," to use a favorite word of our current president [George W. Bush—ed.].

In the last ten to fifteen years another development in our legal system has helped to make the death penalty more entrenched than it has ever been in our history. This is the movement for "victim's rights." As you know, in the United States an appeal to a new *right* is the most effective way to bring about social and political change. With justification we take pride in the role of individual rights in the founding and development of American democracy. However, like every other good thing in this world, the notion of right can be abused. The notion of right has come to have an extraordinary mystique in the United States, a mystique so powerful that it tends to silence all rational debate. In any and all disputes—whether moral or political—each disputant wants to use the notion of right as a weapon to vanquish his or her opponent. So, too, in our legal system. In the case of convictions for murder this means that when there is a sentencing hearing, after the guilt of the accused has been established in the earlier phase of the trial, family members of the victim are invited to speak, as are family members of the convicted. Often family members of the victim passionately demand the death penalty, insisting that their intense suffering will cease only when they have the satisfaction of having the death penalty administered. In excruciatingly emotional pleas they tell the jury and judge that they have a victim's *right* to such release from their suffering. In these circumstances it becomes almost impossible for members of the jury to think rationally about degrees of culpability and about how less culpability would call for punishment less extreme than death. They are put in a position in which it seems that to administer anything less than the death penalty is to violate someone's rights and to force their suffering to continue.

Not only has the death penalty become more entrenched in American society than ever, it has also become more arbitrarily administered than ever, despite the Supreme Court's efforts to remove the arbitrariness in its 1972 decision. To be sure, some of the racial bias has been removed. But still, in some parts of the country, the death penalty is more likely when the victim is white than when he or she is black. But the court is reluctant to attempt to remove the remaining racial bias because the application of the death penalty can be challenged on the grounds of so many additional forms of bias—gender, socio-economic status, national origin, religion, etc. The historically precious American demand for equal treatment can be abused just as the demand for the respect for rights can. The courts see no practical way to remove all those biases, so they permit the arbitrariness to take whatever form it will. Nowadays whether someone is charged with a capital crime is often a matter of whether the prosecutor is up for reelection, whether the budget will permit the enormous expense of a trial, whether any number of factors which are in no legitimate way related to degree of culpability or the moral justification for punishment.

Despite the vehement criticism of America's use of the death penalty from the international community, I doubt that it will be abandoned in the United States in the next twenty-five years. As I have tried to explain, the death penalty over the last thirty years has become virtually inseparable from various other major features of the American legal, moral, and religious landscape so that *all* or *almost all* of these features would have to change if the death penalty is to be abandoned. Strange as it may seem to those in other parts of the world, the statement that an American citizen makes on the death penalty issue has become *the* self-defining statement in the social and political sphere. A person who declares him- or herself opposed to the death penalty is understood by the majority of the US population and its political representatives to declare him or herself "soft on crime." Those who are "soft on crime" have committed a heresy comparable to those in the seventeenth century who were thought to have sided with the devil.

TWENTY

VALUES OF THE AMERICAN
INTELLECTUAL CLASS

The literature on "American exceptionalism" is vast. From colonial times to the present, arguments have been made in favor of the proposition that Americans are unique in their ideals and/or their practices. Most famously, in the 1600s John Winthrop urged that the Puritan community of New England serve as a model for the rest of the world. Many believe that President George W. Bush echoes Winthrop when the he speaks of promotion of American-style "freedom" throughout the world. Critics of the Bush administration argue that American exceptionalism is usually nothing more than propaganda. Such critics sometimes favor an *inverse* or *negative* form of exceptionalism, namely a view, which holds that in some respects, we are uniquely *not* to be emulated by the peoples of the world.

Although I applaud discussion of the relation between American and European values, I am ashamed of how little honest attention we intellectuals have given to our own values. We pen scathing attacks on the values of our society's political, economic, and military leaders. We bitterly complain that our critiques are ignored by those in power. We yearn to possess the power of those we eloquently criticize. Too often we take ourselves to be speaking from the moral high ground. Humility is one of the virtues in short supply among American intellectuals. To be sure, we do not have the same luxury of the "arrogance of power" that our national leaders have in addressing the international community. But our brand of powerlessness does not necessarily render us less arrogant. We have as much confidence in our own moral and intellectual superiority as the Bush administration has in its political, economic, and military superiority.

Some may protest that the self-aggrandizing, imperialistic, and messianic ambitions of the powerful are so abhorrent that the sins of the academy, trivial sins in comparison, do not deserve our attention. To me, that argument is analogous to an argument offered by a police commissioner that there is no pressing need to investigate corruption in the narcotics division because the division's mission is to hunt down drug lords.

I acknowledge that scathing attacks on American intellectuals have been published by such authors as David Horowitz. In *The Politics of Bad Faith: The Radical Assault on America's Future*, Horowitz argues that those who call themselves "liberal" or "progressive" have "ideological agendas" that are "radical and totalitarian." He explains "what it means to be conservative in America, to be 'Right' in a context in which conserving the constitutional foundations means defending a fundamentally liberal framework." "The tradition of the Left," he says, "is intellectually dominant in the American university today in a way that its disciples would never have dreamed possible thirty years ago, as though the human catastrophe produced by its ideas had never taken place."[1] I suggest, however, that the politics Horowitz abhors in the American academy is superficial. Pundits often give lip service—albeit loud lip service—to socialist values, but seldom more than lip service. I personally know scores of academics whom Horowitz would roundly condemn as socialist in their teaching and writing whose everyday conduct is rarely governed by socialist principles of any sort. Call it hypocrisy, call it self-deception, call it dishonesty, call it *akrasia*, call it all of the above, call it what you will; there is a distressing gap between the verbal pronouncements of the professoriate and our everyday behavior.

Not long ago I served for three years as a member of the National Board of Officers of the American Philosophical Association. From firsthand experience I can report that some of the most famous philosophers in

America are also some of the most hypocritical in their politics. They are horrified by any proposal that the APA become politically active.

Let me be careful to be bipartisan. Leftist intellectuals do not have a monopoly on such hypocrisy. There is every reason to believe that hypocrisy is also common among members of the Right. "Bad faith" is as prevalent among Horowitz's friends as among his enemies.

Writing from the Left, Richard Rorty has done a better job than Horowitz of exposing the genuine values of American intellectuals. He does a better job, not because he is on the Left, but because he sees beneath the polarized rhetoric of his colleagues to their everyday conduct. Although I have sometimes been critical of Rorty's views in epistemology and metaphysics, I find myself in agreement with most of the views expressed in his short books, *Achieving Our Country: Leftist Thought in Twentieth-Century America*[2] and *Philosophy and Social Hope*.[3] In those works he faults what he calls the "cultural Left" for its lack of both "social hope" and concrete political action. He calls for the sort of Leftist patriotism earlier espoused by such people as Lionel Trilling, Sidney Hook, and Irving Howe. This is a patriotism that, while recognizing our failings, believes in the American potential for social justice. Without this patriotism of social hope, he says, criticism of American society by the cultural Left loses most of its point. Not surprisingly, when Rorty first published his plea for patriotism in an op-ed piece, many members of the academy were disturbed. Martha Nussbaum, for example, argued that patriotism should be rejected in favor of "cosmopolitanism."[4] Others suppose that this was Rorty's obfuscating way of selling out to the Right. But I believe that Rorty is clearheaded and on target in making a case for a revival of "the reformist Left" and its attendant form of patriotism. To be willing to work hard for social reform, one must be convinced that one's society is genuinely reformable. The more the cultural Left paints a bleak picture of America's possibilities, the less motivated American citizens, including members of the academy, are motivated to carry through the grinding tasks of political change.

Self-absorption is what Rorty believes accounts for American intellectuals of the Left not actively engaging in political reform. Although that explanation is accurate as far as it goes, much more needs to be said about the social context and values that underlie this self-obsession.

Over the course of the twentieth century the number of intellectuals in America grew enormously. Early in the century, for example, the president of the Eastern Division of the American Philosophical Association knew personally almost every person teaching philosophy at a college or university in the United States. Now more than ten thousand people are employed as teachers of philosophy in American institutions of higher education, and even the most gregarious officer of the APA cannot be expected to be acquainted with more than a tiny fraction of that number. One need not be a sociologist of higher education to be aware that the American academy now has many *millions* of members. For reasons of sheer scale, the academy has become a world unto itself, or largely so. Intellectuals have become something like a set of interconnected disciplinary castes that together form a huge caste or what may be called "the American intellectual class." As this intellectual class has grown in size and psychological independence from the society as a whole, it has gradually developed a system of rewards independent of the reward systems prevalent outside its world. I can most easily illustrate this point by reference to the discipline of philosophy.

Some years ago Brian Leiter, then a philosopher at the University of Texas, established what he calls the *Gourmet Report* on doctoral programs in the United States. [Leiter now teaches at the University of Chicago and his *Gourmet Report* still exists—ed.] Leiter said that he intended the report to be helpful to students deciding what doctoral programs to apply to and to enroll in if accepted. He further explained that the report's ranking of graduate programs would be useful because there would be a strong correlation between the rank of the department and the level of success its graduates would have in obtaining teaching positions. He concluded that a PhD from a program not ranked in the top fifty is of so little value on the job market that students who cannot win admission to a department in that elite group are well advised to choose a profession other than philosophy. Not surprisingly, these pronouncements by Leiter angered many members of, or graduates of, programs ranked lower than fifty by his report. But many members of highly ranked departments also protested publicly. There has since been much debate about both the overall aims and the methods of the report and about rankings of particular departments.

From the beginning of these discussions it has been recognized by everyone that there is nothing new about the publication of rankings of American academic departments. Since early in the twentieth century, rankings have proliferated. What is original about Leiter's report—apart from its electronic-only form—is its (exquisite) attention to minute differences and changes in prestige. Through an elaborate network of informants, Leiter painstakingly tracks the activities of individual philosophers. When a philosopher moves from one department to another, that move can have an impact on the rankings of both departments. If a prestigious philosopher is believed by the members of Leiter's advisory panel to be—for one reason or another—no longer likely to be a productive scholar, that belief will immediately and negatively affect the ranking of his or her department.

This obsession within academe is in many respects like the obsession with pedigree characteristic of the American patrician class. Members of America's social elite are exquisitely sensitive to minute differences in "family background." Like members of social elites in other countries for millennia, aristocratic parents in the United States carefully measure the social rank of any prospective spouse for one of their children. Each family uses its own informal *Gourmet* network of informants in an unending effort to move itself higher in the rankings by marriage, business ventures, and any other means available. This obsession over rank flourishes despite widespread belief that in America class status matters much less, if at all, than in other parts of the world. The American obsession with social prestige differs from that found in other parts of the world perhaps most in the level of hypocrisy involved. A society that has persuaded itself that it is fundamentally classless, meritocratic, and egalitarian is far more covert in its fixation on pedigree than other countries where it is deemed acceptable to overtly recognize social class by bestowing titles and the like.

Despite the widespread belief in academe today that the social structure of the intellectual world is largely meritocratic, there is ample sociological evidence to the contrary in such books as Lionel Lewis's *Scaling the Ivory Tower: Merit & Its Limits in Academic Careers.* "Students from elite schools," Lewis reports, "had a 16 percent chance of finding employment at another elite school, while there was only a 2 percent chance of this happening for those whose graduate training was in a school outside the top decile." Where one takes one's doctorate is only one of a formidable set of "ascriptive qualities" and all these qualities have "additive, cumulative, and lasting effects" on a person's career.[5] The pedigree phenomenon is even more powerful in academe than Lewis discusses. The pedigree factor encompasses undergraduate degree, what presses have published your books, what journals have published your articles, the pedigrees of those who write your letters of support, the pedigrees of those who write blurbs for your books, whether the subjects of your research are the current subjects of research of scholars who have the "best" pedigrees, whether institutions at which you have taught are institutions at which people with the best pedigrees teach, whether you have won high-pedigree fellowships, and so on. No one of these is a make-or-break factor in determining a person's status in the pecking order of the American intellectual world, but collectively and cumulatively their grip is powerful indeed. Though meritocracy is by no means extinct in academe, it has become an endangered species.

Am I asking that we intellectuals become superhuman, that we meet a standard of behavior that only a utopian would think feasible? I don't believe so. I am not asking that we cease to be competitive. I am asking that we cease to be such frantic status seekers that we give little attention to intrinsic merit and focus instead on what we like to believe are proxies for merit, namely, pedigrees. Our reputed proxies have become the currency used in the myriad transactions that determine where a person is ranked. To change the metaphor, in the gargantuan social machinery of intellectual caste, pedigrees are believed to be an efficient way to maintain the dauntingly complex status hierarchy. But should we not ask what can be the value of this efficiency if the machine thus maintained is moving in a direction of dubious or at least unexamined merit? If one has served on as many university review boards as I have, one cannot doubt that it is much less time-consuming and stressful to rely on pedigree than it is to read some of a candidate's publications with care. The temptation to employ proxies uncritically is great.

Many causes can be cited for the lack of concrete political action that Rorty deplores. Some of these are so mundane as to be easily overlooked. From my own modest forays in local politics I can report that one reason academics shun political action is that it involves participation in numerous and interminable meetings—meetings of special commissions, meetings of governing bodies, meetings of review boards, not to mention meetings of a host of interest groups that may or may not form alliances. Much of this is so tedious as to require extraordinary patience of its constructive participants. One of my most patient and energetic friends, now retired from her compensated professional work, spends more than eighty hours a week as a local political activist. Her colleagues look on her as almost a freak of nature.

British academics I have spoken to tell me that in the United Kingdom there is a continuing tradition of participation in local politics. They are puzzled and disapproving of the relative lack of participation in the United States. What accounts for the difference? Do Brits have a greater tolerance for tedium? Perhaps. Is it that American academics are lazier? That I very much doubt. In my experience, American academics are workaholics. But the formidable energies of Americans are directed differently. They are more single-mindedly directed toward gaining higher status in their caste.

I am embarrassed to note that philosophers who specialize in pragmatism, as I do, are as reluctant to engage in concrete political reform as any other species of intellectual. Thought, according to pragmatism, can only be understood in relation to action, but we professional pragmatists wish to confine ourselves to thought—leaving action to other people.

Significantly, the quest for higher status in academe has changed radically if gradually over the last several decades. Sociologists of higher education have gathered data showing that the bar for tenure and promotion has steadily risen in terms of number of publications. This accords with my personal experience on review boards. The quantity of publication sufficient to gain full professorial rank at a research university in the 1960s today is insufficient to earn associate rank at an institution of much lower standing. This lifting of the publication bar is closely related to the frenetic status seeking I spoke of earlier in discussing Leiter's *Gourmet Report*. Academic departments and universities to which they belong are striving with every means at their disposal to achieve higher positions in the rankings. Every "cow college," as we say, is anxious to look as much like an elite university as possible. Every elite university dreads a drop in rank. Pity the university president whose institution suffers a plunge in rank. What could be a more natural proxy for quantity of intellectual substance than quantity of published pages? As with the proxy of pedigree, the proxy of quantity of publication becomes more and more remote from what it is supposed to be a proxy for—intellectual achievement. Gradually, what was originally a tool to be used to help measure and maximize intellectual achievement becomes an end itself, and we manage to persuade ourselves that there is a strong correlation between proxy and real achievement. Ditto for citation indices. We find it efficient to believe that if article A has been cited one hundred times more than article B, article A must be much more the intellectually significant of the two. Academic celebrity is an extreme case of this phenomenon. Harold Bloom's pronouncements, for example, are taken to have enormously inflated value—which they would lack if made by a teacher of literature at an obscure college.

You have read a great deal about the use of steroids by athletes. In America baseball players have recently received the most attention in this connection. Commentators have noted that the American public has an insatiable appetite for home runs—single-handed scoring not otherwise possible. Nothing confers more celebrity on a player than the ability to hit home runs, and nothing draws more paying fans than a home run champion. No one should be surprised that Barry Bonds and others use steroids. Analogously, no one should be surprised that academics have become, albeit metaphorically, heavy users of steroids. We "bulk up" our intellectual muscles with few worries about what harm is being done to fundamental intellectual values.

William James famously spoke of "the bitch-goddess success." Academics have little understanding of how thoroughly that goddess has insinuated herself in almost every aspect of intellectual life—little understanding because we indulge in the self-deception that success in our domain is largely meritocratic. Our manic quest for notoriety leaves us little time and energy for the political work that Rorty rightly calls for. There are only twenty-four hours in a day, and if we are obsessively struggling to hitch ourselves higher in the *Gourmet* or other ranking system, little time and energy remains for concrete action that might make more social justice possible. Few doubt that the ever-widening gap between the hyperrich and the poor is a scandal and a serious threat to our democracy, but there are not enough hours left in the week for us to do more than occasionally talk and write about the problem.

To be sure, teaching goes on in the academy, and teaching can be a socially constructive activity. However, the amount of teaching done by the professoriate tends to be inversely related to prestige ranking. Also, often intellectuals fancy that they are playing the role of Socrates in relation to the state. We need to be reminded that America today is not Athens in the fifth century BC. The Bush administration can ignore our pronouncements with impunity, as the rulers of Athens could not ignore the teaching of Socrates.

The most highly educated members of our society would like to find ways to make a political difference that entail modest expenditures of time and energy. Conveniently, we conclude that publication is the appropriate way for citizens of our training and special skills to make political contributions. No elaborate sociological study is needed to show that it is rare for a publication by an academic to make a political difference unless the author is tightly connected to persons who hold major political offices. Op-ed pieces and letters to the editor do much to make their authors feel good about themselves but seldom more than that. "There is no free lunch" in this domain, as in so many others. Solid political effectiveness requires tedious, grinding work. Intellectual brilliance rarely provides an exemption from such demands. That said, it must be acknowledged that the fault also lies in social structures of higher education, which took time to develop and will, with the best intentions and efforts of individuals, take time to change. It must also be recognized that the academic caste of which I am a member is significantly constrained and shaped by the mores of the society as a whole. The academy has absorbed many of the hypocritical and self-serving ways of its national context—and the manic US lifestyle.

In his recent book, *American Mania: When More is Not Enough*, UCLA neuropsychiatrist Peter Whybrow provides an account of the sources of our lifestyle. He cites numerous historical, philosophical, cultural, and neurobiological causes. He shows, for example, how the thought of such Enlightenment thinkers as Adam Smith dovetailed with seemingly unrelated factors. He explains how recent conditions have led to a deepening of our addictions. This is not the place to attempt a summary of Whybrow's contribution to the literature of inverse exceptionalism. Suffice it to mention that one of his most intriguing suggestions is that our mania (first noted by Tocqueville) is partly traceable to the fact that we are a nation of immigrants. What he has in mind is a trait more generic than the desire for ever-greater material wealth. "We are," he says, "the quintessential immigrant nation. Americans, at the bone, are a self-selected group of hard-working opportunists with an insatiable hunger for self-improvement," and our lifestyle becomes ever more manic.[6]

Extending this idea, I suggest that among intellectuals, this mania takes the form of an insatiable desire for a higher position in our caste's intricate hierarchy. Our publications can never attract enough attention to make us feel like winners for more a few days.

I am not merely echoing the claim that colleges and universities are increasingly beholden to the interests of corporations and the government from which so much of their funding comes directly or indirectly. That claim is widely expressed and accepted. I am claiming that something more insidious and distressing has happened. This academy has embraced non-intellectual notions of self-improvement more profoundly than that claim would suggest. The lust for caste status I have described is at most indirectly related to the pursuit of wealth and political power. In our desire for caste prestige we have embraced phony proxies for intellectual values. To a distressing extent we have directed our efforts away from *both* intellectual values and social justice. To blame this misdirection on unfettered capitalism and laissez-faire economics is too simple. Ironically, our sense of ourselves as an intellectual class oppressed by the powers of business and the market has deflected us from genuinely intellectual values. At great cost in time and effort we have created and maintained our own elaborate nonintellectual pecking order to challenge the hierarchy imposed by the economic and political forces of our society. Feeling beaten down by the powerful tradition of anti-intellectualism in American society at large, we intellectuals in desperation have established our alternative class system.

Are there *some* American intellectuals whose everyday actions exhibit dominant values of intellectual excellence and social justice? Of course. I am speaking of *norms* present among intellectuals. Individuals can be found who depart from those norms in varying degrees. Noam Chomsky is an example. Though conservative pundits may think that Chomsky is in the grip of a need to be politically correct, this is a narrowly dismissive estimate of his motives. Anyone who has listened to interviews of him or read his writings with an open mind recognizes that his commitment to intellectual values and social justice is incorporated in his everyday actions. Although it is easy to find passages in his writings in which he seems to lack the patriotic social hope that Rorty believes so valuable, when Chomsky interacts with audiences it is obvious that he believes that grassroots organizing can bring about major reforms in domestic and foreign policy. Day in and day out, he does his best to inspire such organizing. Chomsky is as much a hopeful patriot as Rorty is—or as I would like to be.

Important departures from the norm are not only found on the Left. The recently deceased George F. Kennan was in some respects an even more impressive departure. Kennan, for many years a foreign service officer, was head of the State Department's first Policy Planning Staff in 1947–50 and ambassador to the Soviet Union in 1952. He joined the Institute for Advanced Study in 1953. While he served in the political trenches, the reports he submitted to the highest government officials were some of the most intellectually sophisticated, empirically informed, and well-written documents of the twentieth century. Widely known by political leaders around the world, even those who rejected many of Kennan's conclusions recognized in him an intellect of the highest order and a grasp of world affairs the equal of any of his contemporaries. Although his recommendations were seldom followed, and it is difficult to measure the indirect effects of his work, a strong case can be made for the claim that his subtle and penetrating analyses had greater impact on the course of world history during the Cold War than the work of anyone else who can plausibly be considered an American intellectual.

Except for a brief note about the British, I have made no attempt to compare the values of the US academy with those of European intellectuals. Since I do not know enough about the European intellectual community to do that with any confidence, I leave that to others. My aim has been to raise questions about the academy in my own country in the conviction that, while we have mercilessly analyzed fellow citizens outside our group, we have seldom raised an unflattering mirror to our own faces.

Notes

INTRODUCTION: PRESENT AT THE END?
WHO WILL BE THERE WHEN THE LAST STONE IS THROWN?
Vincent Colapietro

1. While objectivity is dear, so are friends. Thus, I will throughout this essay refer to Peter H. Hare by his first name as I addressed him in life, dropping the barbarity of referring to him, out of misplaced professionalism, by simply his last name.

2. Near the conclusion to his presidential address to the Society for the Advancement of American Philosophy, presented on March 3, 1990, and subsequently published in *Pragmatic Naturalism and Realism*, he floated the idea that we might have a *duty* to believe. While underscoring the dangers such a notion might be used to justify (he cited the example of Henry Luce, who was so convinced that people in the United States had a duty to see the inadequacies of Robert Taft as president of this country that Luce used his power to distort the record of Taft, Peter did not withdraw his suggestion: We have a duty or obligation to form our beliefs in the most rigorous and responsible manner possible or, at least, in a manner commensurate with the importance of the matter about which a belief is to be formed. See Peter Hare, "Problems and Prospects in the Ethics of Belief," in *Pragmatic Naturalism and Realism,* ed. John Shook (Amherst, N.Y.: Prometheus Books, 2003), 239–61.

3. Peter H. Hare and Edward Madden, "Purposes and Methods of Writing the History of Recent American Philosophy," *Southern Journal of Philosophy* 6 (1969): 269–78.

4. As Peter himself explains, the *reliabilist* "judges the epistemic merit of a belief on the basis of the reliability of the mechanisms which produced it. If those mechanisms can be shown to be of a sort that produce true beliefs reliably, then the belief in question is justified. This can be determined, the reliabilist supposes, without consideration of what the believer does or does not have access to; it can be done on a basis *external* to the consciousness of the agent who has the belief."

In contrast, the *responsibilist* "thinks that reliably produced belief is an ideal only and cannot be a requirement of epistemic justification; epistemic justification, the responsibilist says, is instead a question of whether the agent acted responsibly in the context of what was accessible to her." Hare, "Problems and Prospects in the Ethics of Belief," 240.

5. As Peter narrates this history, "responsibilist epistemology is part of a long history in this country of the evaluation of belief in ethical terms. James proposed an ethics of belief, and C. I. Lewis developed such a theory. Dickinson Miller and C. J. Ducasse carried on this work, and Roderick Chisholm, a student of both Ducasse and Lewis, is the most influential current proponent of such a view." Ibid. It is not insignificant, then, that Peter wrote on Miller, Lewis, Ducasse, and Chisholm as well as James.

6. "Philosophy destroys its usefulness," as A. N. Whitehead rightly observes, "when it indulges in brilliant feats of explaining away. It is then trespassing with the wrong equipment upon the field of particular sciences. Its ultimate appeal is to the general consciousness of *what in practice we experience.*" A. N. Whitehead, *Process and Reality*, corrected edition, ed. David Ray Griffin and Donald W. Sherburne (New York: Free Press, 1978 [1929]), 17; emphasis added. Peter was suspicious of cleverness, especially when deployed to explain away what we in practice experience to be of inescapable significance.

7. Pragmatism was designed by Peirce, James, Dewey, Mead, and others from the inaugural period of this intellectual movement to be a form of empiricism more deeply in accord with the disclosures and dynamics of experience itself (see John E. Smith, *America's Philosophical Vision* [Chicago: University of Chicago Press], Chapter 1).

"Pragmatism represents," proclaims James, "a perfectly familiar attitude in philosophy, the empiricist attitude, but it represents it . . . in both a more radical and in a less objectionable form than it has ever yet assumed." William James, *Pragmatism* (Cambridge, Mass.: Harvard University Press, 1975), 31.

8. Peter H. Hare, "William James," in *A Companion to Epistemology*, ed. J. Dancy and E. Sosa (Oxford: Blackwell Publishing, 1992), 228.

9. There are various occasions when Peter uses the expression "pragmatic realism" rather than "natural realism." See, e.g., Hare, "Classical Pragmatism, Recent Naturalistic Theories of Representation, and Pragmatic Realism," in *The Role of Pragmatics in Contemporary Philosophy*, ed. P. Weingartner, G. Schurz, and G. Dorn (Vienna: Hölder-Pichler-Tempsky, 1998), 63.

10. Hare, "Problems and Prospects in the Ethics of Belief," 239.

11. In his presidential address to the Eastern Division of the APA, "Pragmatism, Pluralism, and the Healing of Wounds," Richard J. Bernstein argued that "engaged fallibilistic pluralism" is set in stark contrast to "*fragmenting* plural-

ism," "*flabby* pluralism," "*polemical* pluralism," and "*defensive* pluralism." Richard J. Bernstein, *The New Constellation* (Cambridge, Mass.: MIT Press, 1992), 335–36. Such engaged pluralism "means taking our own fallibility seriously—resolving that however much we are committed to our own styles of thinking, we are willing to listen to others without denying or suppressing the otherness of the other. It means being vigilant against the dual temptation of simply dismissing what others are saying by falling back on one of those standard defensive ploys where we condemn it as obscure, woolly, or trivial, or thinking we can always easily translate what is alien into our own entrenched vocabularies." Ibid., 336; see John E. Smith, *The Spirit of American Philosophy* (Albany: State University of New York Press, 1983), 241–42.

12. Hare, "Problems and Prospects in the Ethics of Belief," 259.

13. "The adoption of empirical, or denotative, method would thus," John Dewey contends, "procure for philosophic reflection something of that cooperative tendency toward consensus which marks inquiry in the natural sciences." Dewey, *Later Works of John Dewey*, vol. 1, *Experience and Nature*, ed. Jo Ann Boydston (Carbondale: Southern Illinois University Press, 1981), 389. Whether this or any other method by itself can procure such a tendency is arguably uncertain. It might, at bottom, be more a question of character—and, thus, of the deliberate cultivation of the Socratic virtues—than a question of method. Peter Hare exemplified—at the level of methodic self-reflection but at the even more fundamental level of self-reflective character—the heuristic necessity of *cooperative* inquiry.

14. Hare, "Classical Pragmatism, Recent Naturalistic Theories of Representation, and Pragmatic Realism," 63.

15. William James, "Philosophical Conceptions and Practical Results," in *Pragmatism and the Meaning of Truth*, 15.

16. Ibid., 49.

17. William James, *The Varieties of Religious Experience* (New York: Scribner Paper Fiction, 1985) 119.

18. William James, *The Principles of Psychology* (Cambridge, Mass.: Harvard University Press, 1981), 1259.

19. Ibid.

20. Ibid., 1260.

21. Cf. John Dewey, *Later Works of John Dewey*, vol. 9, *A Common Faith*, ed. Jo Ann Boydston (Carbondale: Southern Illinois University, 1989), 28, 33.

22. William James, *The Will to Believe and Other Essays* (Cambridge, Mass.: Harvard University Press, 1979), 29, emphasis added.

23. William James, *A Pluralistic Universe* (Cambridge, Mass.: Harvard University Press, 1977), 23.

24. Ibid., 28.

25. Ibid., 23.

26. Ibid., 55–56.

27. Ibid., 143–44.

28. James, *A Pluralistic Universe*, 144.

29. Segal, Hanna, "The Achievement of Ambivalence," *Common Knowledge* 1, no. 1 (spring 1992); *Psychoanalysis, Literature, and War: Papers 1972–1995*, ed. John Steiner. (New York: Routledge, 1997).

30. James, *Pragmatism and the Meaning of Truth* (Cambridge, Mass.: Harvard University Press, 1978), 235.

31. Ibid., 220.

32. Ibid., 221.

33. Ibid., 228.

34. Ibid., 31, emphasis added.

35. Ibid., 310.

36. Ibid., 282.

37. Ibid., 310–11.

38. Ibid., 311.

39. Ibid., 273.

40. In the context of noting Sami Pihlström's enthusiasm for a central figure in analytic philosophy today, Hare asserts: While "Pihlström rightly finds useful support [for his pragmatist program] in a much discussed 1994 work of John McDowell. . . . McDowell's work was anticipated by decades in the work of Will." Such historical points are ones Peter feels need to be made. Hare, "Classical Pragmatism, Recent Naturalistic Theories of Representation, and Pragmatic Realism," 63. Peter had a deep interest in recovering neglected figures in intellectual history, especially North American philosophers whose writings were to date insufficiently mined. Frederick Will was only one example of such a figure.

41. Peter Hare, "Thoughts and Things," 1969 Presidential Address to the Western Division of the APA.

42. Ibid.

43. In "Classical Pragmatism, Recent Naturalistic Theories of Representation, and Pragmatic Realism," (61–62) Peter appeals to Will's distinctive formulation of pragmatic realism, but in doing so quotes one of Will's expositors (Kenneth Westphal) rather than Will himself. In his introduction to *Pragmatism and Realism*, a collection of Will's essays, Westphal astutely observes: "Will shows how without the general and recognizable stability of the things around us, we would not be able to think or speak at all. Will's basic pragmatic point is that human thought is based in and depends on the structure and regularity of the environment, of the world itself in which we live. . . . Our cognitive predicament is not one of establishing a link between our thoughts and their supposed objects, it is instead one of exploiting the links our thinking does and must have with things

in order to discriminate the genuine characteristic of things." Kenneth West-phal, introduction to *Pragmatism and Realism* (Lanham, Md.: Rowman & Lit-tlefield, 1997), xxi–xxiii.

44. James, *Pragmatism and the Meaning of Truth*, 281–82.

45. My reason for saying *misleadingly* is because human experience no less than human knowing are natural processes and, as such, need to be themselves situated in the natural world. Without question, our knowledge of this world is derived from experience, but such experience provides the warrant for identi-fying nature as the context of contexts, the ultimately inclusively context in which all other ones are to be located. On this score, Dewey arguably has the more de-veloped and adequate position.

46. Ibid., 125.

47. This would seem to preclude experience from being a medium in which radical difference can be disclosed. This is, however, not the case. Human expe-rience is a medium in which radical differences of innumerable kinds are refracted in arresting hues. But whatever is disclosed in and through this medium cannot but be intrinsically connected to time, history, fallibility, and the other defining features of this open-ended process.

48. Ibid., 257.

49. Ibid.

50. Ibid., 258.

51. Ibid., 273, emphasis added.

52. Ibid., 258.

53. Cf. John Dewey, *Middle Works of John Dewey*, vol. 10, *Journal Articles, Essays, and Miscellany*, ed. Jo Ann Boydston (Carbondale: Southern Illinois University Press, 1985), 23–24.

54. James, *The Principles of Psychology*, 19.

55. William James, "Remarks on Spencer's Definition of Mind as Correspon-dence," *Journal of Speculative Philosophy* 12 (January 1878): 1–18. It was reprinted in *Essays in Philosophy* (Cambridge, Mass.: Harvard University Press, 1978), 7–22. Though the expression "spectator theory of knowledge" is Dewey's, James in this essay argues for essentially this approach: The "knower is not simply a mirror floating with no foot-hold anywhere, passively reflecting an order that he comes upon and finds simply existing. The knower is an actor, and co-efficient of truth on one side, whilst on the other he registers the truth which he helps to create. . . . In other words, there belongs to mind, from its birth upwards, a spon-taneity, a vote. It is in the game, and not a mere looker-on [or spectator]; and its judgments of the *should-be,* its ideals cannot be peeled off from the body of the *cognitandum* as if they were mere excrescences." *Essays in Philosophy*, 21.

56. In "Context and Thought," Dewey offers this nuanced statement of the most salient points: "Thought lives, moves, and has its being in and through symbols,

and, therefore, depends for meaning upon context as do symbols. We think *about* things, not *by* things. Or rather when we do think by and with things, we are not experiencing the things in their own nature and content. Sounds, for example, and marks in printed books are themselves existential things. But they operate in thought only as they stand for something else; if we become absorbed in them as things, they lose their value for thinking." *Later Works of John Dewey,* vol. 6, *Later Works, 1925–1953,* ed. Jo Ann Boydston (Carbondale: Southern Illinois University Press, 1986), 5.

57. H. S. Thayer, *Meaning and Action: A Study of American Pragmatism* (Indianapolis: Bobbs-Merrill, 1973), 44, 87.

58. James, *Pragmatism and the Meaning of Truth,* 247. James's illuminating account in his *Principles* of skipped intermediaries is far more relevant to his mature account of human cognition than is generally recognized even by informed and sympathetic expositors. See, e.g., *The Principles of Psychology,* 1241.

59. James, *Pragmatism and the Meaning of Truth,* 246.

60. Ibid., 251.

61. James, *The Will to Believe and Other Essays,* 25; Cf. Charles S. Peirce, *Collected Papers of Charles Sanders Peirce,* vols. 1–6, ed. Charles Hartshorne and Paul Weiss, vol. 7 and 8, ed. Arthur W. Burks (Cambridge, Mass.: Belknap Press of Harvard University Press, 1931–58), 5:583.

62. James, *Pragmatism and the Meaning of Truth,* 248.

63. Cf. Ibid., 25.

64. Hare, "William James," 227–28.

65. James, *The Varieties of Religious Experience,* 393.

66. It is almost certainly requisite to draw a distinction between the *temporal* and the *historical* character of this process.

67. While Peirce, Dewey, and Mead were systematically attentive to the role signs and symbols play in the structuring of experience and the acquisition of knowledge, James tended to slight the semiotic dimension of both human experience and human cognition (see, however, *Principles of Psychology,* 796ff). For a naturalistic account of human sign use, albeit one in which the continuity between the signaling of other species of animals, on the one hand, and the distinctively human forms of signification and symbolization, on the other, are stressed, see Dewey, *Middle Works of John Dewey,* vol. 10, 15.

68. Hare, "Classical Pragmatism, Recent Naturalistic Theories of Representation, and Pragmatic Realism," 58.

69. In this paper, Peter examines, albeit rather briefly, the recent contributions of Ruth Millikan and David Papineau—in particular, *Language, Thought, and Other Biological Categories* and *White Queen Psychology and Other Essays* by Millikan and *Reality and Representation* and *Philosophical Naturalism* by Papineau—to argue this point.

70. It is noteworthy that, in this paper, Peter focuses on the contributions of younger scholars (Cheryl Misak, Henry Jackman, and above all Sami Pihlström).

71. An abridged version of this essay appeared in the special issue of the *Transactions* devoted to the memory of Peter Hare.

72. Cf. Peirce, *Collected Papers*, 1:405.

73. Note that, in this context, James writes merely of "the more permanent ideals," not of eternal ones. William James, "The Social Value of the College-Bred," in *Essays, Comments, and Reviews* (Cambridge, Mass.: Harvard University Press, 1987), 110.

74. James, *The Will to Believe and Other Essays*, 141.

75. James, *A Pluralistic Universe*, 129.

76. In "Philosophical Conceptions and Practical Results," James asserts: "Of such postponed achievements do the lives of philosophers consist. Truth's fullness is elusive; ever not quite, not quite!" James, *Pragmatism and the Meaning of Truth*, 259.

77. James, *Pragmatism and the Meaning of Truth*, 234; Cf. Dewey, *Middle Works of John Dewey*, vol. 10, 195.

78. In *Human Nature and Conduct*, Dewey claims: "If it is better to travel than to arrive, it is because traveling is a constant arriving, while arrival that precludes further traveling is most easily attained by going to sleep or dying." *Middle Works of John Dewey*, vol. 14, *Human Nature and Conduct*, Jo Ann Boydston (Carbondale: Southern Illinois University Press, 1985). 195.

79. James, *Pragmatism and the Meaning of Truth*, 290. Earlier, I quoted the text from *Pragmatism* in which James asserts, "All 'homes' are in finite experience; finite experience as such is homeless." This passage concludes, however, with his insistence: "Nothing outside of the flux secures the issue of it. It can hope salvation [or simply success] only from its own intrinsic promises and potencies" (125).

80. It might appear that this makes the quest for certainty, the need to secure indubitable foundations for our epistemic claims, all the more imperative or urgent. But the failure to secure such foundations does not entail the impossibility of obtaining reliable knowledge, only the ever-elusive ideal of obtaining absolutely certain knowledge. There difference between pragmatic fallibilism and thoroughgoing (or textbook) skepticism is unquestionably a difference that makes a difference, even if the absolutist cannot tell the one from the other.

1. THE RIGHT AND DUTY TO WILL TO BELIEVE

1. For recent literature on the question of the meaningfulness of the ethics of belief, see R. M. Chisholm, "Lewis' Ethics of Belief," in *The Philosophy of C. I. Lewis*, ed. P. A. Schilpp (LaSalle, Ill.: Open Court, 1968), 223–27; C. K. Grant,

Belief and Action: Inaugural Lecture of the Professor of Philosophy (Durham, UK: University of Durham Press, 1960); H. H. Price, "Belief and Will," in *Belief, Knowledge, and Truth*, ed. R. R. Ammerman and M. G. Singer (New York: Scribner's, 1970), 57–76; H. H. Price, *Belief* (London: George Allen and Unwin, 1969); Robert R. Ammerman, "Ethics and Belief," *Proceedings of the Aristotelian Society*, New Series, 65 (1964–65): 257–66; Van A. Harvey, "Is There an Ethics of Belief?" *Journal of Religion* 49 (1969): 41–58.

2. He had apparently borrowed the expression from Charles Renouvier, always the major philosophical influence on James, and whom he had first read in 1868. See Wilbur Long, "The Philosophy of Charles Renouvier and Its Influence on William James" (unpublished PhD dissertation, Harvard University, 1925), 369n2.

3. Ralph B. Perry, *The Thought and Character of William James*, 2 vols. (Boston: Little, Brown, 1935), 1:529. Hereafter cited as *TC*.

4. *TC*, 1:531–532.

5. This essay may be found, among other places, in William James, *Essays on Faith and Morals* (Cleveland: Meridian, 1962). Hereafter cited as *EFM*.

6. *EFM*, 201.

7. *EFM*, 209.

8. E.g., "There is some believing tendency wherever there is willingness to act at all" (*EFM*, 34).

9. James's recognition of the distinction between actions and habits of action is most evident in *The Principles of Psychology*, 2 vols. (New York: Dover, 1950), 2:321–22. Hereafter cited as *PP*. Sometimes James writes of belief as *causing* action; cf. *PP*, 2:309.

10. This essay may be found in *EFM*. The paper was first delivered in 1895.

11. Around this time, A. J. Balfour, H. G. Wells, and F. C. S. Schiller were all, to varying degrees, advocating a rather extreme liberality with respect to belief and its connections with fact.

12. William James, *Pragmatism* (Cleveland: Meridian, 1955), 168. It is Wilbur Long who suggests that the title was taken from Renouvier; see Long, "The Philosophy of Charles Renouvier," 369.

13. *PP*, 2:486.

14. See for example, *PP*, 2:296; *EFM*, 40.

15. *EFM*, 195.

16. *PP*, 2:288–89.

17. *EFM*, 39.

18. *EFM*, 39.

19. For a vivid illustration of how such incompatibilities arise, see *PP*, II, 289–90.

20. *PP*, 2:321.

21. Cf. *PP*, 2:321–22.

22. Bk. II, Chap. 4 of the *Nicomachean Ethics*. See also James's note to the literature in *PP*, 2:322.

23. William James, *Some Problems of Philosophy* (New York: Longmans, Green and Co., 1911), 224.

24. Ibid.

25. Chauncey Wright got James to agree to this condition in 1875: "[James] agreed that attention to all accessible evidence was the only duty involved in belief" (*TC*, I, 531). We try to show, of course, that this is *not* the *only* duty, given the whole of James's philosophy.

26. E.g., James says: "We cannot control our emotions" (*PP*, II, 321); "[Man's desires] are the lowest terms to which man can be reduced" (*TC*, I, 301).

27. *TC*, 2;222.

28. E.g., *EFM*, 105ff.

29. *TC*, 1:301.

2. WILLIAM JAMES, DICKINSON MILLER, AND C. J. DUCASSE ON THE ETHICS OF BELIEF

1. *The Thought and Character of William James*, vol. 2 (Boston: Little, Brown, and Company, 1936), 240. Dickinson S. Miller (1868–1963) was a student of William James. James was instrumental in getting him an appointment at Bryn Mawr College in 1893, the year after Miller's graduation from Harvard. Miller left Bryn Mawr in 1898 to teach at Harvard and later at Columbia. He received a D. D. at Berkeley (California) Divinity School and in 1911 started to teach apologetics at the General Theological Seminary in New York City. Later he occasionally served as a Unitarian minister in the Boston area. Miller's was an extremely penetrating and constructively critical mind. His article provocatively entitled "Free Will as Involving Determinism and Inconceivable Without It" (1934), published, for obscure reasons, under the name of R. E. Hobart, has become a *locus classicus* of the free-will controversy. Until now, however, little has been known about his views on the will to believe issue. Cf. Herbert Feigel, *The Encyclopedia of Philosophy*, ed. Paul Edwards (New York: The MacMillan Company and The Free Press, 1967), vol. 5, 323–24.

2. *The Letters of William James* (Boston: The Atlantic Monthly Press, 1920), vol. 2, 48. In another letter about the will to believe, James calls Miller "illustrious friend and joy of my liver," *Letters*, vol. 2, 84.

3. "'The Will to Believe' and The Duty to Doubt," *International Journal of Ethics* 9 (1898–99): 169–95.

4. Unpublished letter of Miller to Ducasse, September 10, 1952. We are grateful to Professor Ducasse for giving us his correspondence with Miller and for permitting us to publish here those parts which concern the will to believe.

5. "James's Doctrine of 'The Right to Believe,'" *Philosophical Review* 51 (1942): 552. Miller published a number of articles dealing with one aspect or another of James's philosophy: "Professor James on Philosophical Method," *Philosophical Review* 8 (1899): 166–70; "Some of the Tendencies of Professor James's Work," *Journal of Philosophy* 7 (1910): 645–64; "Mr. Santayana and William James," *Harvard Graduates Magazine* 29 (1920–21): 348–64; Review of Bixler's *Religion in the Philosophy of William James, Journal of Philosophy* 24 (1927): 203–10; "Dr. Schiller and Analysis," *Journal of Philosophy* 24 (1927): 617–24; "James's Philosophical Development; Professor Perry's Biography," *Journal of Philosophy* 33 (1936): 309–18; "A Debt to James," in *In Commemoration of William James, 1842–1942* (New York: Columbia University Press, 1942), 24–33; and "William James, Man and Philosopher," in *William James: The Man and the Thinker* (Madison: University of Wisconsin Press, 1942), 31–52.

6. "James's Doctrine of 'The Right to Believe,'" 541–58.

7. Letter of Ducasse to Miller, January 18, 1943.

8. Letter of Miller to Ducasse, January 20, 1943.

9. Letter of Miller to Ducasse, September 10, 1952.

10. Letter of Ducasse to Miller, September 11, 1952.

11. "'The Will to Believe' and The Duty to Doubt," 173.

12. C. J. Ducasse, *A Philosophical Scrutiny of Religion* (New York: The Ronald Press Company, 1953), 163–64.

13. Ibid., 165.

14. Ibid., 166.

15. Ibid., 166.

16. Ibid., 166–67.

17. See E. H. Madden, *Chauncey Wright and the Foundation of Pragmatism* (Seattle: University of Washington Press, 1963), 43–50.

3. PROBLEMS AND PROSPECTS IN THE ETHICS OF BELIEF

1. Presidential Address to the Society for the Advancement of American Philosophy, March 3, 1990, Buffalo, New York. Readers should note that in this paper are to be found the broad brushstrokes and exhortation appropriate to writing in the genre of the presidential address, a genre as close to that of the sermon as to that of the journal article. Also, this quasi sermon is intended for an audience firmly committed to the development of the classical American philosophy of Peirce, James, Royce Dewey, Mead, Whitehead, Lewis, et al. For earlier discussions of related issues in a different genre, see Peter H. Hare and Edward H. Madden, "William James, Dickinson Miller, and C. J. Ducasse on the Ethics of Belief," *Transactions of the C. S. Peirce Society* 4 (1968): 115–29; Peter Kauber and Peter H. Hare, "The Right and Duty to Will to Believe," *Canadian Journal of*

Philosophy 4 (1974): 327–43; and Peter H. Hare, "Toward an Ethics of Belief," in *Philosophie et Culture: Actes du XVIIe congrès mondial de philosophie / Philosophy and Culture: Proceedings of the 17th World Congress of Philosophy* (Montreal: Editions Montmorency, 1988), vol. 3, 428–32.

2. Lorraine Code, *Epistemic Responsibility* (Hanover, N.H.: University Press of New England, 1987), 8.

3. Ibid., 69.

4. James Montmarquet, "Epistemic Virtue," *Mind* 90 (1987): 483.

5. Ibid., 484.

6. Ibid.

7. Ibid.

8. Ibid, 485.

9. Stewart Cohen, "Knowledge, Context and Social Standards," *Synthese* 73 (1987): 3–26.

10. Hilary Kornblith, "Some Social Features of Cognition," *Synthese* 73 (1987): 31.

11. Ibid., 32.

12. Ibid., 33.

13. Ibid., 33.

14. Frederick F. Schmitt, "Justification, Socialty and Autonomy," *Synthese* 73 (1987): 43–85.

15. Morton White, "Pragmatism and the Revolt against Formalism: Revising Some Doctrines of William James," *Transactions of the C. S. Peirce Society* 26 (1990): 3–4.

16.Ibid., 5–6.

17. Ibid., 9–10.

18. Ibid., 10.

19. Richard Foley, *The Theory of Epistemic Rationality* (Cambridge, Mass.: Harvard University Press, 1987), 213.

20. Ibid., 218.

21. Ibid., 219.

22. Ibid., 224.

23. Ibid.

24. Ibid, 226.

25. Paul K. Moser, *Empirical Justification* (Dordrecht: D. Reidel, 1985), 224–25.

26. Ibid., 230.

27. Kornblith, "Some Social Features of Cognition," 36.

28. Shelley E. Taylor, *Positive Illusions: Creative Self-Deception and Healthy Mind* (New York: Basic Books, 1989).

29. Ibid., xi.

30. Ibid., 10–11.

31. Ibid., 71.

32. Ibid., 74.

33. Ibid., 89–90.

34. Ibid., 121.

35. Ibid., 124.

36. Quoted by Taylor, *Positive Illusions*, 145.

37. Ibid., 157.

38. Hilary and Ruth Anna Putnam, "Epistemology as Hypothesis," *Transactions of the Charles S. Peirce Society* 26 (1990): 407–33.

39. Newton Garver, "The Ambiguity of the Police Role," *Social Praxis* 2 (1974): 320.

40. Ibid., 321.

41. Ibid., 321–22.

42. Ibid., 322.

43. H. H. Price, "Belief and Will," *Proceedings of the Aristotelian Society Supplement* 28 (1954): 1–26, reprinted in *Philosophy of Mind*, ed. Stuart Hampshire (New York: Harper and Row, 1966), 101.

44. David Halberstam, *The Powers That Be* (New York: Dell, 1979), 133.

45. Jonathan Harrison, "Some Reflections on the Ethics of Knowledge and Belief," *Religious Studies* 23 (1987): 328–29.

4. A CRITICAL APPRAISAL OF JAMES'S VIEW OF CAUSALITY

1. James, "Against Nihilism," in Ralph Barton Perry, *The Thought and Character of William James*, 2 vols. (Boston: Little, Brown and Co., 1935), 1:525.

2. Ibid.

3. Ibid., 525–26.

4. Ibid., 526.

5. Ibid., 525.

6. Ibid.

7. Ibid.

8. Cf. James's chapter on "Reasoning" in *The Principles of Psychology*, 2 vols. (New York: Henry Holt and Co., 1896), 2:323–71.

9. We have developed this concept ourselves in "The Powers That Be," *Dialogue* 10 (1971): 12–31. Cf. also E. H. Madden, "A Third View of Causality," *Review of Metaphysics* 23 (1969): 67–84, and "Hume and the Fiery Furnace," *Philosophy of Science* 38 (1971): 64–78.

10. For a thorough treatment of the relation between Renouvier and James, see Wilbur H. Long, "The Philosophy of Charles Renouvier and Its Influence on William James" (unpublished doctoral dissertation, Harvard University, 1925).

Unfortunately what appears to be the only copy extant of this useful piece of scholarship is in the Hoose Library of Philosophy, University of Southern California.

11. "Against Nihilism," in Perry, *The Thought and Character of William James*, 526.

12. Ibid.

13. Cf. William James, "The Feeling of Effort," in *Collected Essays and Reviews* (New York: Longmans, Green and Co., 1920), 151ff; "The Experience of Activity," in *Essays in Radical Empiricism [and] A Pluralistic Universe* (New York: Longmans, Green and Co., 1947), 155ff; and "Novelty and Causation—the Conceptual View" and "Novelty and Causation—the Perceptual View," in *Some Problems of Philosophy* (London: Longmans, Green and Co., 1916), 189–207 and 208–19, respectively.

14. James, *Essays in Radical Empiricism [and] A Pluralistic Universe*, 186.

15. James, *Some Problems of Philosophy*, 199.

16. Ibid.

17. Ibid., 213.

18. James, *Essays in Radical Empiricism [and] A Pluralistic Universe*, 186–86.

19. Cf. James, *Some Problems of Philosophy*, 208–19.

20. Ibid., 218–19. He refers to panpsychism as a "complication" and the discussion rather abruptly ends.

21. Later Whitehead, accepting the same premises as James, drew the panpsychic consequence.

22. Sterling Lamprecht, *The Metaphysics of Naturalism* (New York: Appleton-Century-Crofts, 1967), 136–37.

23. A. Michotte, *The Perception of Causality* (New York: Basic Books, 1963), esp. "Commentary" by T. R. Miles, 373–415.

24. Association of James's theory of causality with Bergson's metaphysical intuitionism and romantic evolutionism has regrettably discredited it with some readers who might otherwise have recognized its basic soundness. For James's generous but seriously misleading acknowledgement of Bergson, see *Some Problems of Philosophy*, 219, footnote.

25. Madden and Hare, "The Powers That Be," 28–31.

26. Fred I. Dretske, *Seeing and Knowing* (London: Routledge and Kegan Paul, 1969); W. D. Joske, *Material Objects* (London: Macmillan, 1967).

27. A. J. Ayer, *The Origins of Pragmatism* (San Francisco: Freeman, Cooper, 1968), 215–324, passim.

28. In R. B. Perry, *The Thought and Character of William James*, 2:370.

29. James, *Essays in Radical Empiricism [and] A Pluralistic Universe*, 76.

30. Cf. Robert G. Meyers, "Natural Realism and Illusion in James's Radical Empiricism," *Transactions of the Charles S. Peirce Society* 5 (1969): 211–23.

31. Cf. C. J. Ducasse, *Nature, Mind, and Death* (La Salle, Ill.: Open Court, 1951), 246–90; *Truth, Knowledge, and Causation* (London: Routledge and Kegan Paul, 1968), 42–60, 60–72, 90–131; and Roderick M. Chisholm, *Perceiving: A Philosophical Study* (Ithaca, N.Y.: Cornell University Press, 1957); "Theory of Knowledge" in *Philosophy, The Princeton Studies* (Englewood Cliffs, N.J.: Prentice-Hall, 1964), esp. 261–86, 312–44.

5. IN MEMORIAM: FREDERIC HAROLD YOUNG (1905–2003) AND THE FOUNDING OF THE PEIRCE SOCIETY

1. Frederic Harold Young was born March 2, 1905, in Indiana, the eldest of five children of Rev. Harold E. Young and Gertrude Young. His father was an itinerant clergyman in Maine, and Frederic as raised and attended schools in Kennebunkport, Maine. He received a BA from Bates College in 1927, a Masters of Divinity from Harvard Divinity School in 1930, and a PhD in Philosophy from Columbia University in 1948. He served as Acting Head of the Music Department and English Master at Phillips Academy, Andover, Mass., 1930–31. Having been earlier ordained a Congregational minister, he was ordained an Episcopal deacon in 1937 and a priest in 1938. He was pastor-rector of Congregational and Episcopal Parishes in Montana, Massachusetts, Maine, and New Jersey, 1931–48. While a captain-chaplain in the National Guard, 1940–41, marital troubles and divorce led to advice from his bishop that his prospects as a full-time priest were limited, so he "decided to resume my original intention of becoming a professor of philosophy and religion," while continuing to serve as a minister "on a demand-and-supply basis" ("Personal Sketch for the Rt. Rev'd Frederick H. Borsch," by F.H.Y., undated). His first wife was Myrna Hawkes; his second was Valesca von Heidt Herzog. In 1961 he married a third time, to Diana Boyce. Beyond the publications discussed in the text above, Young's chief publications were *Contemporary Philosophy in the USA 1900–1950* (published in Spanish, 1960) and "Historical Survey of Oriental Philosophy in America," *The Indian Philosophical Annual* (1971). Poems and other essays were published in various magazines. His alma mater Bates College published an obituary at www.bates.edu/x35142 .xml. His successes as an undergraduate were many. He won the freshman prize for debate, the sophomore prize for speaking, and the junior prize for declamation. He was a choir organist and debater. To the experience of college debating Young credited "the mental critical habits that have served me well in my career." Elected to Phi Beta Kappa, he wrote a philosophy honors thesis, "A Study of the Conscience of Man," that is a historical and critical essay of impressive maturity.

2. Accompanying Young's letter to Joseph Brent (see note 15 below) was a copy of his address and a note titled "A Pleasant Detail": "After giving my Milford ad-

dress to the Pike County Historical Society, I visited 'Arisbe,' and as I talked with the people living there then, in 1945, they graciously offered me any souvenir I might desire. I chose a tile from the French tiles that once surrounded the frame of the main fireplace. (Probably chosen by Juliette. All of the tiles were of scenes of the New Testament.)"

3. Max Fisch, in a letter of February 25, 1970, asked Young: "Do you know the source of the creditors-attic-ladder story? Mrs. Quick said there was nothing to it; neither in the house nor in the barn was there any attic or other room which could have been used in that way." Young replied: "I do not know the source of the 'creditors-attic-ladder story.' (I think I read it first in Weiss's (?) account in *Dict. of Amer. Biog.*[)]" Whether or not Young first learned of the story in Weiss's biography, the tale does, in fact, appear in Weiss's DAB article.

4. Norman B. Lehde, President of the Pike County Historical Society, in a letter of April 23, 1949, told Max Fisch that the Society had purchased all the books recommended for purchase by Young, and had presented them to the public library in Milford. On April 25, 1946, the *Milford Dispatch*, in an article titled "Peirce Society Formed," reported: "Recently there has been established by members of the American Philosophical Society a special group known as the Peirce Society. . . . The new society has plans to extend appreciation of the genius of Prof. Peirce, as was suggested by Reverend Frederic H. Young of Newark and Princeton, who has become known to Milford residents by his several visits here. His paper on the life and attainments of Peirce, which he read at a meeting last autumn before the Pike County Historical Society, has been published by that society, and is having interested purchasers, the proceeds from its sale will benefit Milford High School as a prize for a student excelling in mathematics." Today the Pike County Historical Society has a Peirce Room in its museum. The Milford Public Library has a Peirce Corner.

5. Letter of Young to Mr. Terwilliger of the Pike County Historical Society, January 14, 1946.

6. Although the Peirce Society's constitution recognizes Young as "Founder," and the narrative I have given demonstrates the appropriateness of that title, it should be acknowledged that Young sometimes hesitated to give himself that title (using instead "Founder Member," "Co-Founder," or "Founding Member") when preparing a curriculum vitae or other autobiographical sketch. I surmise that, though proud of what he had accomplished, he was a little embarrassed, as a "student" of Peirce, not an "authority," to call himself by such a grand title. Let us add humility to the long list of Reverend Young's virtues.

7. Frederic Harold Young, *The Philosophy of Henry James, Sr.* (New York: Bookman Associates, 1951).

8. Ibid., vii.

9. Ibid., 179–80.

10. Philip P. Wiener and Frederic H. Young, ed., *Studies in the Philosophy of Charles Sanders Peirce* (Cambridge, Mass.: Harvard University Press, 1952), v.

11. Letter of Young to Max Fisch, June 10, 1972.

12. Letter of Young to Kathie O'C Hodge, dean, Emeritus Institute, Saddleback College, February 11, 1990.

13. Letter of DuBridge to Lee McGrew, dean, Saddleback Community College, August 1, 1978.

14. *Charles Sanders Peirce: A Life* (Bloomington: Indiana University Press, 1993). IUP published a revised edition in 1998.

15. Letter of Young to Joseph Brent, July 22, 1993.

16. Letter of Young to Nathan Houser, August 27, 2001. Nathan Houser and Christian Kloesel, ed., *The Essential Peirce: Selected Philosophical Writings, Volume I (1867–1893)* (Bloomington: Indiana University Press, 1992).

17. PHH interview of Gloria Tucker, February 3, 2004. For help in preparing this paper, I wish to extend my thanks not only to Gloria Tucker but also to Nathan Houser, general editor of the Peirce Edition Project; Joseph Brent; the staff of the Pike County Historical Society; and the staff of the Muskie Archives and Special Collections of Bates College. Joseph Brent and Nathan Houser have generously given permission to quote from Young's letters to them.

7. PROPOSITIONS AND ADVERBIAL METAPHYSICS

1. C. J. Ducasse, "Propositions, Opinions, Sentences, and Facts," *Journal of Philosophy* 37 (1940): 704; page 183 of this article was reprinted in C. J. Ducasse, *Truth, Knowledge, and Causation* (London: Routledge and Kegan Paul, 1968).

2. Of historical significance is the fact that Ducasse first formulated this philosophical method as early as 1924 in his first book, *Causation, and the Types of Necessity*. See reprint of *Causation, and the Types of Necessity*, with an introduction by Vincent Tomas (New York: Dover Publications, 1969), 119–30.

3. Cf. C. A. Baylis, "Facts, Propositions, Exemplification and Truth," *Mind* 57 (1948): 459–79.

4. It is interesting that many years ago Roderick Chisholm suggested to Ducasse that he adopt an adverbial theory of propositions. After several times in earlier letters (June 25, 1944; May 24, 1945; and June 25, 1945) expressing doubt that we need to suppose that there are propositions, Chisholm wrote Ducasse (November 29, 1951) that "one of your views. I believe might be formulated by saying that propositions are alien accusatives of believings. I think one could plausibly argue, applying Occam's razor, that propositions

are merely *connate* accusatives of believings. Possibly you would regard this as an abuse of the technique [the technique of reducing allegedly alien accusatives to connate accusatives]—though I am inclined to feel that it may be applied to propositions quite as legitimately as to sense data." Ducasse's reply to Chisholm (November 30, 1951) is interesting though somewhat inconclusive: "Your suggestion that propositions may be merely connate accusatives of believing is interesting, and, offhand, I do not see any particular reason why this could not be the case. The test would be whether any propositions 'exist' or 'subsist' while not being believed, disbelieved, or doubted. Also is there such a thing as belief, disbelief, or doubt having no proposition as 'content' or 'object'? The instances of 'folie du doute,' and of 'conviction' as a bare feeling or emotion (as in the mystic trance or the 'anesthetic revelation') might be cases in point. As to existence or subsistence of propositions independently of their being believed, disbelieved, or doubted, the first thing needed, of course, would be agreement as to what exactly a proposition is. If, as Baylis believes, a proposition is a particular kind of concept, then the answer would seem to be that they have no independent existence. If, on the other hand, in 'this table weighs 300 lbs.,' the table which the words 'this table' denotes is, as I think, a literal constituent of the proposition that sentence formulates, then it would seem that at least some constituents of some propositions exist independently of their being believed, disbelieved, or doubted. As you say, it turns out to be a long story."

I am grateful to Professors Ducasse and Chisholm for permitting me to refer to this correspondence.

5. Ducasse's earliest statements of this adverbial theory appear in "On the Attributes of Material Things," *Journal of Philosophy* 31 (1934) and "Introspection, Mental Acts, and Sensa," *Mind* 45 (1936); the former is reprinted in *Truth, Knowledge, and Causation*, 42–60. Cf. Peter Hare and Richard Koehl, "Moore and Ducasse on the Sensa Data Issue," *Philosophy and Phenomenological Research* 28 (1968): 313–31.

6. Wilfrid Sellars, *Naturalism and Ontology* (Atascadero, Ca.: Ridgeview Publishing Co., 1979), 137.

7. Cf. Bruce Aune, "Statements and Propositions," *Noûs* 1 (1967): 215–29.

8. C. J. Ducasse, "Symbols, Signs, and Signals," *Journal of Symbolic Logic* 4 (1939), reprinted in *Truth, Knowledge, and Causation*, 73–89; Also see C. J. Ducasse, *Nature, Mind and Death* (La Salle, Ill.: Open Court, 1951), 354–99.

9. C. J. Ducasse, "Some Comments on C. W. Morris's 'Foundations of the Theory of Signs,'" *Philosophy and Phenomenological Research* 3 (1942): 43–52.

10. C. J. Ducasse, "Objectivity, Objective Reference, and Perception," *Philosophy and Phenomenological Research* 2 (1941); page 117 of this article was reprinted in *Truth, Knowledge and Causation*.

8. THICKENING HOLISTIC PRAGMATISM

1. *Holism: A Shopper's Guide*, ed. J. Fodor and E. Lepore ({PUB CITY: Wiley-Blackwell, 1992) and *Holism: A Consumer Update*, ed. Fodor and Lepore, Grazer Philosophische Studien 46 (Amsterdam: Rodopi, 1993).

2. Henry Jackman, "Moderate Holism and the Instability Thesis," *American Philosophical Quarterly* 36, no. 4 (1999): 361–64.

3. Jackman, "Holism, Context, and Content," http://www.yorku.ca/hjackman /papers/Locality.pdf.

4. Ibid.

5. Ibid.

6. W. V. Quine, "Two Dogmas of Empiricism," in *From a Logical Point of View* (Cambridge, Mass.: Harvard University Press, 1953), 41.

7. Morton White, *Toward Reunion in Philosophy* (New York: Atheneum, 1963), 256.

8. Morton White, *What Is and What Ought To Be Done: An Essay on Ethics and Epistemology* (New York: Oxford University Press, 1981), 15.

9. Morton White, "Normative Ethics, Normative Epistemology, and Quine's Holism," in *The Philosophy of W. V. Quine*, ed. Lewis E. Hahn and Paul A. Schilpp (Chicago: Open Court, 1998), 651.

10. Ibid., 652–53.

11. Ibid., 652–53.

12. Ibid., 654.

13. Ibid., 661.

14. Ibid., 664–65.

15. White, *What Is and What Ought To Be Done*, 109.

16. Morton White, personal communication with the author, May 10, 2004.

17. Loc. cit.

18. Morton White, "The Psychologism of Hume and Quine Compared," in *Proceedings of the Twentieth World Congress of Philosophy* (Bowling Green, Oh.: Philosophy Documentation Center, 2000), 156.

19. Loc. cit.

20. Alvin Goldman, "The Unity of Epistemic Virtues," in *Virtue Epistemology: Essays on Epistemic Virtue and Responsibility*, ed. Abrol Fairweather and Linda Zagzebski (Oxford: Oxford University Press, 2001), 31.

21. Ibid., 38.

22. Ibid., 43.

23. Ibid., 44–45.

24. White, "Normative Ethics, Normative Epistemology, and Quine's Holism," 665.

25. Hilary Putnam, *The Collapse of the Fact/Value Dichotomy and Other Essays* (Cambridge, Mass.: Harvard University Press, 2004).

26. Mark Bross, *Externalism and Understanding: Toward a Unified Account of Epistemic Justification* (PhD Dissertation, State University of New York at Buffalo, 2003), 242.

27. Morton White, *A Philosophy of Culture: The Scope of Holistic Pragmatism* (Princeton: Princeton University Press, 2002), 6.

28. Linda T. Zagzebski, *Virtues of the Mind: An Inquiry into the Nature of Virtue and the Ethical Foundation of Knowledge* (Cambridge: Cambridge University Press, 1996), 222.

29. Michael Rouse, *How Scientific Practices Matter: Reclaiming Philosophical Naturalism* (Chicago: The University of Chicago Press, 2002).

30. Cf. Rom Harre and Edward H. Madden, *Causal Powers: A Theory of Natural Necessity* (Oxford: Basil Blackwell, 1975).

31. Rouse, 27.

32. Ibid., 183.

33. Ibid., 285.

34. Clifford Geertz, *The Interpretation of Cultures* (New York: Basic Books, 1973), 5, 14.

35. Andy Clark, *Being There: Putting Brain, Body, and World Together Again* (Cambridge, Mass.: MIT Press), 1997, 220-21.

36. Mark Johnson, *The Meaning of the Body: Aesthetics of Human Understanding* (Chicago: University of Chicago Press, 2007), xii, 25; see also George Lakoff and Mark Johnson, *Philosophy in the Flesh: the Embodied Mind and Its Challenges to Western Thought* (New York: Basic Books, 1999).

37. Ibid., 117.

38. Cf. Abner Shimony, *Search for a Naturalistic World View*, vol. 2, *Natural Science and Metaphysics* (Cambridge: Cambridge University Press, 1993).

9. ON THE DIFFICULTY OF EVADING THE PROBLEM OF EVIL

1. Karl Barth, *The Epistle to the Romans*, trans. Edwyn C. Hoskyns, 6th ed. (London: Oxford University Press, 1933); *Dogmatics in Outline*, trans. G. T. Thomson (New York: Philosophical Library, N. D.); *Church Dogmatics*, vol. 1, trans. G. T. Thomson (Edinburgh: T. & T. Clark, 1936).

2. In this connection Barth speaks of "temptation," "illegitimate desire," and "unhealthy pride." *Church Dogmatics*, 1:186.

3. In *God Here and Now* (New York: Harper and Row, 1964, 31), Barth writes that "because it is free grace, the proclamation of the Church cannot deal with any characteristics, capacities, points of contact, and the like which might be credited on the human side, or with any human potentialities or merits which should

be taken into consideration. It is grace for creatures to whom God owes nothing, nothing at all."

4. Barth, *Church Dogmatics*, 1:214, 280. Cf. *Faith and the Philosophers*, ed. John Hick (New York: St. Martin's Press, 1964), 159–222.

5. Edward A. Dowey, "'But Is It Barth?,'" in Hick, *Faith and the Philosophers*, 204–5.

6. Paul Tillich, *Systematic Theology*, vol. 1 (Chicago: University of Chicago Press, 1951), 8.

7. Ibid., 9.

8. Ibid., 56–57. Cf. 16–18, 150–53.

9. Ibid., 57.

10. See Peter Winch, *The Idea of a Social Science and Its Relation to Philosophy* (London: Routledge and Kegan Paul, 1958). Cf. Alasdair MacIntyre's "Is Understanding Religion Compatible with Believing?" in Hick, *Faith and the Philosophers*, 119–24.

11. Winch, *The Idea of a Social Science*, 100–1; quoted by MacIntyre.

12. See Norman Malcolm's "Is It a Religious Belief that 'God Exist'?" in Hick, *Faith and the Philosophers*, 103–10, and his "Anselm's Ontological Arguments," *Philosophical Review* 69 (1960): 41–62. Cf. John Hick's "Sceptics and Believers" in *Faith and the Philosophers*, 235–42, and Antony Flew's *God and Philosophy* (London: Hutchinson and Co., 1966), 173–77. Also Flew, 79–81.

13. H. J. Paton, *The Modern Predicament* (New York: Collier Books, 1962), 52.

14. Tillich, *Systematic Theology*, 3:372.

15. J. L. Austin, *Philosophical Papers* (London: Oxford University Press, 1961), 224.

16. Tillich, *Systematic Theology*, 1:15.

17. MacIntyre, "Is Understanding Religion Compatible with Believing?," 121–22.

18. Ibid., 121.

19. Tillich, *Systematic Theology*, 3:372–74.

20. Ibid., 372–73. Tillich's quasi theism has appealed to many of the now widely discussed "Death of God" theologians. Much of John A. T. Robinson's *Honest to God* (Philadelphia: The Westminster Press, 1963) is an exposition of Tillich; *Radical Theology and The Death of God* by Thomas J. J. Altizer and William Hamilton (Indianapolis: Bobbs-Merrill, 1966) is dedicated to Tillich. They are drawn to Tillich's famous polemic against theism (i.e., against belief in God as a being). Many of these theologians use Tillich's metaphysics of "the ground of being" to develop what is supposed to be a nontheistic version of Christianity. Of course, insofar as the "Death of God" theologians are simply humanists with the addition of a little traditional religious language we have no quarrel

with them. It is only when they attempt to reintroduce by means of a novel metaphysics many of the elements of a traditional theism in what amounts to a quasi theism that we object. For a criticism of Tillich's own attempt to do this, see Peter H. Hare, "Religion and Analytic Naturalism," *Pacific Philosophy Forum* 5 (1967): 52–61.

21. Tillich, *Systematic Theology*, 3:372.

22. Ibid., 373.

23. Ibid., 374.

24. Ibid., 1:150.

25. Ibid., 1:151. Cf. Tillich's "The Meaning and Justification of Religious Symbols" in *Religious Experience and Truth*, ed. S. Hook (New York: New York University Press, 1961), 3.

26. Tillich, *Systematic Theology*, 1:152–53.

10. RELIGION AND ANALYTIC NATURALISM

1. An example of the latter is the position in which the view that all events are caused (at least in the usual sense) is denied in order to defend free will and repudiate causal explanation of human actions.

2. P. F. Strawson, *Individuals* (London: Methuen and Co., 1959), 9.

3. John Wisdom, *Philosophy and Psychoanalysis* (Oxford: Basil Blackwell, 1953), 248–82.

4. Stephen Pepper, *World Hypotheses* (Berkeley: University of California Press, 1961), 91.

5. Ibid., 77.

6. Ibid., 82, f.

7. Cf. W. H. Walsh, *Metaphysics* (London: Hutchinson University Library, 1963), Chap. 10.

8. Holmes, Arthur, "Philosophy and Religious Belief," *World Futures: The Journal of Global Education* 5 (1967): 35.

9. Ibid., 50.

10. John Herman Randall Jr., *Nature and Historical Experience* (New York: Columbia University Press, 1958), Part II.

11. Paul Tillich, *Systematic Theology*, vol. 1 (Chicago: University of Chicago Press, 1951), 20–21.

12. Ibid., 21.

11. BUCHLER'S ORDINAL METAPHYSICS AND PROCESS THEOLOGY

1. For a comparison between Buchler's and Whitehead's critiques of traditional substance, see Beth J. Singer, "Substitutes for Substance," *Modern Schoolman* 53 (1975): 19–38.

2. For a helpful discussion of the relations between Buchler and many other metaphysicians, see Stephen David Ross, *Transition to an Ordinal Metaphysics* (Albany: State University of New York Press, 1980).

3. Justus Buchler, *Metaphysics of Natural Complexes* (New York: Columbia University Press, 1966), 1.

4. Ibid., 8.

5. Ibid., 95.

6. Ibid., 22.

7. For a detailed discussion of Buchler's treatment of identity, see Marjorie C. Miller, "The Concept of Identity in Justus Buchler and Mahayana Buddhism," *International Philosophical Quarterly* 16 (1976): 87–107.

8. Buchler, *Metaphysics of Natural Complexes*, 8.

9. Ibid., 24, 56, and 102.

10. Ibid., 31.

11. A. N. Whitehead, *Process and Reality*, corrected edition, ed. David Ray Griffin and Donald W. Sherburne (New York: Free Press, 1978 [1929]), 343/521.

12. See Buchler's "On a Strain of Arbitrariness in Whitehead's System," *Journal of Philosophy* 66 (1969): 589–601.

12. NEGLECTED AMERICAN PHILOSOPHERS IN THE HISTORY OF SYMBOLIC INTERACTIONISM

1. Talcott Parsons, "Interaction: Social Interaction," in *International Encyclopedia of the Social Sciences*, ed. David L. Sills (New York: Macmillan and Free Press, 1968), vol. 7, 434.

2. John W. Petras, "The Genesis and Development of Symbolic Interactionism in American Sociology" (unpublished PhD dissertation, University of Connecticut, 1966). Petras makes only a footnote reference to Royce (151) and no reference at all to Peirce and Wright; his forty-five-page bibliography includes only James Harry Cotton's *Royce on the Human Self* (242). That Petras gives so little attention to Royce is especially surprising in light of the fact that Charles W. Morris in the introduction to his edition of Mead's *Mind, Self, and Society* (Chicago: University of Chicago Press, 1934) mentions Royce as a teacher of Mead who had a social theory of self (xiii). Fay Berger Karpf, *American Social Psychology: Its Origins, Development and European Background* (New York: McGraw-Hill, 1932) refers several times to Royce (e.g., 269, 280, and 290) but makes no references to Wright or Peirce.

3. George Herbert Mead, *Selected Writings*, ed. Andrew J. Reck (Indianapolis: Bobbs-Merrill, 1964), 95.

4. John Clendenning, introduction to *The Letters of Josiah Royce*, ed. by John Clendenning. (Chicago: University of Chicago Press, 1970), 24–25. Indeed, Royce's

emphasis on the social can be traced to his doctoral dissertation in 1878. See Bruce Kuklick, *Josiah Royce: An Intellectual Biography* (Indianapolis: Bobbs-Merrill, 1972), 14–15fn.

5. George Herbert Mead, "Cooley's Contribution to American Social Thought," *American Journal of Sociology* 35 (1930): 693–706, reprinted in Charles Horton Cooley, *Human Nature and the Social Order* (New York: Schocken Books, 1964), xxi–xxxviii.

6. George Herbert Mead, "Josiah Royce—A Personal Impression," *International Journal of Ethics* 27 (1917): 169. Royce is made to appear an un-American metaphysician in Mead's "The Philosophies of Royce, James, and Dewey in Their American Setting," *Selected Writings*, 371–91.

7. Josiah Royce, *The Basic Writings of Josiah Royce*, ed. John J. McDermott, 2 vols. (Chicago: University of Chicago Press, 1969). From the point of view of symbolic interactionism, the most useful of the studies of Royce is Peter Fuss, *The Moral Philosophy of Josiah Royce* (Cambridge, Mass.: Harvard University Press, 1965). Fuss makes use of Royce's numerous unpublished papers in social psychology.

8. Kuklick, *Josiah Royce: An Intellectual Biography.*

9. Charles W. Morris, *Six Theories of Mind* (Chicago: University of Chicago Press, 1932), 322fn.

10. Edward H. Madden, *Chauncey Wright and the Foundations of Pragmatism* (Seattle: University of Washington Press, 1963), 183–86. Madden's Chapter 7 is an excellent account of Wright's views on self-consciousness.

11. Chauncey Wright, "Evolution of Self-Consciousness," *North American Review* 116 (1873): 245–310. Parts of this monograph are reprinted in *The Philosophical Writings of Chauncey Wright: Representative Selections*, ed. Edward H. Madden (New York: Liberal Arts Press, 1958), 71–97.

12. Philip P. Weiner, *Evolution and the Founders of Pragmatism* (New York: Harper Torchbooks, 1965), 31.

13. Wright, "Evolution of Self-Consciousness," 262.

14. Ibid., 263.

15. For an account of the "Metaphysical Club" of which they were all members, see Wiener, *Evolution and the Founders of Pragmatism*, 18–30, and Max H. Fisch's "Was There a Metaphysical Club in Cambridge?," *Studies in the Philosophy of Charles Sanders Peirce, Second Series*, ed. Edward C. Moore and Richard S. Robin (Amherst: University of Massachusetts Press, 1964), 3–32. The secondary literature on Peirce by philosophers is vast, but some of the more useful works from the point of view of symbolic interactionism are Charles Morris, "Peirce, Mead, and Pragmatism," *Philosophical Review* 47 (1938): 109–27; Morris, *The Pragmatic Movement in American Philosophy* (New York: George Braziller,

1970); and John E. Smith, *Royce's Social Infinite* (New York: Liberal Arts Press, 1950), 19–31, 68–73. Especially helpful in explaining the technicalities of Peirce's theory of signs is Douglas Greenlee, *Peirce's Concept of Sign* (The Hague: Mouton, 1973).

16. Charles Sanders Peirce, *Collected Papers*, vols. 1–6, ed. Charles Hartshorne and Paul Weiss; vols. 7–8, ed. Arthur Burks (Cambridge, Mass.: Harvard University Press, 1934–58), 5:13.

17. Cf. Max H. Fisch, "General Introduction: The Classical Period American Philosophy," *Classic American Philosophers*, ed. Max H. Fisch (New York: Appleton-Century Crofts, 1951), 29–30.

18. Peirce, *Collected Papers*, 5:314.

19. Duane H. Whittier, "Language and the Self," in *Studies in Philosophy and the History of Science: Essays in Honor of Max Fisch*, ed. Richard Tursman (Lawrence, Kansas: Coronado Press, 1970), 168–81. Whittier's comparisons between Peirce and such philosophers as Wittgenstein are also valuable. It should be of interest to historians of symbolic interactionism to know that there has been a rebirth of many of the ideas of Wright, Peirce, Royce, and Mead in very recent Anglo-American philosophy of language and self. An illuminating account of the relations between earlier and later symbolic interactionism in philosophy is Tom Clifton Keen, "George Herbert Mead's Social Theory of Meaning and Experience" (unpublished PhD dissertation, Ohio State University, 1968). Surprisingly, John Searle says that he has no acquaintance with kindred thinkers in the social sciences or in the history of American philosophy, though he has often been told that his ideas are like Mead's (conversation with Peter H. Hare, summer 1971).

20. G. H. Mead, *The Philosophy of the Present* (LaSalle, Ill.: Open Court, 1932).

21. Quoted by Fuss, *The Moral Philosophy of Josiah Royce*, 93–94, originally published in "The External World and the Social Consciousness," *Philosophical Review* 3 (1894): 532.

22. Josiah Royce, "Some Observations on the Anomalies of Self-Consciousness," *Psychological Review* 2 (1895): 443, and *Studies of Good and Evil* (New York: Appleton, 1898; reprinted, Hamden, Conn.: Archon Books, 1964), 180–81.

23. Josiah Royce, "Self-Consciousness, Social Consciousness and Nature," *Philosophical Review* 4 (1895): 468, and *Studies of Good and Evil*, 201.

24. Josiah Royce, *The Problem of Christianity*, with a new introduction by John E. Smith (Chicago: University of Chicago Press, 1968), originally published in two volumes by MacMillan Company, New York, 1913. Smith's introduction to the one-volume edition is a useful supplement to Fuss's book.

14. WHAT ARE POETS FOR? CONTEXTUALISM AND PRAGMATISM

1. Garrison Keillor, *Good Poems* (New York: Penguin Books, 2003), xxii.

2. Ibid., xix.

3. Wallace Stevens, *Opus Posthumous: Poems, Plays, and Prose* (New York: Vintage, 1990), 158.

4. Jeffrey Walker, *Rhetoric and Poetics in Antiquity* (Cambridge: Oxford University Press, 2000), 168.

5. Ibid., 169.

6. William James, *The Correspondence of William James*, vol. 5, ed. Ignas K. Skrupskelis and Elizabeth Berkeley (Charlottesville: University Press of Virginia, 1997), 233.

15. MISUNDERSTANDINGS BETWEEN POET AND PHILOSOPHER: WALLACE STEVENS AND PAUL WEISS

1. The best source for information about the life and thought of Paul Weiss is Lewis Edwin Hahn, ed., *The Philosophy of Paul Weiss* (Chicago: Open Court, 1995).

2. *Wallace Stevens, Collected Poetry and Prose*, ed. Frank Kermode and Joan Richardson (New York: The Library of America, 1997), 666–85.

3. Paul Weiss, quoted in *Letters of Wallace Stevens*, ed. Holly Stevens (New York: Alfred A. Knopf, 1977), 476.

4. Ibid.

5. Ibid., 587.

6. Peter Brazeau, *Parts of a World: Wallace Stevens Remembered: An Oral Biography* (New York: Random House, 1983), 185–86.

7. Ibid., 186.

8. Letter of August 15, 1951, Special Collections, Morris Library, Southern Illinois University.

9. Letter of December 7, 1951, Special Collections, Morris Library, Southern Illinois University.

10. Letter of December 8, 1951, Henry E. Huntington Library, San Marino, California.

11. Letter of January 21, 1952, Henry E. Huntington Library, San Marino, California.

12. Letter of January 24, 1952, Henry E. Huntington Library, San Marino, California.

13. Brazeau, *Parts of a World*, 212–13.

14. Stevens, *Collected Poetry and Prose*, 851.

15. Ibid., 862.

16. Ibid.

17. Ibid., 863.

18. Brazeau, *Parts of a World*, 212.

19. Interview by Peter Brazeau, Henry E. Huntington Library, San Marino, California.

20. Brazeau, *Parts of a World*, 213.

21. Stevens, *Collected Poetry and Prose*, 296. Cf. Paul Weiss, *Beyond All Appearances* (Carbondale: Southern Illinois University Press, 1974), 142–43.

22. Interview by Peter Brazeau, Henry E. Huntington Library, San Marino, California. Weiss is by no means the only commentator who has noted that in his poetry Stevens appears to endorse contradictory epistemologies—in this case the offending contradiction is found in a single poem. In my view, it is a mistake to suppose that in his poetry, philosophical though it may be, Stevens is asserting epistemological propositions. He is, instead, using epistemologies as metaphorical structures. No one reasonably expects all the metaphors a poet uses to form a logically consistent set.

23. Ibid.

24. Paul Weiss, *First Considerations: An Examination of Philosophical Evidence* (Carbondale: Southern Illinois University Press, 1977), 210–11.

16. DEEP CONCEPTUAL PLAY IN WILLIAM JAMES

1. Charlene Haddock Seigfried, *William James' Radical Reconstruction of Philosophy* (Albany: State University of New York Press, 1990), 105.

2. Ibid., 165.

3. Ibid.

4. Ibid.

5. Megan Mustain, "Metaphor as Method: Charlene Haddock Seigfried's Radical Reconstruction," accessed at http://williamjamesstudies.org/1.1/mustain.html. Section 6.

6. Ibid.

7. Ibid., Section 7.

8. Ibid., Section 11.

9. Ibid., Section 14.

10. Ibid., Section 16.

11. William James, *The Correspondence of William James*, vol. 5, ed. Ignas K. Skrupskelis and Elizabeth Berkeley (Charlottesville: University Press of Virginia, 1997), 233.

12. William James, *The Letters of William James*, vol. 2, ed. Henry James (Boston: Atlantic Monthly Press, 1920), 39.

13. Gertrude Stein, "A Substance in a Cushion," *Selected Writings of Gertrude Stein* (New York: Vintage, 1990), 461.

14. Gertrude Stein, "Roastbeef," *Tender Buttons* (Mineola, N.Y.: Dover Publications, 1997), 20.

15. Richard Rorty, *Contingency, Irony, and Solidarity* (Cambridge: Cambridge University Press, 1989), 20.

16. William James, *The Varieties of Religious Experience* (Cambridge, Mass.: Harvard University Press, 1903), 369.

17. George Lakoff and Mark Johnson, *Metaphors We Live By* (Chicago: University of Chicago Press, 1980), 4.

18. Ibid., 8.

19. Charles Peirce, "Esthetics, Ethics, and Logic," in *The Collected Papers of Charles Sanders Peirce*, ed. Paul Weiss and Charles Hartshorne (Cambridge, Mass.: Belknap Press of Harvard University Press, 1932), 196.

20. Daniel Campos, "Peirce on the Role of Poietic Creation in Mathematical Reasoning," *Transactions of the Charles S. Peirce Society: A Quarterly Journal in American Philosophy* 43, no. 3 (summer 2007): 470–89.

21. Charles Peirce, "The Neglected Argument for the Reality of God," in *The Collected Papers of Charles Sanders Peirce*, 458.

17. REFLECTIONS ON CIVIL DISOBEDIENCE

This is a revised version of a paper read at a meeting of the Fullerton Club held at Temple University on October 11, 1968.

1. In "Essence and Ethics of Civil Disobedience," *Nation*, March 16, 1964, 258, Carl Cohen argues that Thoreau's action is not "civil disobedience in the strict sense."

2. Cf. Sidney Hook, "Neither Blind Obedience Nor Uncivil Disobedience," *New York Times Magazine*, June 5, 1966, 53; Charles E. Wyzanski Jr., "On Civil Disobedience," *Atlantic*, February, 1968, 58–60; American Civil Liberties Union, "Statement on Civil Disobedience," *Civil Liberties: Monthly Publication of the A.C.L.U.*, March-April, 1968, 4; and Harriet F. Pilpel, "Civil Disobedience: Arguments for Rescinding the A.C.L.U. Policy Statement," *Civil Liberties*, May 1968, 2.

3. There may be some question of *how premeditated* the illegal act must be to count as civil disobedience. The answer is that it need not be *planned*, though it must be consciously and rationally accepted before being committed. A demonstration may be entirely lawful until the crowd is asked to disperse, at which time some individuals, believing the request to be harassment, may refuse and be arrested for disturbing the peace. Such acts constitute civil disobedience if they meet all the other criteria.

4. In "The Moral Grounds of Civil Disobedience," *Ethics* 76 (1965): 142–45, Darnell Rucker considers an act not accompanied by willingness to accept penalties to be "defiance of law" and not civil disobedience.

5. Cf. Hugo A. Bedau, "On Civil Disobedience," *Journal of Philosophy* 58 (1961): 656; and Stuart M. Brown Jr., "Civil Disobedience," *Journal of Philosophy* 58 (1961):

678. Bedau excludes violence by definition, but Brown includes some violent acts as genuine, if not justified, civil disobedience.

6. For a discussion of "Natural Law" as a justification, see Christian Bay, "Civil Disobedience," in *International Encyclopedia of the Social Sciences*, ed. David L. Sills, vol. 2 (New York: MacMillan, 1968), 477.

7. Cf. Harry Prosch, "Limits to Moral Claim in Civil Disobedience," *Ethics* 75 (January, 1965): 103–11; Darnell Rucker, "The Moral Grounds of Civil Disobedience," *Ethics* 76 (January, 1966): 142–45; Michael Walzer, "The Obligation to Disobey," *Ethics* 77 (April 1967): 163–75; Harry Prosch, "Toward an Ethics of Civil Disobedience," *Ethics* 77 (April 1967): 176–92; Harry Prosch, "More About Civil Disobedience," *Ethics* 77 (July 1967): 311–13.

8. It is impossible to distinguish precisely between civil disobedience with a violent element and insurrection since at some middle spot they would shade into each other. There might be instances falling in this "middle spot" which would be difficult to classify one way or the other. But clearly it is possible to give a rough distinction that would make it possible in almost all cases to distinguish examples of these different types of defiance. A distinction between insurrection and civil disobedience can be made by saying that insurrection or terrorism, though premeditated and perhaps focused on specific issues, is an action in which those resisting the government, instead of minimizing and controlling violence for its dramatic effect as in civil disobedience, employ the most violent weapons they can lay their hands on to do as much damage as they can. The only limitation on the use of violence for insurrectionists (for example, in Algeria) is that imposed by their desire to avoid being caught and imprisoned, which would prevent them from using violence against the government another day.

9. Abe Fortes, *Concerning Dissent and Civil Disobedience* (New York: New American Library, 1968), 34.

10. Ibid., 64.

11. Martin Duberman, "Black Power in America," *Partisan Review* 35 (1968): 38.

12. Martin Luther King Jr., *Where Do We Go from Here: Chaos or Community?* (New York: Harper and Row, 1967), 82.

20. VALUES OF THE AMERICAN INTELLECTUAL CLASS

1. David Horowitz, *The Politics of Bad Faith: The Radical Assault on America's Future* (New York: Simon & Schuster, 1998), 14 and 48.

2. Richard Rorty, *Achieving Our Country: Leftist Thought in Twentieth-Century America* (Cambridge, Mass.: Harvard University Press, 1998).

3. Richard Rorty, *Philosophy and Social Hope* (London: Penguin Books, 1999).

4. Martha Nussbaum, *For Love of Country?* (Boston: Beacon Press, 1996).

5. Lionel Lewis, *Scaling the Ivory Tower: Merit & Its Limits in Academic Careers* (New Brunswick, N.J.: Transactions Publishers, 1998), 120.

6. Peter Whybrow, *American Mania: When More Is Not Enough* (New York: W. W. Norton, 2005), 46.

Index

AMERICAN PHILOSOPHY

Douglas R. Anderson and Jude Jones, series editors

Kenneth Laine Ketner, ed., *Peirce and Contemporary Thought: Philosophical Inquiries.*

Max H. Fisch, ed., *Classic American Philosophers: Peirce, James, Royce, Santayana, Dewey, Whitehead, second edition.* Introduction by Nathan Houser.

John E. Smith, *Experience and God, second edition.*

Vincent G. Potter, *Peirce's Philosophical Perspectives.* Edited by Vincent Colapietro.

Richard E. Hart and Douglas R. Anderson, eds., *Philosophy in Experience: American Philosophy in Transition.*

Vincent G. Potter, *Charles S. Peirce: On Norms and Ideals, second edition.* Introduction by Stanley M. Harrison.

Vincent M. Colapietro, ed., *Reason, Experience, and God: John E. Smith in Dialogue.* Introduction by Merold Westphal.

Robert J. O'Connell, S.J., *William James on the Courage to Believe, second edition.*

Elizabeth M. Kraus, *The Metaphysics of Experience: A Companion to Whitehead's "Process and Reality," second edition.* Introduction by Robert C. Neville.

Kenneth Westphal, ed., *Pragmatism, Reason, and Norms: A Realistic Assessment—Essays in Critical Appreciation of Frederick L. Will.*

Beth J. Singer, *Pragmatism, Rights, and Democracy.*

Eugene Fontinell, *Self, God, and Immorality: A Jamesian Investigation.*

Roger Ward, *Conversion in American Philosophy: Exploring the Practice of Transformation.*

Michael Epperson, *Quantum Mechanics and the Philosophy of Alfred North Whitehead.*

Kory Sorrell, *Representative Practices: Peirce, Pragmatism, and Feminist Epistemology.*

Naoko Saito, *The Gleam of Light: Moral Perfectionism and Education in Dewey and Emerson.*

Josiah Royce, *The Basic Writings of Josiah Royce.*

Douglas R. Anderson, *Philosophy Americana: Making Philosophy at Home in American Culture.*

James Campbell and Richard E. Hart, eds., *Experience as Philosophy: On the World of John J. McDermott.*

John J. McDermott, *The Drama of Possibility: Experience as Philosophy of Culture.* Edited by Douglas R. Anderson.

Larry A. Hickman, *Pragmatism as Post-Postmodernism: Lessons from John Dewey.*

Larry A. Hickman, Stefan Neubert, and Kersten Reich, eds., *John Dewey Between Pragmatism and Constructivism.*

Dwayne A. Tunstall, *Yes, But Not Quite: Encountering Josiah Royce's Ethico-Religious Insight.*

Josiah Royce, *Race Questions, Provincialism, and Other American Problems, expanded edition*. Edited by Scott L. Pratt and Shannon Sullivan.

Lara Trout, *The Politics of Survival: Peirce, Affectivity, and Social Criticism*.

John R. Shook and James A. Good, *John Dewey's Philosophy of Spirit, with the 1897 Lecture on Hegel*.

Josiah Warren, *The Practical Anarchist: Writings of Josiah Warren*. Edited and with an Introduction by Crispin Sartwell.

Naoko Saito and Paul Standish, eds., *Stanley Cavell and the Education of Grownups*.

Douglas R. Anderson and Carl R. Hausman, *Conversations on Peirce: Reals and Ideals*.

Rick Anthony Furtak, Jonathan Ellsworth, and James D. Reid, eds., *Thoreau's Importance for Philosophy*.

James M. Albrecht, *Reconstructing Individualism: A Pragmatic Tradition from Emerson to Ellison*.

Mathew A. Foust, *Loyalty to Loyalty: Josiah Royce and the Genuine Moral Life*.

Cornelis de Waal and Krysztof Piotr Skowroński (eds.), *The Normative Thought of Charles S. Peirce*.

Dwayne A. Tunstall, *Doing Philosophy Personally: Thinking about Metaphysics, Theism, and Antiblack Racism*.

Erin McKenna, *Pets, People, and Pragmatism*.

Sami Pihlström, *Pragmatic Pluralism and the Problem of God*.

Thomas Alexander, *The Human Eros: Eco-ontology and the Aesthetics of Existence*.

John Kaag, *Thinking Through the Imagination: Aesthetics in Human Cognition*.

Kelly A. Parker and Jason Bell (eds.), *The Relevance of Royce*.

W. E. B. Du Bois, *The Problem of the Color Line at the Turn of the Twentieth Century: The Essential Early Essays*. Edited by Nahum Dimitri Chandler.

Nahum Dimitri Chandler, *X—The Problem of the Negro as a Problem for Thought*.

John Lachs, *Freedom and Limits*. Edited by Patrick Shade.

Morris Grossman, *Art and Morality: Essays in the Spirit of George Santayana*. Edited by Martin A. Coleman.

Peter Hare, *Pragmatism with Purpose: Selected Writings*. Edited by Joseph Palencik, Douglas R. Anderson, and Steven A. Miller.